STUDIO
GANG
ARCHI-
TECTS
REVEAL

STUDIO GANG ARCHITECTS

REVEAL

Princeton Architectural Press *New York*

Published by
Princeton Architectural Press
37 East Seventh Street
New York, New York 10003

For a free catalog of books, call 1.800.722.6657.

Visit our website at www.papress.com.

Printed and bound in China

14 13 12 11 4 3 2 1 First edition

Editor: Dan Simon
Creative Direction & Design: Elizabeth Azen

Typeset in Foundry Gridnik and Akkurat
Paper: 128 gsm Japanese Matte and 70gsm Ensolux

Special thanks to: Bree Anne Apperley, Sara Bader, Nicola Bednarek Brower,
Janet Behning, Megan Carey, Becca Casbon, Carina Cha, Tom Cho,
Penny (Yuen Pik) Chu, Russell Fernandez, Pete Fitzpatrick, Jan Haux, Linda Lee,
John Myers, Katharine Myers, Dan Simon, Andrew Stepanian, Jennifer Thompson,
Paul Wagner, Joseph Weston, and Deb Wood of Princeton Architectural Press
—Kevin C. Lippert, publisher

Library of Congress Cataloging-in-Publication Data

Gang, Jeanne.
Reveal : Studio Gang Architects / Jeanne Gang.
—1st ed. p. cm.
ISBN 978-1-56898-993-8 (alk. paper)

1. Studio Gang Architects (Firm)—Catalogs. 2. Architecture—
United States—History—20th century—Catalogs.
 3. Architecture—United States—History—21st century—
Catalogs. 4. Architecture—Environmental aspects—United
States—Catalogs. I. Title. II. Title: Studio Gang Architects.
NA737.S742A4 2011

720.92'2—dc22

2010027916

To Mark

STEEL

STONE

CONCRETE

BRICK

Architecture is a practice of amnesia. When projects are completed, the numerous ideas, thoughts, and research that supported their making are most often purged as the project is narrowed down to its essence—typically leaving behind only a set of final photographs and, maybe, a single sketch. Piles of cardboard models, binders of sketches, over-loaded servers, and endless communications become invisible. Even the voices of the project's participants, no matter how present during design and construction, are forgotten as the messy process of all that goes into making architecture is whisked away into archives. To most observers, the hard work of making an architectural project is incomprehensible as chaotic design morphs into polished professionalism.

Reveal is a book that rescues ideas, including those paths-not-taken, from the dominant design trajectory and completes them as independent thoughts. It pays attention to the tangential information, the people, the places, and the lore that surround every project. The book's chapters are organized by project and include traditional project photographs, but they are also full of additional content: essays, drawings and diagrams, and interviews—the flurry of information that defines and creates the context of an architectural project for the many involved. These pieces of information are more like the genetic markers of the project that may or may not express themselves in the final, featured work.

Though it is always tempting to include everything in a book like this, especially when it's the first, *Reveal* focuses on a subset of Studio Gang's work. All of the projects selected share a particular idea, exhibiting a common interest played out in a different way. These works (organized by material rather than by time) strive to expose something that is not normally seen, is underrepresented, or is frequently overlooked, whether it's a quality of a physical material, an unusual building type, a pattern in an ecological system, or a social mechanism. Future books will include projects organized around other themes, but for now—in the spirit of "reveal"—it seemed appropriate to show a selection and save a little something for later.

—*Jeanne Gang*

Hyde Park Housing

Ex-PLA chief downplays threat

The Visible and the Tangible: The Work of Studio Gang Architects

Mohsen Mostafavi

Architecture has always been about veiling, the covering of things—so why the urge to reveal? The work of Studio Gang is of course not the first instance of architecture's fascination with procedures of exposure. The origins of the use of glass as curtain wall in Chicago, the studio's home city, can be attributed not just to technical and financial expediencies and logics but also to the transparent qualities of the material: like an X-ray, it reveals the truth. But unlike Chicago's earlier tradition, the focus of the work addressed in this book is not on the literal transparency of buildings. The interrelationship between inside and outside, while important, is not the main subject either. Rather, it is the processes that have resulted in the shaping of the architecture that is the primary point of reference.

In this sense the book constitutes a way of unraveling the steps undertaken during the evolution of a building. It documents the material that is invariably left behind, subsumed within the image of the completed project. *Reveal*, as an archive of recent work, exposes an approach that simultaneously provides its origins and its rationale. More than with most other practices, to understand the work of Studio Gang is to understand the steps they took to get there.

Despite this approach, each project accepts its own finitude as a product, as a performative artifact received, encountered, and judged by its audience. And yet each artifact retains traces of all the issues and concerns—the research—that is particular to its formation. This entanglement between autonomy and process is one of the key characteristics of the work of Jeanne Gang and of her Studio.

Why should this matter? Why should a practice be so concerned with revealing these formative processes? Part of the answer lies in the value of a mode of working that at least at the outset is more akin to detection than visualization. Architects generally start the design of a new building by considering what it will look like. And in the case of many architects, a new building invariably looks like something they might have designed before.

Studio Gang consider each project a new beginning— a new opportunity to learn about a site, a phenomenon, a technique, and to explore its impact on the architecture, including its visual characteristics and qualities. This sense of discovery is what makes *Reveal* a kind of detective enterprise, where the scientifically gathered evidence is laid bare in front of us. It is this evidence that is supposed to present the facts of the case, facts that help to resolve the mystery of each project: to reveal its findings and the logic of its conclusions.

The image of the carcasses of thousands of birds of various species meticulously collected by the Canadian Fatal Light Awareness Program, and reproduced in the book, demonstrates the devastating results of migrating birds' collisions with glass buildings. But the hazard of

glass is only one of the factors that has helped shape the design of the Ford Calumet Environmental Center, among the studio's recent projects. Other factors include the environmental and ecological conditions of the location's part-industrial, part-postindustrial habitat.

The architects' research even extends to an analysis of birds' nests, their various techniques of weaving and their durability. They seem to be thinking that a study of how birds protect themselves might provide good clues as to how we may protect them as well. The visitor center is therefore not just for us but literally for the local bird population too.

This kind of sensitivity toward the environment as an ecosystem that includes birds as well as humans applies to other aspects of the construction process, such as the choice of materials. The visual inventory of salvaged materials and the decision to provide a metal mesh edge to the building create a building that both protects birds and is in keeping with the "wasteland" tonality of its industrial surroundings. Also, the project's "seductively malleable" fences and gates made of perforated plates (the salvaged leftover from the metal-stamping process) could be considered a reminder of—an homage to—the work of the British architects Alison and Peter Smithson, in particular their concept of the "as found." The Smithsons argued against covering up architecture with representational elements. Instead they assigned a visual role to the performative and functional aspects of their buildings, such as the "functional" details of the bathrooms at Hunstanton School.

Studio Gang shares with the Smithsons their hesitation about the immediacy of the visual. This is a sensibility that has its lineage in avant-garde art, in particular the Russian Constructivists' concept of *faktura*, the visual demonstration of properties inherent to materials. Instead of the visual being something that is first imagined and then made of materials (whether appliqué or otherwise),

there is in this way of designing buildings an inseparable reciprocity between the materials and methods of construction and their visual potentials.

The Marble Curtain project, exhibited in 2003 at the National Building Museum in Washington, D.C., uses stone to develop a design that relies on the inherent properties of a material as the basis for construction. Here the focus is less on the conventional and symbolic qualities associated with this important building material and more on a desire to discover it anew. The team worked with Matthew Redabaugh, a master craftsman. The research part of the project developed new ideas for the use of stone, not as a heavy load-bearing material in compression but as a "light and thin" material in tension.

Experimenting with different types of marble with variations in thickness and internal structure, the collective of architects, craftspeople, and engineers had to deal with many uncertainties, yet against all the odds they were able to construct (on time) a translucent, shell-like structure. The Marble Curtain also points to the value of the knowledge that can be gained from experiments in making. Had the architects not been able to benefit from the experience and expertise of the other members of the team this structure in all likelihood would have failed. This process also underscores the interrelationship between the idea of the limits of construction and the appearance of the Marble Curtain installation.

This approach is also consistent with the design and construction of the SOS Children's Villages, completed in 2007 in Chicago. This is a relatively simple building that fulfills its programmatic requirement despite the fact that the architects had to rely on donated materials for its construction. This meant that Studio Gang had to consider an ever-changing palette of materials, and in response, recalibrate the design of the building. This uncertainty regarding the availability of building materials might be common in some parts of the world, but is unusual with the U.S. construction industry. Here, the availability of mass-produced materials tends to dictate the visual aesthetic of the vast majority of building projects— a condition that leads to a much greater degree of homogeneity than might be desirable.

The results of Studio Gang's chance acquisition of materials are perhaps best demonstrated by the exterior, originally planned in brick, but ultimately made of leftover concrete. The firm used the pressure to save on resources as an opportunity to both create a new facade and record the "accidental" history of the building's construction. This is achieved on the outside through undulating bands of varying shades of concrete, somewhat akin to a series of sedimentations below the Earth's surface.

In some ways the circumstances surrounding the construction of this building, perhaps more than any other of Gang's projects, exemplify the notion of rendering the invisible visible. But the issue at stake in Studio Gang's work is not a simple one-way movement from the invisible to the visible but rather a process of open questioning between the two conditions. This process reinstates the need for the interrogation of architecture as a perceptual project caught in the ambiguity between certitude and incertitude.

This form of interrogating architecture also implicates the viewer in the process of making things visible. They can no longer rely on assumed meanings but instead must be open to perceiving things in ways that are more sensitive to the becoming of a building, an installation, a high-rise. But the perceptual experience of the work of Studio Gang is in many respects inseparable from our sense of the tactile qualities of their buildings. The relation between the visible and the tactile is a topic well articulated by the philosopher Maurice Merleau-Ponty, who wrote, "We must habituate ourselves to think that every visible is cut out in the tangible, every tactile being in some manner promised to visibility and that there is encroachment, infringement,

not only between the touched and the touching but also between the tangible and the visible, which is encrusted in it, as, conversely, the tangible itself is not a nothingness of visibility, is not without visual existence."[1]

The inseparability of the visual from the tactile, of the perceptual from the experiential, is a hallmark of the way in which the buildings and projects of Jeanne Gang's studio distinguish themselves from earlier manifestations of unveiling. There is little emphasis on the use of transparent materials as a device for exposing the interior of buildings. Instead, Reveal is a way of both making and experiencing architecture that finds clues where most others would see none. The results, though often based on highly rational procedures that include substantial information about the site, the choice of materials, and technologies of fabrication, invariably induce a strong visceral response from their audience.

Their high-rise, Aqua, is no exception. Considered as a kind of "topographic tower," the building's curvilinear balconies provide its inhabitants with a variety of unconventional external spaces. Yet these same balconies provide the viewer of the building with the sense of an ever-changing, even illusory, vertical landscape of dunes and lakes.

The disjuncture between the engineering objectivity behind the design and construction of the balconies and the emotional experience of the building as a total object further demonstrates the consistency of Gang's approach. And perhaps it is not a coincidence after all that Chicago, the site of some of the world's most rational and innovative architectural projects, should now be the location for yet another set of groundbreaking experiments that reveal the intertwining between the visual and the tactile. **S/G/A**

Notes
1 Maurice Merleau-Ponty, The Visible and the Invisible (Evanston, IL: Northwestern University Press, 1983), 134.

Reveal

Jeanne Gang

Inside NASA's giant metal warehouse the walls were lined with wooden crates stacked to the ceiling, their parallel rows seeming to continue into infinity. Painted sky blue, each had been carefully stenciled with black identification numerals and put in its proper place within the high bays: relics stacked within a cathedral dedicated to organizational precision. One crate had been placed on the floor and opened, its delicate contents of miniature aircraft carefully deposited on top of custom foam packing. Daylight from the open door behind us glinted off this shiny object, drawing us toward it for closer inspection.

Prior to designing an exhibit for the architecture gallery at the Art Institute of Chicago entitled "Aerospace Design," I had the rare opportunity to visit NASA's Langley Research Center and explore their collection of wind tunnel test models, some of which were to become part of the exhibition. Langley's meticulously crafted prototypes for the study of flight ranged in dimension from thimble-size to full-scale components and even to full-scale aircraft. Examining and learning about these remarkable artifacts led me to contemplate how the process of their creation focused on revealing invisible forces (in this case, the wind) and how this potentially paralleled our own architectural design process.

In aerospace design, information about the forces of wind, gravity, and temperature is gathered through wind tunnel testing or computer simulation and analyzed in order to determine each factor's impact on flight. The results are then combined to directly shape the exterior body of an aircraft and its parts, such that seeing a model aircraft is almost like seeing the wind itself in relief. These sensuous prototypes appeal to us on an aesthetic level because, in so clearly exposing their function, they are a striking example of formal purity. Architecture too can be iteratively shaped to improve performance and respond to functional criteria. Design in both cases is an activity that aims to reveal, and it is this seemingly similar goal and design process that makes it tempting for our architecture to borrow more and more from purely technological methods and tools.

Under closer comparison, however, a major difference between the scientific and architectural notions of reveal becomes apparent: in aerospace design, reveal is focused on answering the question of "how?" while in architecture, reveal opens up the more complex questions of "why?" and "about what?" This is because science must rely on technology alone to reveal nature; it cannot operate through abstract ideas. Although the designs of aircraft are a reflection of our society (be they commercial jets or military bombers), it is difficult for these objects to express a position with respect to that society. They must focus on how to overcome gravity and air currents, not why. To express anything more in their design (a cultural position, for example) would be detrimental to their purpose. Art, on the other hand, which is not bound to fulfilling any certain purpose, can reveal nature using representation, language, and ideas.

Architecture navigates the interesting territory between these realms. It can fully utilize technological methods, but can also structure itself on an idea. It can explore making many kinds of forces visible, not only physical ones. Because the scope of architecture's subject matter is very broad, reveal becomes a multifaceted concept. Shelter, the city, religion, justice, networks of capital, entire ecological systems, and many other issues—all are available architectural currency. But in order to tap into reveal's conceptual potential, architecture must not limit itself to its own profession-centric vocabulary, in which the heterogenous significance of the word is reduced to the control joint between two materials.

2

fig. 1 The exhibition design highlights NASA's proto-types, protected by heat-bent acrylic vitrines arrayed across the curved gallery wall.

fig. 2 Wallpaper-scale photography taken from inside the wind tunnels gives presence to this typically behind-the-scenes architecture.

To liberate the concept of reveal is to leave behind this narrow definition and instead employ it as an idea: exploring its many connotations, allowing it to be mined for its meanings in different contexts, and exposing its paradoxes. In religion, for example, reveal is divine inspiration. In pornography, it is a strip tease. Reveal can mean both to display something and to betray someone. It is an aperture whose degrees of dilation are infinite.

In our work, reveal is a potent concept and its multiple, sometimes paradoxical meanings hold together the select-ed projects presented in this book. For two early works, the Solar Sequins Project and Aerospace Design Exhibition, reveal refers to a perceivable presence given to a force that is typically invisible. The solar sequins gently move in the wind, allowing their changing patterns to visibly ani-mate the facade while simultaneously producing power for the building. The Aerospace Design Exhibition, in addi-tion to displaying the finely crafted prototypes, emphasized previously behind-the-scenes wind tunnel architecture

by using wallpaper-scale photography from inside the tunnels themselves. Patterns of the wind's invisible streamlines were made visible when they were drawn directly onto the gallery walls.

At the Ford Calumet Environmental Center, reveal calls attention to frequently unnoticed events such as bird migration and networks of the salvage steel industry present in the region. Here, a basket-like mesh made from salvaged rebar protects migrating birds from glass that they cannot see, and markings on salvaged steel column-bundles tell visitors that they were fabricated nearby. For the Marble Curtain and the SOS Community Center, reveal makes known the secret qualities of a physical material. Stone's secret is betrayed when it is revealed in tension, and concrete at SOS is caught off guard when its once-fluid state is preserved in the building's final form.

The meaning of reveal is closer to a strip tease in the Brick Weave House, where the selective subtrac-tion of mass in the outer wall offers glimpses into the

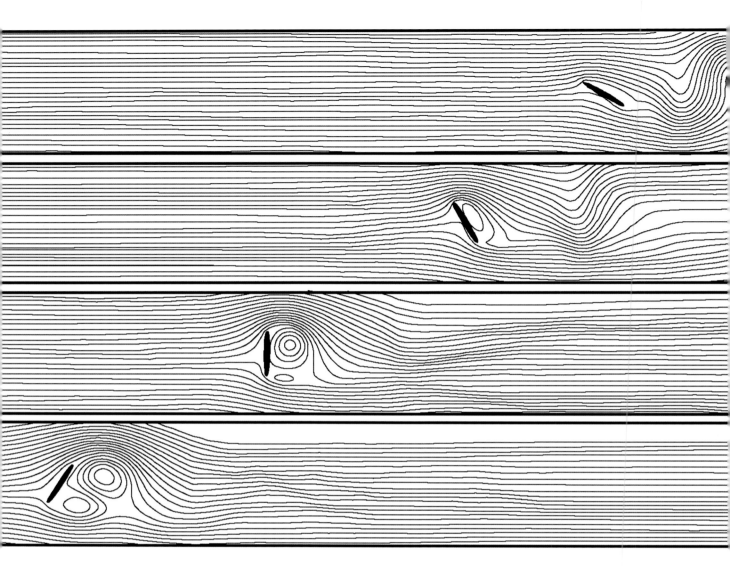

fig. 3 Visualization of streamlines encountering an oblique plate and vortex shedding

home's inner sanctum; for Maisonette, on the other hand, it implies a didactic demonstration of the way metal is fabricated. At Aqua Tower it acts like a map, pointing out landmarks in the city and providing habitable topography on the facade from which to see them, while at the Blue Wall Center, reveal metaphorically magnifies nature that is otherwise too camouflaged to be appreciated.

With much of contemporary architecture concerned with technologies that produce effects, a concept as potent as reveal should provide a welcome alternative trajectory. This book is intended to open up a host of ideas with the potential to move beyond effects toward the possibilities latent in architecture's structural, programmatic, and narrative ingredients. Going beyond the "how," reveal begins to address the question "why?"; thereby becoming an idea which recognizes that pleasure and discovery often stem from looking at the world with openness, as if we are seeing it for the first time. S/G/A

Very useful to the clarification of thoughts for this essay was The Veil of Isis: an Essay on the History of the Idea of Nature by Pierre Hadot, translated by Michael Chase (Cambridge, MA: Harvard University Press, 2006), a volume that elaborates on the history of revealing nature. Also important was Aerospace Design: Aircraft, Spacecraft and the Art of Modern Flight (London: Merrell in association with NASA, 2003), edited by Anthony M. Springer, who collaborated on the Aerospace Design Exhibition.

5

Anxious to observe the powerful and sometimes menacing forces they were unable to see with the naked eye, engineers crafted the wind tunnel to reveal the invisible effects of wind on aircraft. Though they can be architectural in scale, wind tunnels (like the forces of wind they attempt to expose) are hardly familiar forms. They are a behind-the-scenes kind of single purpose architecture whose design evolved rapidly from simple rickety contraptions into highly calibrated instruments. The Wright brothers and others assembled the early wind-pipes (as wind tunnels were then called) in order to understand lift on air foils. In 1919, the National Advisory Committee for Aeronautics, NACA (which later became NASA) began building its first wind tunnel at Langely.

Wind tunnels were considered critical to the development of flight and their design occupied noteworthy engineers. Gustave Eiffel, for example, known for showy, iconic structures, devoted years to working on improvements to these devices that would only be seen by fellow engineers. Eventually, wind-pipes were fashioned into closed circuit loops, enabling higher speeds of air to be used with more control. NASA's wind tunnel experiments took both tunnel making and test model making to new heights—especially after formulas were discovered that could scale up wind forces with great accuracy.

The simulation of wind over a prototypical aircraft makes it possible to experiment with form in an environment closer to the extreme conditions that real aircraft experience in flight. Currents of air are sucked through the tunnel by a large fan and guided around by vanes to a test chamber in the loop where the scale model is mounted. The internal environments of the tunnels have expanded to include cryogenic operations and magnetic fields. Pressure sensors on the prototype allow engineers to analyze lift, drag, stability, and controllability. To further aid visualization, coatings can be applied to the test models that reveal flow. A few examples include thermosensitive paint that turns Day-Glo colors when exposed to wind, coatings of oil whose streaks reveal flow patterns, and smoke inside the test chamber that shows streamlines or turbulence across the prototypes. In addition to wind tunnel testing, computer simulations and actual test flights are all employed in the design process. Improvements to the performance of the aircraft are achieved through iteratively adjusting test models' shape.

fig. 4 NACA's first wind tunnel was a five-foot long straight duct constructed at the Langley Memorial Aeronautical Laboratory.

fig. 5 Langley's model shop in 1944; expert model making for wind tunnel testing has long been critical to aeronautical research.

6

7

fig. 6 Drawings made on the curved wall of the exhibition represent a flow of streamlines.

fig. 7 A view of the test chamber of the full-scale tunnel at Langley

RKS

Jiang Ren/ImagineChina

GATHERING IS
THE BEGINNING
OF NEST MAKING

FORD CALUMET ENVIRONMENTAL CENTER

The City of Chicago Department of Environment and the State
of Illinois partnered to develop a new environmental center in the
Calumet area of Chicago. On Earth Day 2004, Studio Gang's winning
entry to the international design competition for the center was
announced. When completed, the Ford Calumet Environmental Center
will educate the public about the industrial, cultural, and ecological
heritage of the Calumet area, and will provide an operational
base for research activities, volunteer stewardship, environmental
remediation, and ecological rehabilitation.

OWNER: City of Chicago Department of Environment, Public Building
Commission of Chicago

LOCATION: Hegewisch Marsh in the Calumet Region
Torrence Avenue at 134th Street, Chicago, USA

SIZE: 28,000 SF

COMPLETION DATE: 2011

This is Calumet.

1.2 (previous page) Rendering of the building's south porch during winter

1.3 The remnants of wetland habitats between industrial sites and railways define the landscape of the Calumet region.

BEST NEST

What if a building were more like a nest? If it were, it would be made out of local, abundant materials. It would be specific to its site and climate. It would use minimal energy but maintain comfort. It would last just long enough and then would leave no trace. It would be just what it needed to be.

The Ford Calumet Environmental Center uses a nest as its construction model. By employing plentiful and leftover materials found nearby in its design, it demonstrates the important environmental principle of re-use. By proposing a building made from materials at hand, the project introduces an entirely new paradigm for a project delivery process that has not changed substantially in the last fifty years. It radically alters the way a building is both conceived and made: form follows availability.

Existing Process

While project delivery or construction has remained constant, the design process has changed significantly over time. It gradually shifted from the architect custom-designing everything, to selecting and designing premade components. When the first structural steel buildings were attempted in the 1890s, architects and engineers designed everything down to the columns themselves.[1] They used rudimentary steel pieces connected together to create columns. As the uses of steel developed, it became possible to select a wide-flange column in select sizes with known structural qualities. After World War II, building product standardization expanded. Windows, for example, were once custom-designed frames that held a piece of glass. Later, windows became pre-made technical assemblies of pre-determined sizes from which to choose. Details of contemporary window assemblies are ready-made, saving architects drawing time and eliminating uncertainty through warranties.

Standardization and worldwide availability has made specifying pre-made parts for buildings more effortless in recent years. Through websites, trade shows, and eager sales representatives, all of the critical information, including details, dimensions, and samples for globally produced building components, are available upon demand.

Though the idea of prefabrication offers potential environmental benefits, shipping building parts around the world, for example, is less appealing from an ecological point of view than sourcing from one fabricator. On another level, specifying finished products from across the globe has effectively separated designers from raw materials and has ultimately taken some of the fun out of architecture. What's missing is the sense of discovery at finding something useful, and perhaps unexpected, closer to home. Material opportunities could potentially arise if architects were more like hunters and gatherers.

If the hunter-gatherer archetype provides an additional model for architectural practice, new systems for locating materials would become necessary. In any city, a massive variety of building materials exists between the buildings being pulled down and ordinary scrap yards. From leftover steel to pulverized rubber, bulk quantities of useful things pass through metropolitan areas. But as fascinating as it is to contemplate, these local materials currently require a great deal of effort to locate. Rather than a simple point-and-click from a desktop, finding appropriate scrap requires persistent gathering. Like gleaning, gathering currently involves the physical action of visiting scrap yards or buildings to be razed in order to locate materials. Making architecture from nearby scrap, however, seems both elementary and urgent in a world that is overflowing with waste.

>page 38

  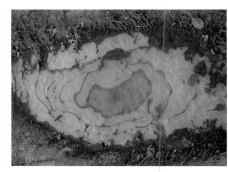

1.4 Bits of evidence of the post-industrial landscape in Calumet on
and near Hegewisch Marsh: rusted car skeletons, lush habitat, animal
castings, invasive phragmites, frozen puddles, abandoned railroad
tracks, ATV tire ruts, a beaver-gnawed tree, and steaming landfill.

     PROJECT / FORD CALUMET ENVIRONMENTAL CENTER

1.5

1.6

1.7

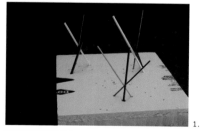

1.8

1.9

1.10

Calumet Industry

Calumet is a great place to gather. This is where Chicago's once-mighty steel mills burnt coke, and melted and rolled steel as some of the world's leading producers. Calumet's location proved to be advantageous for steel mills: producers could purchase raw materials from the vast iron ore deposits in the Great Lakes region. A well-connected rail network, coupled with an abundance of local water, made Calumet ideal for steel production. Other industries took advantage of similar resources and set up shop in Calumet. As the heyday of steel production came to an end in the 1970s, many remnant structures were left decaying on their sites.

Today, hulking structures of the former steel industry—defunct ore unloaders, pusher cars, and quench towers—dot every vista in the Calumet region. In between are mounds of black slag, a byproduct of steel production, which lend an eerie contour to the otherwise flat landscape. Other industries remain in operation alongside the derelict ones. Automakers such as Ford, building-material suppliers, and scrap industries still call Calumet their home. The combination of abandoned structures and contemporary salvage offers a plethora of materials for making buildings.

Habitat

Imagining the industrial presence and history of Calumet provides only half the picture. Today, Calumet is dually important as a resting stop for migratory birds and as a habitat for many other species. Because many sites were left untouched, and because little area was developed with the usual residential landscape of chemically treated monocultural lawns, a great variety of species have been able to thrive here. Twenty-six different endangered birds have been sighted on the site itself. Migratory birds follow the waterways of Calumet and make stops here to refuel for their long journey south in the fall and back north in the spring. It is a crucial nesting ground or stopping place for the Yellow-headed Blackbird, the Yellow-crowned Night Heron, and the Little Blue Heron.

> page 41

1.5 With steel replacing wrought iron, massive invention and creativity occurred in the first twenty years of high-rise design. Without standard shapes to choose from, engineers competed to design and patent steel column shapes that were compared and contrasted in terms of eccentric loading, weight, workmanship, cost, and availability. The array of column types reveals a fascinating moment in time in which the engineer's search for "form follows function" produced both incredible variety as well as specificity and rigor in design. Steel manufacturers, like those in Calumet, flourished under these new developments, creating products with versatile uses.

Column Forms, Showing Required Punching Operations
Starting from top left, across:
a. Larimer column, 1 row of rivets
b. Plate and angles, 2 rows
c. Z-bar column, without covers, 2 rows
d. 4-section Phoenix column, 4 rows
e. Channel column, with plates or lattice, 4 rows
f. Gray column, 4 rows
g. Z-bar column, with single covers, 6 rows
h. Channels, web-plate, and angles, 6 rows
i. Box column of plates and angles, 8 rows
j. Latticed angles, 8 rows
k. 8-section Phoenix column, 8 rows
l. Z-bar column with double covers, 10 rows

Source: Figure and column descriptions reprinted from Joseph Freitag, Architectural Engineering (New York: John Wiley & Sons, 1909).

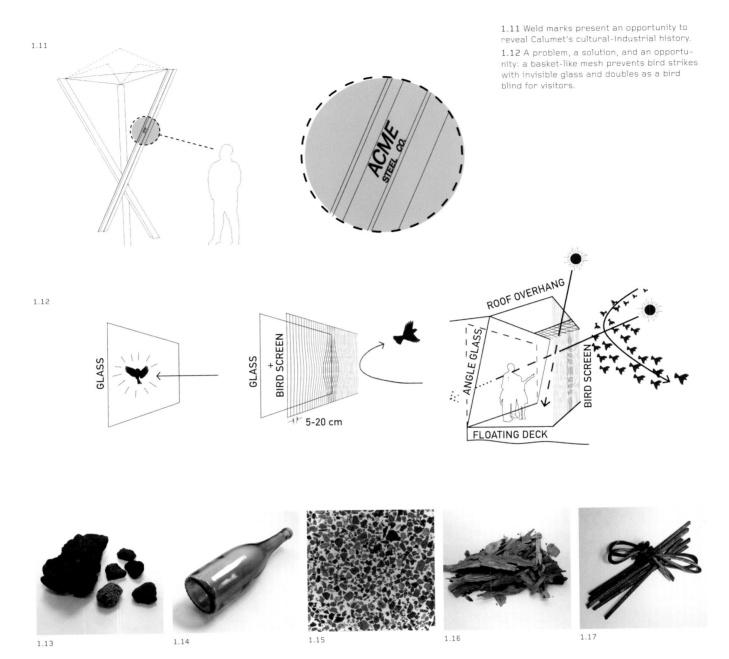

1.11

1.12

1.11 Weld marks present an opportunity to reveal Calumet's cultural-industrial history.

1.12 A problem, a solution, and an opportunity: a basket-like mesh prevents bird strikes with invisible glass and doubles as a bird blind for visitors.

1.13 1.14 1.15 1.16 1.17

< **1.6** Calumet's location on the Mississippi Flyway migration route

1.7 As many as 26 endangered or threatened bird species have been sighted at Hegewisch Marsh, near the former sites of heavy steel production.

1.8 Steel columns reveal their manufacturing origin to the visitor through weldmarks on the metal.

1.9 Model of column-bundles. Dissimilar salvaged steel piles found near the site to be driven into its wet, clayey soil. The splay gives lateral stability to the structure.

1.10 A model of the Ford Calumet Environmental Center depicts the column-bundle supports along with a bird blind running the full length of the center's exterior porch.

^ **1.13** Piles of slag, a byproduct of steel production, are abundant in Calumet.

1.14 Colorful glass: a highly recyclable inert material with many uses

1.15 Test sample of terrazzo made with a combination of slag and broken glass

1.16 Biomass from roadside clippings or fallen trees can be used for fuel in highly efficient and clean bio-mass boilers.

1.17 Copper wire, recycled rebar, and metal bar-stock are abundant in salvage yards near the site.

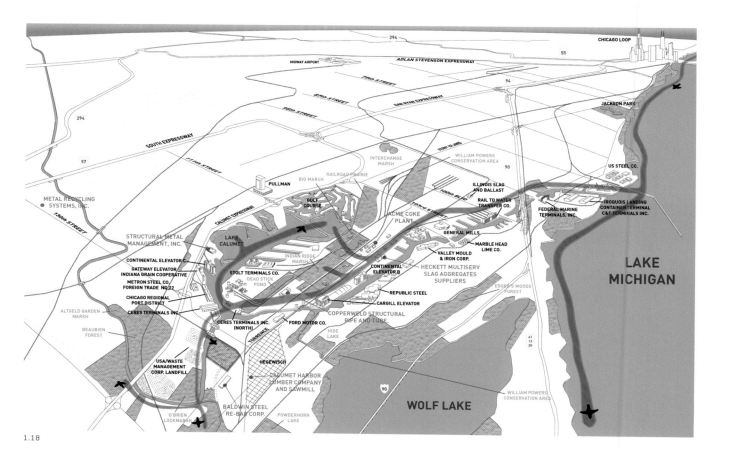

1.18

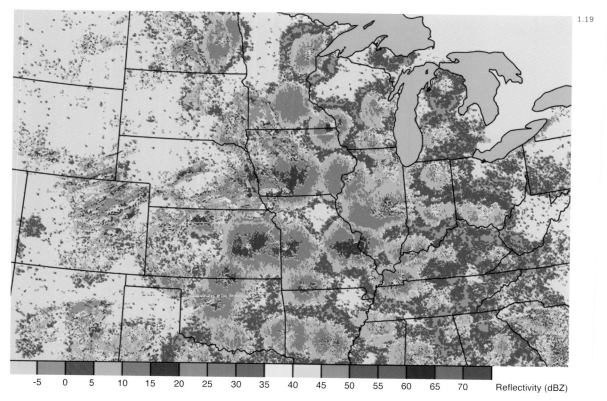

1.19

-5 0 5 10 15 20 25 30 35 40 45 50 55 60 65 70   Reflectivity (dBZ)

1.18 A map showing the overlap of the ecological and industrial context of the Calumet region: the waterways, wetlands, and green spaces attract migratory birds and a host of other species. Current industrial companies also make use of the area's supply of fresh water as well as its multiple transportation networks. Indicated in red are industries near the site that supply materials with potential for use in architecture.

1.19 As discussed on the Clemson University Radar Ornithology Lab website (http://virtual.clemson.edu/groups/birdrad/comment.htm), weather surveillance radar initially captured images of bird migration inadvertently. Now, better Doppler radars with higher sensitivity are being utilized to show density and direction of peak migratory movements over the radar stations. This information will allow ornithologists to determine if migratory flights are decreasing, stable, or increasing for different regions of the country.

The image is similar to a NEXRAD (NEXt generation RADar) base reflectivity map. NEXRAD maintains an extensive network of stations providing near complete radar coverage of the continental United States, Alaska, and Hawaii. These radars transmit microwave signals into the atmosphere and listen for return echoes from objects. Converting this quantity to reflectivity in dBZ (or decibels of Z) gives a representation in different colors based on density in relation to the location of the radar.

The doughnut shaped splotches show high densities of migratory birds just after take-off at dusk. The splotches on the map are stopover sites in which migrant birds have spent the day feeding and resting in preferred habitat.

Map courtesy of the National Weather Service (NOAA), http://radar.weather.gov/Conus/centgrtlakes.php

Notes
1 Joseph Freitag, Architectural Engineering (New York: John Wiley & Sons, 1909).
2 Salvaged steel is steel that has been rejected from other construction sites for non-structural reasons such as arriving in the wrong size or where visual defects such as flash rusting has occurred. Using salvaged material saves the energy of re-melting and reforming the sections.
3 Below the building, the steel acts as foundation piles. This structural strategy of angled column bundles provides the lateral bracing required for the entire building.

The Center

Reconciling these divergent identities, the 'nest' concept produces a building made of gathered re-used materials such as salvaged steel and slag, and simultaneously establishes the site's current and future role as a wildlife habitat. Visitors will come here to learn about the importance of both aspects of this region and how the two can coexist.

Recycled materials are employed in new ways throughout the building. The structure itself is made of reused steel. Salvaged steel sections of appropriate sizes are gathered from nearby yards.[2] Instead of a regular grid of identically sized columns, the design is created from a variety of column types based on what is available for collection. Rammed into the earth at inclined angles, several steel pieces come together to form column-bundles.[3]

Utilizing diverse sizes of tube, wide-flange, and pipe, each steel piece, weld-marked with its fabricator's name, will reveal the wide diversity of the material as well as its local origin. A walk through the building's exhibit spaces will present a virtual library of recycled steel and make a visual connection to the region's industrial past.

At the south facade, a finer grain of steel is deployed to create a basket-like mesh wrapping the building's expansive exterior porch. The mesh, made of rebar and bar stock, protects birds from collisions with glass they cannot see in this critical nesting spot and habitat. At the same time, it creates an outdoor viewing area or bird blind for visitors to inhabit. The mesh allows the building to function as a transparent pavilion in the industrial-natural landscape without killing the birds that people are coming to see.

Below the high roof plane, a series of lower program pods enclose classrooms and service functions. Work areas, exhibition space, and an auditorium are connected through the tall space that winds between the pods. The pods' placement and height differences allow air to flow between them and through the building, while hot air rises for extraction through the roof.

Other abundant local materials are recycled to shape the building. Slag and broken bottles find a new purpose as aggregate in the terrazzo floors. Wood used to form the roof plane is left in place as finish material. Leftover punched metal scrap is employed as site fencing. Old melted milk cartons are reformed into boardwalk planks for outdoor trails.

Availability also guides the site strategy and energy. By placing the building close to the existing road, it gains easy physical and infrastructural access while reducing disturbance to the site. The building's orientation and environmental systems take advantage of what is already there. Passive solar power and geothermal temperature are used to minimize energy use, and air is exhausted through natural displacement ventilation. Rainwater is collected for reuse in flushing toilets and is then cleaned through living plants. Clippings from nearby roads and scrap from a local sawmill feed a biomass boiler, producing heat in extreme winters and cool air in the summer. These systems are revealed through educational and stewardship programs that the building will house.

The structure's interconnected systems work with the fluidity of an organism rather than a mechanically heated and cooled building. By using minimal energy and what is available nearby, the environmental center reveals the site's industrial past, while hinting at what it means to make architecture that is akin to a nest. S/G/A

What about nests?

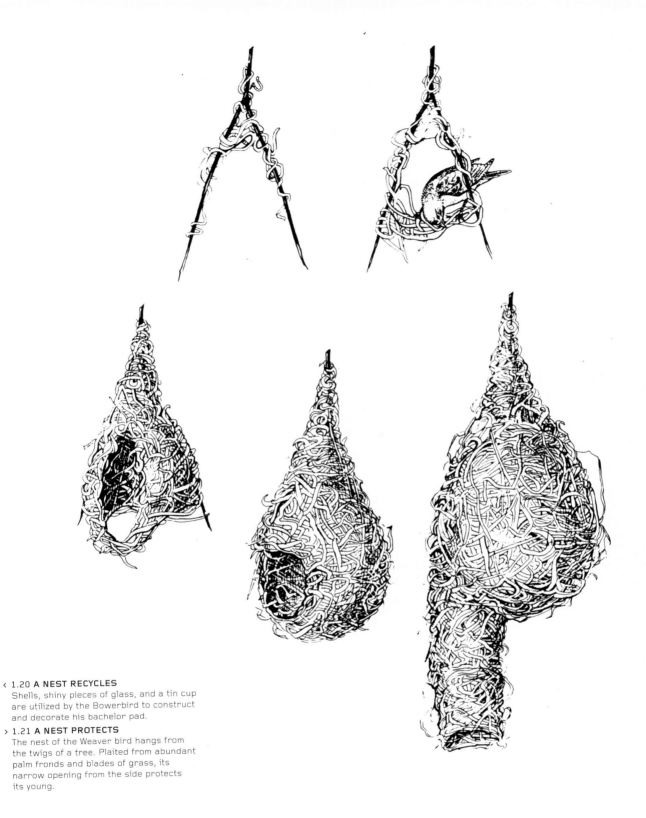

1.20 **A NEST RECYCLES**
Shells, shiny pieces of glass, and a tin cup
are utilized by the Bowerbird to construct
and decorate his bachelor pad.

1.21 **A NEST PROTECTS**
The nest of the Weaver bird hangs from
the twigs of a tree. Plaited from abundant
palm fronds and blades of grass, its
narrow opening from the side protects
its young.

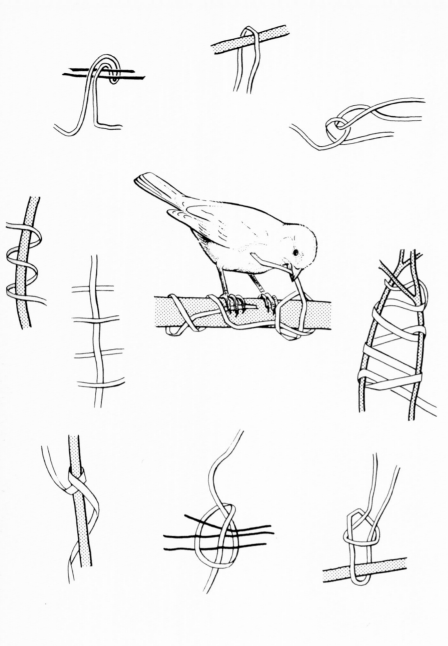

‹ 1.22 **A NEST IS WELL MADE**
Durability of the Weaver bird's knotted
nest comes from both the material it uses
as well as its craftsmanship. These nests
can last for years due to their meticulous
construction, and their flexibility allows
for expansion.

∨ 1.23 **A NEST IS GREEN**
Some birds use earth as the insulation
for their nests. The Brush-turkey, for
example, uses the heat generated by
decaying leaves to create the perfect
temperature for hatching its eggs.

› 1.24 **A NEST IS WELL PLACED**
A fork near the trunk of a tree is chosen
by squirrels to avoid shaking during
storms. Squirrels also make use of a cavity in an existing tree to save themselves
the energy of building an outer structure.

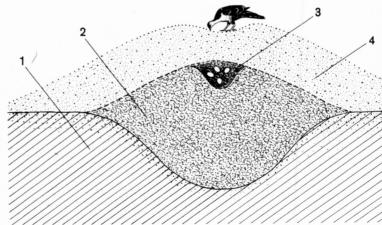

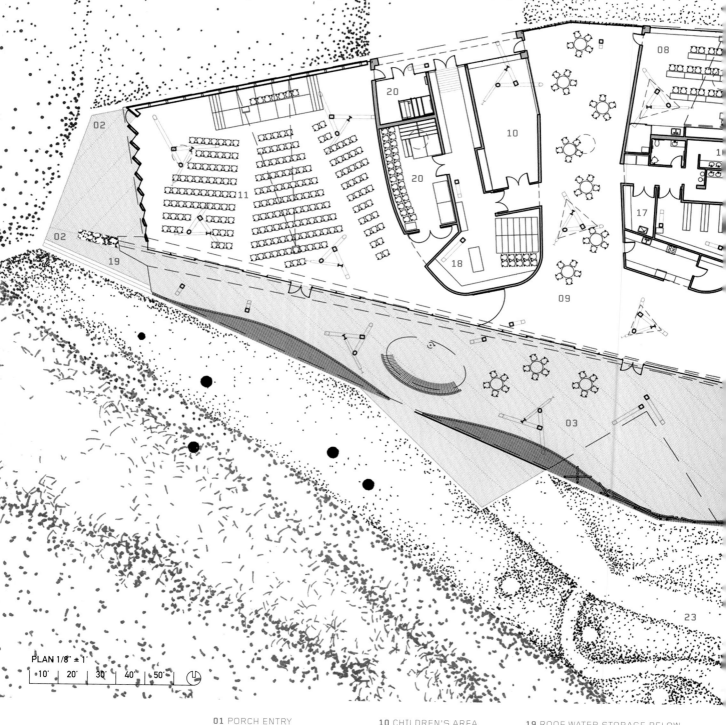

PLAN 1/8" = 1'

10' 20' 30' 40' 50'

01 PORCH ENTRY
02 TRAIL HEAD
03 EXTERIOR PORCH
04 VERTICAL FLOW WETLAND
05 LOBBY
06 MAIN EXHIBIT
07 MEDIA ORIENTATION
08 CLASSROOM
09 CAFE / DINING

10 CHILDREN'S AREA
11 AUDITORIUM
12 LAB
13 STAFF OFFICE
14 CONFERENCE
15 VOLUNTEERS
16 TOILETS
17 RECYCLING
18 STORAGE

19 ROOF WATER STORAGE BELOW
20 MECHANICAL
21 PARKING
22 BIKE PARKING
23 SLAG GRASS GARDEN / PATH
24 STORAGE FOR BIOMASS FUEL
25 GEOTHERMAL BOREHOLE FIELD
26 EARTH TUBE FIELD
27 DEMONSTRATION GARDEN

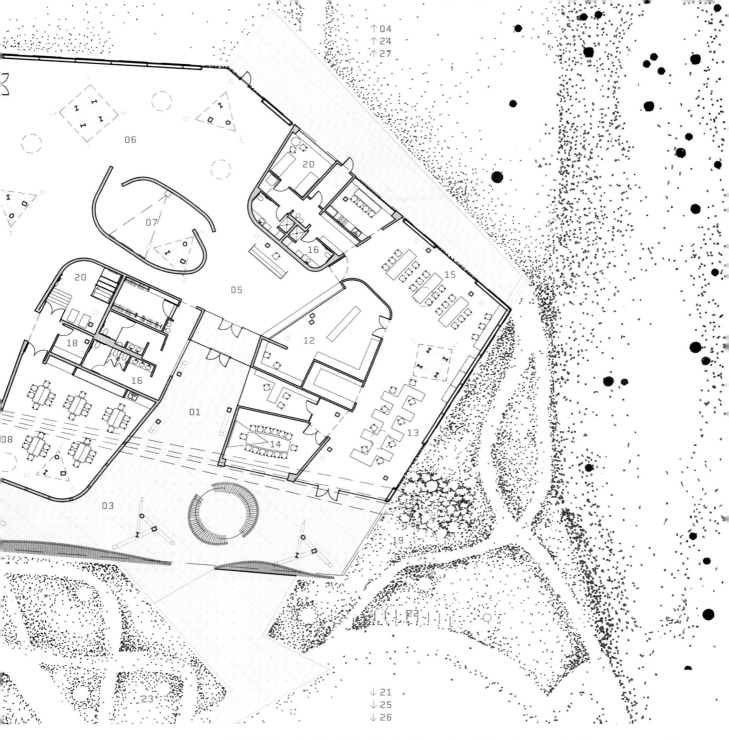

1.25 Walk Through: Enter the building from the south porch through an opening in the woven screen-like mesh. The porch doubles as a meeting space and outdoor classroom with smaller spaces defined by screens and columns clusters. Once inside, on the right, watch live lab work by scientists examining the site. To the left, move through the exhibition that interprets Calumet's unique industrial and natural heritage. Enclosed classrooms are organized into "pods" along the way. At the west end the auditorium space opens onto an open air deck and trailheads, leading to outdoor exhibits on the site.

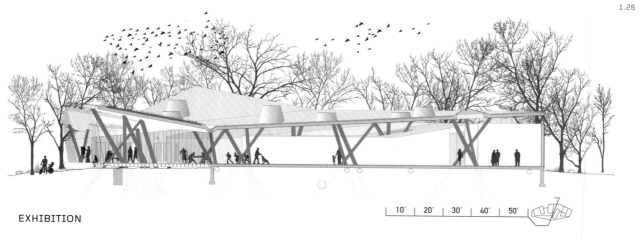

EXHIBITION

| 10' | 20' | 30' | 40' | 50' |

LAB

| 10' | 20' | 30' | 40' | 50' |

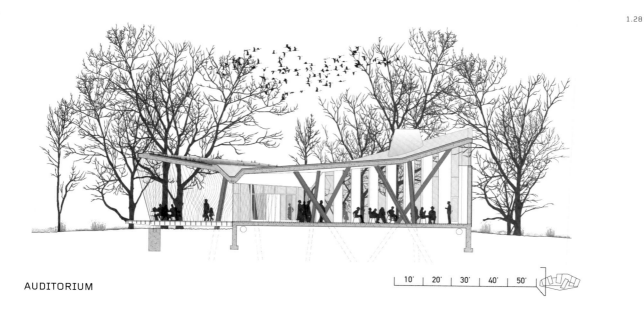

AUDITORIUM

| 10' | 20' | 30' | 40' | 50' |

1.26–28 A continuous concrete roof hovers above the indoor and outdoor spaces. Pitched toward a central fold-line, the roof functions like a leaf, funneling rainwater to cisterns for later use, as well as providing a surface for solar power collection. The roof's pitch permits winter sun angles and shades against summer sun. Underneath the roof canopy, exhibition space flows around a series of pods that house classrooms, lab space, exhibition storage, and services. At the auditorium, the roof tilts up to create a high ceiling to allow views to the surrounding woods.

1.29–30 Constructed of salvaged steel rebar, the mesh enclosing the south porch protects birds from striking the structure's transparent facade. At the same time, it defines an engaging space for visitors to explore and a "blind" for them to observe the surrounding wildlife. On the north elevation, the building insulates against winter cold by employing solid walls with intermittent windows. Clad with reclaimed barrel wood, the walls have a linear texture which transitions to slats in front of windows to prevent bird strikes.

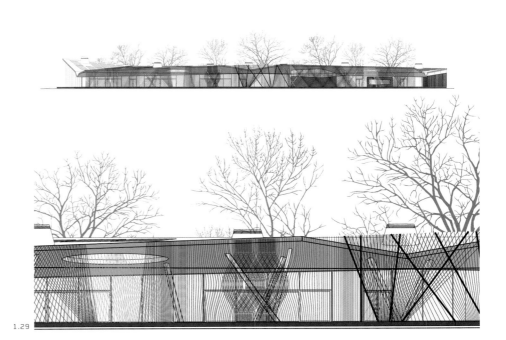

1.29

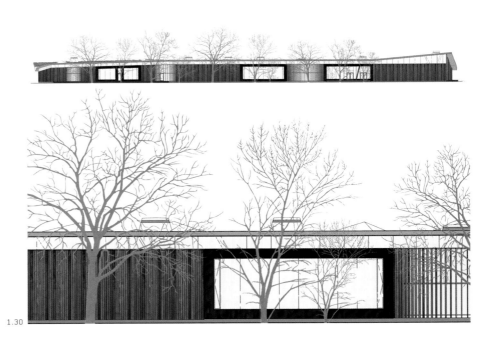

1.30

SHEET GLASS: AN INVISIBLE AND LETHAL HAZARD FOR BIRDS
MAKING OUR HOMES AND WORKPLACES SAFE FOR BIRDS

DANIEL KLEM, JR., Department of Biology, Muhlenberg College, Allentown, PA

THE FACTS

The dead and dying victims of glass are most often hidden from view in vegetation surrounding human dwellings. They are either killed outright, injured and struggling to recover, or quickly taken by predators and scavengers. Lethal collisions are possible wherever birds and glass mutually occur. Glass casualties have been recorded the world over with panes of all sizes in residential homes and single- or multistory buildings. Fatal or injurious collisions occur when flying birds attempt to reach habitat visible on the other side of clear panes, or by attempting to reach illusions of habitat and sky reflected in the glass surface. Intensive studies at single homes reveal one out of every two strikes results in a fatality. Glass is an indiscriminate killer that takes the fit as well as the unfit of a species population. Attrition at glass is an additive rather than a compensatory avian population mortality factor.

Researchers differ in their evaluations of the magnitude of the toll that glass exacts on individual species and bird populations overall. Before much was known, annual deaths attributable to windows were hypothesized to be 3.5 million in the 1970s. Since then, extensive studies over the past three decades have been used to estimate the annual toll to be between one hundred million to one billion birds in the U.S. alone. To put these numbers in perspective, annual U.S. bird populations are estimated to be 20 billion in the fall, and annual glass kills are estimated to be 0.5 to 5.0 percent of this figure. By comparison, each year U.S. hunters are estimated to take 120.5 million birds, and free-ranging domestic cats are suspected to kill hundreds of millions to over a billion songbirds. Some researchers suggest that the overall avian mortality rate attributable to glass is likely to be much greater than what is attributable to cats: reasoning that cats are active predators that most often capture vulnerable prey while sheet glass is an indiscriminate killer that takes the strong as well as the weak and is astronomically more numerous than cats. Minimally, from an ethical and moral perspective, any unintended and unnatural killing associated with human presence in the environment should be addressed and reduced if not eliminated. Guilt and anxiety are common feelings among an increasing number of people who discover an accidental fatality beneath the window of their home, workplace, or any other structure.

Birds behave as if clear and reflective glass is invisible to them (Klem, 1989; Klem, 1990; O'Connell, 2001). The sex, age, or resident status of a bird in any locale has little influence on their vulnerability to windows. There is no season or time of day, and almost no weather conditions during which birds elude glass. Transparent or reflective panes of various colors are equally lethal to birds. Strikes occur at sheet glass of various sizes, heights, and orientation in urban, suburban, and rural environments, but birds are more vulnerable to large ($>2 m^2$) panes near ground level and at heights above 3 m in suburban and rural areas. Strikes are more frequent during winter when birds are attracted to feeders in larger numbers than at any other time of the year, including the spring and fall migratory periods when glass casualties typically attract the most human attention because they are often more visible on sidewalks or around workplaces.

Currently, there are many solutions that effectively reduce or eliminate bird strikes, but none that are universally applicable or readily acceptable for all human structures. Protective measures range from physical barriers that keep birds from striking to detractants that protect by transforming the area occupied by glass into uninviting space or a recognizable obstacle to be avoided. The manufacture of new varieties of sheet glass is recommended: panes having external patterns that alert birds to its presence but retain the current unaltered view from inside. Placement of bird feeders within one meter of the glass surface eliminates the hazard for visitors to these attractants. S/G/A

> 1.31 Some fatalities of window collisions become specimens in museum collections donated by the individuals who find them. A physical record can provide important information should the species suddenly go into decline. These specimens from the Smithsonian include a Hudsonian Godwit collected by Charles Darwin, a Cedar Waxwing from Theodore Roosevelt, a Rock Wren and Rufous-sided Towhee from John James Audubon, and an Orange-throated Tanager of a genus named after the sixth Smithsonian secretary, Alexander Wetmore.

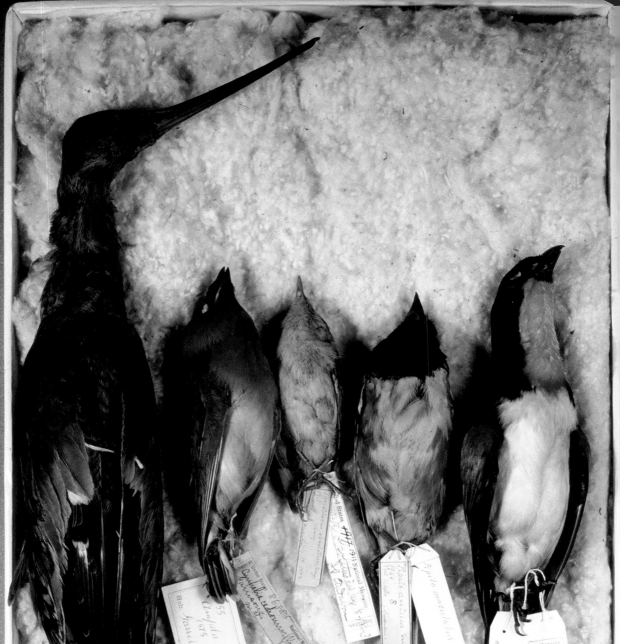

REFERENCES

American Ornithologists' Union. 1975. Report of the ad hoc committee on scientific educational use of wild birds. Auk 92 (Suppl.): 1A–27A.

Banks, R. C. 1979. Human related mortality of birds in the United States. U.S. Fish and Wildlife Service Special Report 215: 1–16.

Corcoran, L. M. 1999. Migratory Bird Treaty Act: strict criminal liability for nonhunting caused bird deaths. Denver University Law Review 77: 315–358.

Dunn, E. H. 1993. Bird mortality from striking residential windows in winter. J. Field Ornithology 64(3): 302–309.

Gelb, Y. and N. Delacretaz. 2006. Avian window strike mortality at an urban office building. The Kingbird 56(3): 190–198.

Graham, D. L. 1997. Spider webs and windows as potentially important sources of hummingbird mortality. J. Field Ornithology 68(1): 98–101.

Klem, D., Jr. 1981. Avian predators hunting birds near windows. Proceedings Pennsylvania Academy of Science 55: 90–92.

Klem, D., Jr. 1989. Bird-window collisions. Wilson Bulletin 101(4): 606–620.

Klem, D., Jr. 1990. Bird injuries, cause of death, and recuperation from collisions with windows. J. Field Ornithology 61(1): 115–119.

Klem, D., Jr. 1990. Collisions between birds and windows: mortality and prevention. J. Field Ornithology 61(1): 120–128.

Klem, D., Jr. 1991. Glass and bird kills: an overview and suggested planning and design methods of preventing a fatal hazard. In Wildlife Conservation in Metropolitan Environments NIUW Symposium Series 2, L. W. Adams and D. L. Leedy, Eds., National Institute for Urban Wildlife, MD, 99–104.

Klem, D., Jr. 2006. Glass: a deadly conservation is for birds. Bird Observer 34(2): 73–81.

Klem, D., Jr. 2007. Windows: an unintended fatal hazard for birds. In Connecticut State of the Birds Connecticut Audubon Society, Fairfield, CT, 7–12.

Klem, D., Jr., D. C. Keck, K. L. Marty, A. J. Miller Ba E. E. Niciu, and C. T. Platt. 2004. Effects of window angling, feeder placement, and scavengers on avi mortality at plate glass. Wilson Bulletin 116(1): 69

O'Connell, T. J. 2001. Avian window strike mortalit at a suburban office park. The Raven 72(2): 141–1

Ogden, L. J. E. 1996. Collision course: the hazards of lighted structures and windows to migrating bir World Wildlife Fund Canada and the Fatal Light Av ness Program.

Veltri, C. J. and D. Klem, Jr. 2005. Comparison of fa bird injuries from collisions with towers and windo J. Field Ornithology 76(2): 127–133.

BIRD COLLISIONS: CAUSES FOR INJURY AND ANTIDOTES

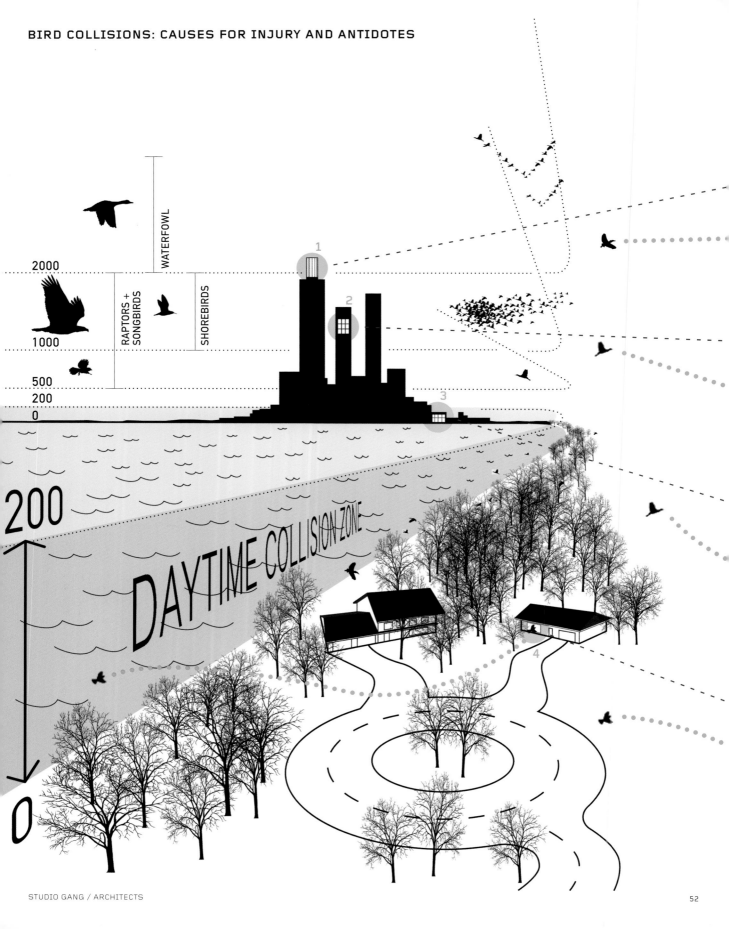

WATERFOWL

RAPTORS + SONGBIRDS

SHOREBIRDS

2000

1000

500

200

0

1

2

3

4

200

0

DAYTIME COLLISION ZONE

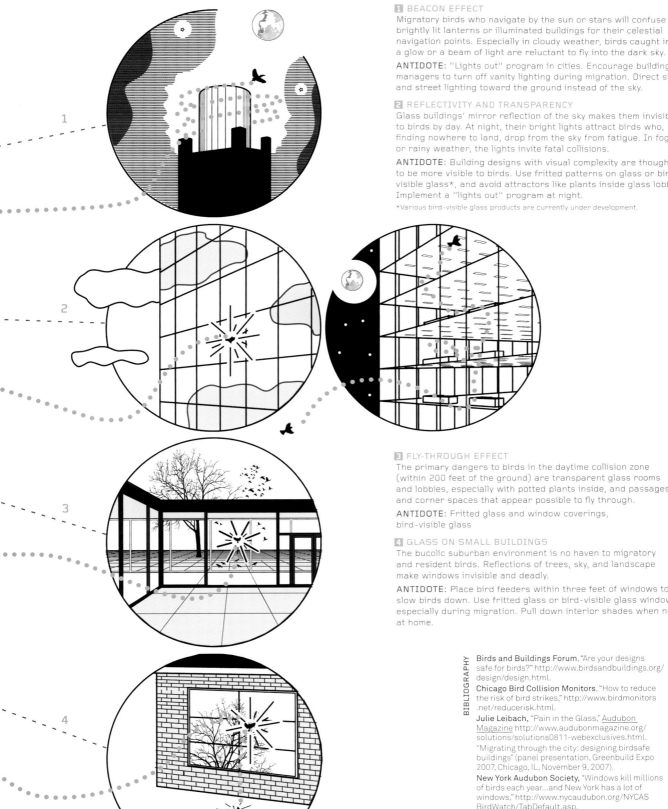

1 BEACON EFFECT

Migratory birds who navigate by the sun or stars will confuse brightly lit lanterns or illuminated buildings for their celestial navigation points. Especially in cloudy weather, birds caught in a glow or a beam of light are reluctant to fly into the dark sky.

ANTIDOTE: "Lights out" program in cities. Encourage building managers to turn off vanity lighting during migration. Direct site and street lighting toward the ground instead of the sky.

2 REFLECTIVITY AND TRANSPARENCY

Glass buildings' mirror reflection of the sky makes them invisible to birds by day. At night, their bright lights attract birds who, finding nowhere to land, drop from the sky from fatigue. In foggy or rainy weather, the lights invite fatal collisions.

ANTIDOTE: Building designs with visual complexity are thought to be more visible to birds. Use fritted patterns on glass or bird visible glass*, and avoid attractors like plants inside glass lobbies. Implement a "lights out" program at night.

*Various bird-visible glass products are currently under development.

3 FLY-THROUGH EFFECT

The primary dangers to birds in the daytime collision zone (within 200 feet of the ground) are transparent glass rooms and lobbies, especially with potted plants inside, and passages and corner spaces that appear possible to fly through.

ANTIDOTE: Fritted glass and window coverings, bird-visible glass

4 GLASS ON SMALL BUILDINGS

The bucolic suburban environment is no haven to migratory and resident birds. Reflections of trees, sky, and landscape make windows invisible and deadly.

ANTIDOTE: Place bird feeders within three feet of windows to slow birds down. Use fritted glass or bird-visible glass windows, especially during migration. Pull down interior shades when not at home.

BIBLIOGRAPHY

Birds and Buildings Forum, "Are your designs safe for birds?" http://www.birdsandbuildings.org/design/design.html.

Chicago Bird Collision Monitors, "How to reduce the risk of bird strikes," http://www.birdmonitors.net/reducerisk.html.

Julie Leibach, "Pain in the Glass," Audubon Magazine http://www.audubonmagazine.org/solutions/solutions0811-webexclusives.html.

"Migrating through the city: designing birdsafe buildings" (panel presentation, Greenbuild Expo 2007, Chicago, IL, November 9, 2007).

New York Audubon Society, "Windows kill millions of birds each year...and New York has a lot of windows," http://www.nycaudubon.org/NYCAS BirdWatch/TabDefault.asp.

Toronto Fatal Light Awareness Program (FLAP), "How to make windows safe for birds," http://www.flap.org/new/prefr.htm.

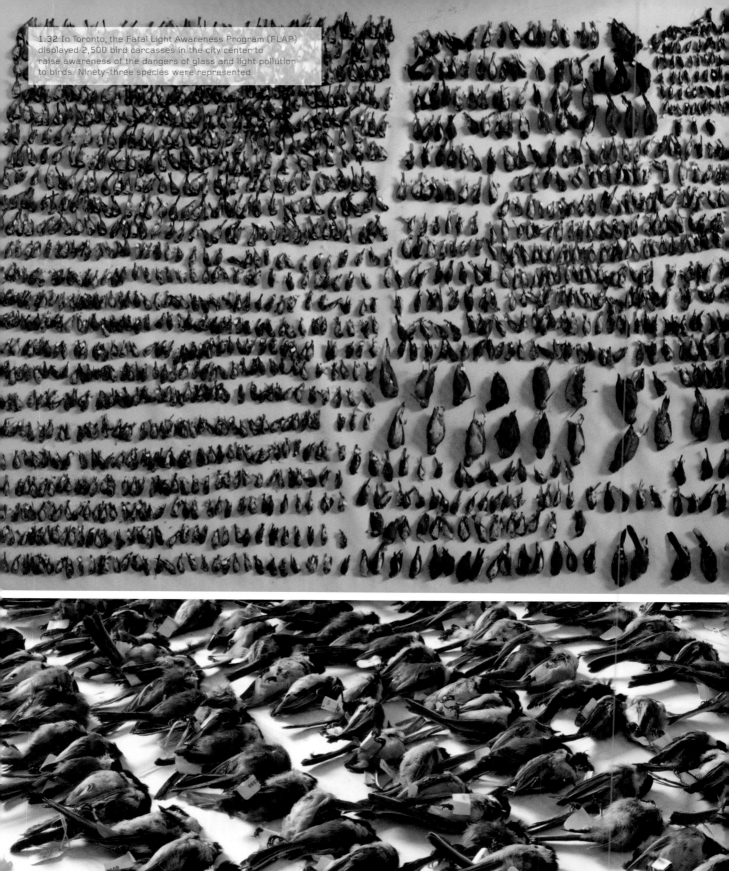

1.32 In Toronto, the Fatal Light Awareness Program (FLAP) displayed 2,500 bird carcasses in the city center to raise awareness of the dangers of glass and light pollution to birds. Ninety-three species were represented.

INTERVIEW / 6:00 AM MAY 1
MONITORING BIRD COLLISIONS IN THE CHICAGO LOOP

It was partly cloudy when I met up with Annette Prince, director of the Chicago Bird Collision Monitors. She had offered to take me along on her rounds in the Loop because I wanted to learn more about the particulars of bird strikes with buildings during the spring migration season. It was easy enough to spot her; she was wearing a khaki vest with a bright green bird collision monitor name tag around her neck, holding a bag with a butterfly net protruding from the back. We said "hello" and without any chitchat she moved into her ritual as if I weren't there. She advanced along the gridded blocks of downtown Chicago, scanning ahead for fallen birds.

Within a minute we were at the base of a tall building, approaching a small, gray lump on the ground. Annette had me stay back as she approached the fallen bird. With a swoop of her net she captured it, though it was immediately obvious that this unfortunate bird was going nowhere. Even though it was already dead, Annette pulled out a brown paper bag and inserted the carcass. With a marker she labeled the bag with the some vital information: the type of bird, time, date, and address, and a big "D" for dead. She placed it into her duffel bag and started off again.

A few doors down we descended into a plaza surrounded by lush vegetation and glass: a lethal combination for birds, according to Annette. In the plaza there were a few fallen birds lying near the glass. Again she netted and bagged the birds. Some were alive and some dead. She collected them quickly before the hovering gulls and crows could feast on them. Over the next hour Annette bagged eight more birds at both modern and historic-style buildings. By 6:55 her parking meter was about to expire. As we walked toward her car, she explained:

Annette Prince [AP] You know, one of the significant things is that birds die in any kind of a population. There's natural death, but when birds are killed by glass, it's indiscriminate. In nature, it's the weaker bird that dies, or the bird that doesn't survive the winter very well, or the slower bird. But the birds that hit windows could be the best breeding pair of a particular species, so we feel when we rescue some of these birds we're helping birds that the species could not really afford to lose; they aren't poor members of the species, they just don't understand what glass is.

Photographs by Mark Jackson (www.markjackson.ca)

Annette's cell phone rings and she answers, "Chicago Bird Collision Monitors....It's Kelly, he's coming around the corner."

A man approaches us carrying an enormous dead Brown Thrasher, one of the extraordinary variety we had collected that morning. Kelly, a well-dressed, forty-something environmental consultant, exemplified the fact that volunteers come from many walks of life. I was impressed that he took time to collect (with his bare hands) this victim and call the monitors. Annette manages over ninety volunteers with seven to ten patrolling every day during migration, which lasts several months. The monitors collect approximately 5,000 birds in a year. Around 2,000 are rescued and released while over half are found dead. Annette bags the bird Kelly found and we climb in the car as she responds to calls on her cell phone.

Jeanne Gang [JG] So have you ever found birds that are rare or endangered?

AP Yes, a lot of birds we find are. One of the birds we find most often is the Brown Creeper, and a couple years ago that was a threatened species. We've gotten rare birds like Yellow Rails; we've had both live and dead. We've gotten a Least Bittern, which is another species that's on the endangered species list in Illinois. We got a Least Bittern last year. We get birds that are seldom found, like a Worm-eating Warbler. We've collected a Clay-colored Sparrow, which is not often seen.

JG And Annette why are these birds important to people, why is it important to rescue them?

AP There's the aspect that they're an important part of the balance of nature. They're major controllers of insect populations. They're involved in pollination of plants and distribution of seeds, so they're an important part of the environment and that connection. They certainly just have the aesthetic value; people enjoy having them. And we do get birds, things like hawks, colliding with buildings; we're talking about a bird that controls rodent populations, as do owls; we have had owls that hit buildings. So birds are an indicator species: they're indicative of the overall health of an ecosystem. Besides the fact that people enjoy them, they're part of the balance.

And there are aspects we don't even know. They're a part of the puzzle and you don't want to throw any parts away. And these birds, many of them that we're finding are already being stressed by loss of habitat and the species can't afford to lose individuals. They say that after habitat loss—it's the second largest cause of death for birds—is migratory bird collisions. So it's right up there in the ranks.

We stop to pick up Janet Pellegrini, another volunteer and an environmental scientist with the United States Environmental Protection Agency. The first call-in we respond to is from a building manager that has found a bird. Janet and Annette work together like rehearsed professionals. Janet jumps out to pick up the bird while Annette stays with the car until she returns.

Janet Pellegrini [JP] That bird was stunned, but it either got away or, well, we couldn't find it.

JG So that was another call from a building manager? Your phone seems to be ringing constantly now.

AP Yes, when I have a busy morning we get lots of calls from the public and building people, that was staff—maintenance staff—and people on their way to work who see things. We try and encourage people who are there to do something about it because they're right on the spot.

JG Are some buildings worse than others? I can imagine it could be damaging for a building to be known as a particularly deadly building and they might not want to help you.

AP They do help; they pick the birds up. We have really cooperative relationships, and buildings have come to us and said, "Help us fix our building." That's why we don't name names, or want buildings listed in the stories we do tell; we don't attack buildings. There are a lot of people who want us to be very adversarial, slam the dead bird down and tell people what they're doing to these birds. But we don't take pictures of buildings. Others have been adversarial and buildings say they don't want to work with them. But buildings come to us and say that they want to work with us because they appreciate the fact that we know they don't want these birds to die. You, as an architect, understand that it's not intentional. There's a place for protest but that's not our approach. We've rescued more birds because we have people who are allies in this cause who we're helping to find solutions. It makes a big difference.

AT THE RENDEZVOUS LOCATION, 7:30 AM

We head to East Wacker Drive where other volunteers are gathering and loading their bird bags into the "day captain's" car. She will be driving them to a wildlife rehabilitation center where the live ones will recover and later be released into the wild. Some of the volunteers are consulting a guide book to identify the birds they have found. According to the U.S. Fish and Wildlife Service, there are over five hundred different species in the Midwest region, including migratory birds. Even for birders they can be hard to identify. Each of the volunteers will later enter their information into a database. I find myself mesmerized by a strange triangular-bodied bird with a yellow beak and silvery green legs. It's an amazing-looking creature, but unfortunately it's dead. It's called a Sora, I'm told.

JG Do you ever call to find out whatever happened to your birds? Do you get a report?

JP We get a report usually at the end of the season, sometimes at the start of the next season because they've had to process so many birds. We don't bother them trying to follow up, we'll find out later. The report just says whether they survived or not. We enter it into a database. When we get reports, then we know what the outcome of the bird was. Sometimes we don't know the ID, and you're not supposed to take a lot of time to ID it, you're supposed to just get it in the bag—so you might think that it's some kind of funny sparrow and then later you get the ID back from whoever rehabbed it and the day it was found, so then you know exactly.

JG What time do you have to get up to volunteer with the bird monitors?

AP Normally, I start work at about 8:00 AM. But on Tuesdays when I volunteer, I get up at 3:30 AM because I have to catch the train, and the Brown line, and then I transfer to the Red, and then Sarah picks me up down here at five. That's why I only do it one day a week. It's tough when I have important meetings scheduled for Tuesday.

JG Why do you do this? There are so many bird collisions, do you feel like you're making a difference?

JP Oh definitely. Every bird you pick up, you're making a difference in that particular bird's life and helping the species overall. I mean, these birds have so many hurdles during migration, it's a shame that they have to deal with glass, too. And they've almost made it; it's like they're on third base; they're almost home when they get to Canada.

AP Exactly. They've traveled all these miles, they fly all night, and there's weather and thunder and all that, and then they hit a window. The birds that we see in the spring are birds that made it all the way south safely, survive on wintering grounds with all the perils that are there with habitat loss and predation, and pesticides—and then they made it this far north past a bunch of other cities and then they hit a window. So these birds somehow, to me, seem even more tragic. These are the survivors; these are the birds that survived all kinds of other things. Each travels hundreds or thousands of miles, not just once in their life, they do it twice a year, every year. And I just find it astounding.

JG It is amazing.

AP They're troopers. They're little birds that weigh only a few ounces. I always say that if you asked me to walk to Mexico, and gave me all the time I wanted, I wouldn't do it, I'd get so far and I'd stop. And then you'd tell me that when I got there I would have to turn around and walk back. Because that's what these birds are essentially doing, they're getting down there and—

JP Wait, but first they have to have babies, and raise them and THEN come all the way back. [They laugh.]

AP All different people help with the rescue: retired people, working people, young people. There's something really amazing just about coming into contact with these animals—that they've been so far and they're so precious. I see it as a privilege that I can save these birds. They're part of this amazing migration. And if there's something that we can do to help that, it's simply a privilege. S/G/A

∧1.33 Rescued birds are taken to a rehabilitation center to recover and be released back into the wild.
›1.34 A bird rescuer uses a guide to identify the Swamp Sparrow that was found dead.

SECTION THROUGH CONSTRUCTION ASSEMBLY

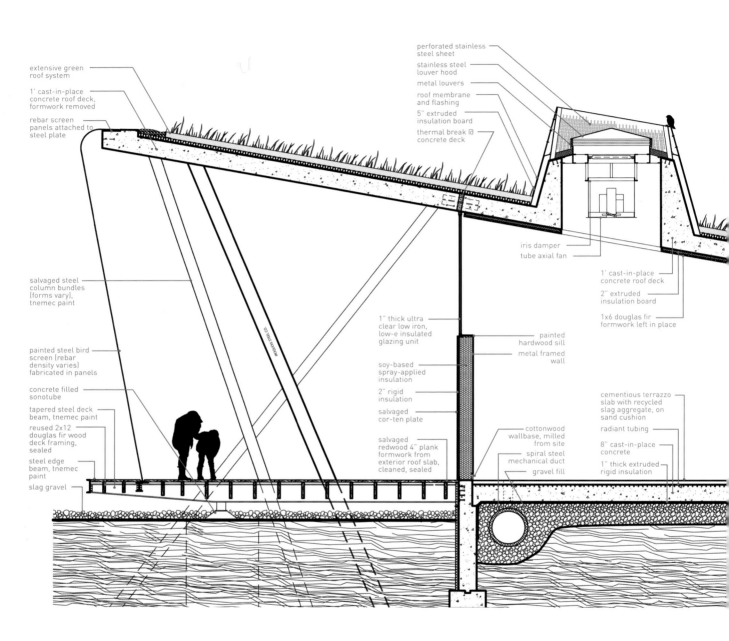

extensive green
roof system

1' cast-in-place
concrete roof deck,
formwork removed

rebar screen
panels attached to
steel plate

salvaged steel
column bundles
(forms vary),
tnemec paint

painted steel bird
screen (rebar
density varies)
fabricated in panels

concrete filled
sonotube

tapered steel deck
beam, tnemec paint

reused 2x12
douglas fir wood
deck framing,
sealed

steel edge
beam, tnemec
paint

slag gravel

perforated stainless
steel sheet

stainless steel
louver hood

metal louvers

roof membrane
and flashing

5" extruded
insulation board

thermal break @
concrete deck

iris damper
tube axial fan

1' cast-in-place
concrete roof deck

2" extruded
insulation board

1x6 douglas fir
formwork left in place

1" thick ultra
clear low iron,
low-e insulated
glazing unit

soy-based
spray-applied
insulation

2" rigid
insulation

salvaged
cor-ten plate

salvaged
redwood 4" plank
formwork from
exterior roof slab,
cleaned, sealed

painted
hardwood sill

metal framed
wall

cottonwood
wallbase, milled
from site

spiral steel
mechanical duct

gravel fill

cementious terrazzo
slab with recycled
slag aggregate, on
sand cushion

radiant tubing

8" cast-in-place
concrete

1" thick extruded
rigid insulation

1.35 Detailed cross section through exhibition space and porch

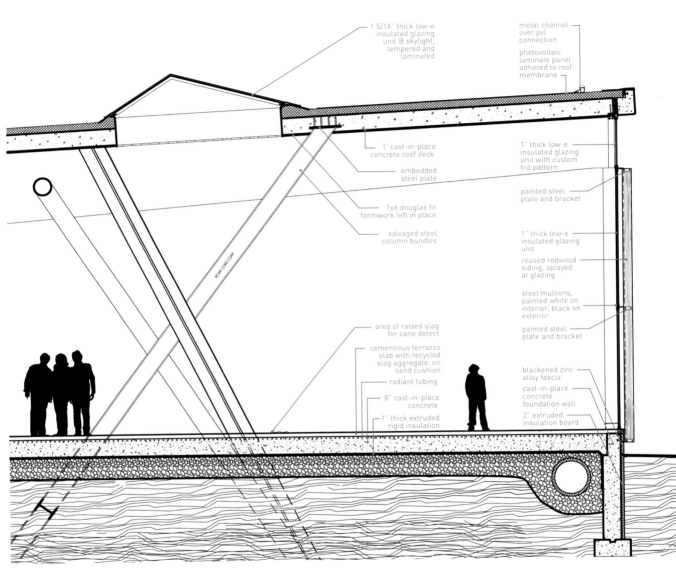

1 5/16" thick low-e insulated glazing unit @ skylight, tempered and laminated

metal channel over pvl connection

photovoltaic laminate panel adhered to roof membrane

1' cast-in-place concrete roof deck

embedded steel plate

1x6 douglas fir formwork left in place

salvaged steel column bundles

1" thick low-e insulated glazing unit with custom frit pattern

painted steel plate and bracket

1" thick low-e insulated glazing unit

reused redwood siding, splayed at glazing

steel mullions, painted white on interior, black on exterior

painted steel plate and bracket

area of raised slag for cane detect

cementious terrazzo slab with recycled slag aggregate, on sand cushion

radiant tubing

8" cast-in-place concrete

1" thick extruded rigid insulation

blackened zinc alloy fascia

cast-in-place concrete foundation wall

2" extruded insulation board

2'   4'   6'   8'   10'

PROJECT / FORD CALUMET ENVIRONMENTAL CENTER

1.36 Night view across slag garden

FORD CALUMET INDUSTRIAL LANDSCAPE
A VISUAL INVENTORY OF SALVAGED MATERIALS

Materials of all sorts find their way into a recycling circuit that exists out of sight on Chicago's South Side. Inside large warehouses, materials are collected, sorted, smashed, traded, and sold. Outside, abandoned structures from a bygone era of industrial production wait for their turn to be dismantled and scrapped. Photographed September 2007.

1.37 Aluminum pipe, various diameters
1.38 Solid aluminum sections; machine parts
1.39 Uncoiled electrical copper cables
1.40 Radiators from automobiles
1.41 Stamped parts from metal plates leave behind useful grillage for use as fencing.
1.42 Tiny stainless steel discs
1.43 Brass stamped plate and rod
1.44 Solid steel rod, flash rusted
1.45 Corrugated copper tubes
1.46 Trimmings from flat copper sheet
1.47 Sorted copper bundles
1.48 Copy machine rollers
1.49 Bundled steel highway signs
1.50 Galvanized steel wire
1.51 Aluminum juice and soda cans
1.52 Reclaimed wooden timber

1.37

1.38

1.39

PROJECT / FORD CALUMET ENVIRONMENTAL CENTER

1.40

1.41

1.42

1.43

1.44

1.45

1.46

1.47

1.48

1.49

A BRIEF HISTORY *of the* CALUMET AREA

WHEN PREHISTORIC LAKE CHICAGO RECEDED, A SERIES OF FRESHWATER FINGER LAKES FORMED IN THE CALUMET REGION, CREATING A ECOLOGICALLY DIVERSE AREA WITH THREE MAJOR BIOMES: EASTERN DECIDUOUS FORESTS, BOREAL REMNANTS, AND TALL GRASSLAND. THE GREATER CALUMET WET-LANDS EXTEND EAST FROM LAKE CALUMET TO INDIANA AND CONTAIN MARSHES, SHRUB SWAMPS, AND PRAIRIE REMNANTS.

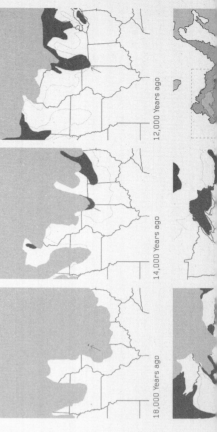

12,000 Years ago

14,000 Years ago

18,000 Years ago

Native Americans once tracked through this region on trails that were later replaced by diagonal streets and highways running contrary to the Chicago grid. The first major man-made intrusions into the Calumet region, however, came from railroad development and commercial and industrial growth along the Calumet River. After the Civil War, America's iron and steel industries came to Calumet, lured by cheap, vacant land, access to water transportation, rail connections, available labor, and space to dump waste materials. Other industries came to the region, including a Ford Motor Company assembly plant, a General Mills grain elevator, flour and cereal mills, and the State Line Generating Station's power plant.

The region's heavy industry had huge environmental consequences. Between 1869 and 1921, industrial wastes such as phenols, cyanides, pickle liquor, and sulfuric acid were dumped directly into the river, and much of the solid waste from the mills was dumped on vacant marshland. By 2007 there were 423 hazardous waste sites and 460 hazardous storage tanks around the river, causing the Environmental Protection Agency to label it an "area of concern."[1]

The greatest detriments to the landscape, however, came from the extension of the shoreline

ATLANTIC

The great lakes basin is a glacial memory and a rich aquatic landscape of wetlands.

10,000 Years ago

8,000 Years ago

BWQ-3-33

II-1438

dredging spoils, and slag (a byproduct of steel production). These materials stabilized Chicago's soft soil for future roads, railroads, and buildings, leaving only 500 of the original 20,000 acres of wetlands.

Landfills developed in the Calumet region in the 1940s. A landfill is a waste-disposal technique that utilizes a bottom liner to create a tub that is covered daily by a layer of soil. If the bottom liner fails, waste migrates into the groundwater. Landfills have posed numerous environmental threats in Calumet. The Paxton 2 landfill, for example, was opened in 1976 and closed in 1992 due to cover problems. In 1999, Paxton 2 was in danger of collapsing into a neighboring business. Leachate, a toxic substance, had to be pumped out to relieve the pressure on the sides of the landfill.

Because of the ecological damage by heavy industry and by landfills, a strong grassroots environmental movement in Calumet gained momentum in the 1970s. The citizenry, accustomed to organizing labor negotiations, proved to be particularly effective at mobilizing for environmental causes. Many environmentalist groups formed, giving former steel workers and their families a new identity as the mills started to disappear.

In 1988, a referendum that prohibited future landfills on Chicago's southeast side overwhelmingly passed in the 10th ward, and a proposal for an airport in the region was defeated in 1992. In 1993, the Calumet Ecological Park Association formed, in 1998 the National Park Service designated the Calumet region a National Heritage area, and the Chicago Department of Environment announced plans to build an environmental center there. Despite the fact that the mills and other heavy industry have either closed down entirely or have reduced operations, little remediation has rectified the widespread environmental contamination in the region. Meanwhile, invasive plant species, such as purple loosestrife, garlic mustard, and phragmites, have altered native wetlands.

To balance the future of economic and environmental interests in the region, the City's Department of Environment developed the Lake Calumet Economic-Ecosystem Initiative Project, which has provided the groundwork for cleaning up abandoned industrial sites while restoring the ecology of adjacent natural areas.

In June 2000, Mayor Daley and then-Governor Ryan announced a plan that called for the creation of the Calumet Open Space Preserve to protect 3,000 acres from development. It includes the cleanup of sites near the Paxton landfill and creating renewable energy. In an effort to maintain bird migration through the area, the City of Chicago in conjunction with several state and national agencies implemented a plan in June 2007 to create "a road map for protecting plants and wildlife" while the Calumet area is restored.[2] The plan begins at the site of the new Ford Calumet Environmental Center and will guide the preservation of wildlife, bird migration, and natural environment in an area once contaminated by toxic sludge.

SGA

BIBLIOGRAPHY

Greenberg, Joel. A Natural History of the Chicago Region. Chicago: The University of Chicago Press, 2002.
Sellers, Ron. Chicago's Southeast Side Revisited. Chicago: Arcadia Publishing, 2001.

Notes

1. United States Environmental Protection Agency. "Grand Calumet River Area of Concern." http://www.epa.gov/glnpo/aoc/grandcal.html.
2. "Mayor Daley Announces Protocol for Protecting Calumet Region's Plants and Animals," (press release, City of Chicago Department of the Environment, Chicago, IL, June 9, 2007).

1.56

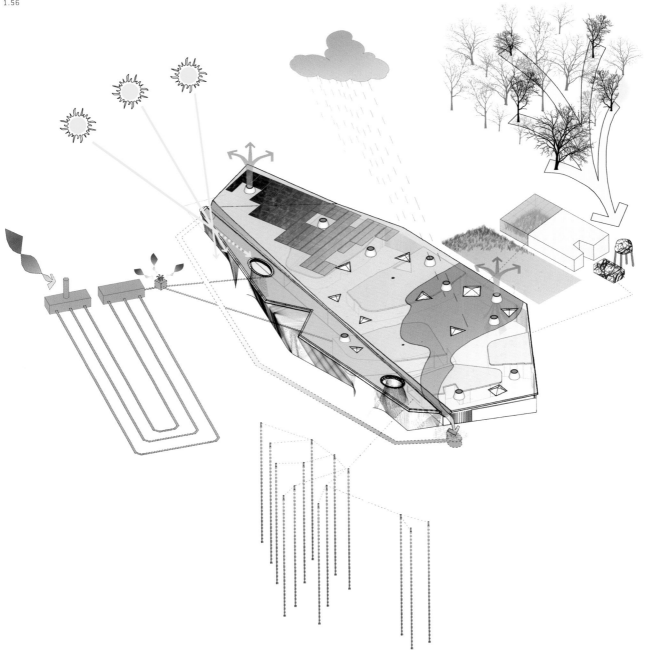

< **1.53** (page 69, above fold) Workers laid tracks through Hyde Lake to connect Chicago's East Side neighborhood with Hegewisch in 1915. Railroads generally followed the sand ridges that existed between cattail marshes. Image courtesy of the Southeast Chicago Historical Society.

1.54 (page 69, on fold) Recession of the last glaciation of the Great Lakes region

1.55 (page 70) This aerial photograph from 1938 shows a newly straightened Little Calumet canal running adjacent to the faint arc of the filled-in river bed. Across Torrance Avenue, street outlines indicate the growth of the Hegewisch community. Illinois Aerial Photograph collection, University of Illinois at Urbana-Champaign Library.

1.56 A synthesis of environmental systems allows the building to act more like a living organism by using minimal energy to maintain comfort. It starts with the simple orientation of the building with its long dimension along an east-west axis. The south-facing facade is shaded by a large overhanging roof tilted to allow winter sun inside while keeping summer sun out. Earth's moderate temperature is tapped through geothermal boreholes to reduce both heating and cooling loads. In addition, an earth tube circles laterally at a shallower depth to pick up the moderate temperature for air distribution. Inside air is distributed low and exhausted up high through the roof using natural displacement ventilation. Solar panels produce the energy needed for the building from a renewable source. Extra heating or cooling for extreme outdoor temperatures is offered by a biomass boiler fed by wood chips and roadside clippings. Rain water is collected on the roof and used for flushing. Waste water is then treated metabolically and through plants prior to being released onto the site.

MATERIAL REPORT: SAMURAI SWORDS OF STEEL
METALLURGY MADE VISIBLE

Steel is an unusual material. Unlike many metals, it can assume different types of crystalline structures depending on its chemistry, temperature, and rate of cooling. Strength, ductility, and other properties of steel depend on which crystalline structure has formed. Samurai sword craftsmen masterfully manipulated the properties and visual qualities of steel over a thousand years ago without modern tools or industry.

Today, high-heat furnaces and precise rates of cooling are used to transform the desired crystal structure. Chemically, the amount of carbon in steel is critical to its character. Carbon can be added or subtracted from the mixture at any time during the process with heat, and can also be physically forced out. Hammering steel breaks up large pieces of slag, reduces the carbon content, and increases its hardness by reducing the impurities that get in between the crystal structures. While modern metallurgy and the electron microscope have aided widespread understanding of crystal structures of steel, samurai sword makers working centuries ago had already started to discover these properties and to manipulate them for the production of their steel blades.

The intricate beauty of the sword begins with the raw material. Japanese smiths smelted iron ore and extracted the impurities to make ingots. Because of the moderate temperature of their furnaces, sword makers could never fully extract carbon and impurities from the iron and had to melt the varying ingots they produced with steel plates to achieve the right balance of strength and ductility. During a second firing, the layered composition melted together into a solid block of steel that visually retained its variegated layers.

The newly fused block, called kawagane, became the outer layer of a two-part composite sword blade through a lengthy process of forging and folding. Experienced smiths could "read" the steel mixture as they folded and hammered it onto itself up to 20 times to produce a material of approximately 32,000 layers. Between each fold the blade was repeatedly hammered, increasing the strength of the steel at every turn. If the smith sensed that too much carbon was being hammered away, he could coat it with plant or organic material before reheating it in the furnace. Ultimately, folding a layered piece of steel resulted in a strong and solid block with fine strata of darker and lighter layers. This created a grainy pattern, not unlike a wood grain, that became a permanent visible feature of the sword blade that was manipulated by the sword smith for intensity and contrast.

One of the secrets behind the excellence of Japanese swords was the composite blade. In addition to the kawagane, a softer piece of steel became the core of the blade. The softer steel core with a harder steel edge made the sword blade an optimal weapon: extremely strong for fighting, flexible for agility, and light for wielding. The kawagane steel was folded into a V and then folded around the core to create the sword edge.

To further harden the blade edge, the steel had to reach extreme temperatures and be cooled quickly. The smiths added another level of refinement to this step that produced the most distinctive and effective features of the samurai sword. The blade was coated in a clay mixture that was reheated in the furnace and then quickly quenched in cold water. When quenched, the heated steel molecules turned into distinctive forms of crystal microstructures. The clay insulated the steel from the cold temperature of the water so that thinly coated areas around the blade cooled faster than areas with a thicker coating and took on the hardest form of crystal structure called martensite. Those with a thicker coating took the form of a moderately hard micro-structure called austenite. A meandering line formed between these juxtaposed crystal structures and traced the smith's gesture when patterning the clay.

This meandering line is called the hamon and tells a great deal about the sword. Primarily, it resists shear across the transition of harder and softer metals and offers more resistance to shear parallel to the blade than a straight line. The particular character of the line can be used to identify the smith or the school under which he trained. Because the lightness of the line depended on the intensity of the smith's furnace, a variable that usually varied from region to region, the hamon could even be used to place the work geographically.

Despite its graphic beauty, the samurai sword was not purely decorative. The metal smith's understanding of raw material at a microscopic level, combined with the process of working that material, created an artifact and a formidable weapon. Every step in the process of making the blade is critical to technical performance. Although the samurai sword exemplifies a process of experimentation and design that we quaintly call craft, its development is remarkable because it foreshadows, by a thousand years, the science that we know today as material engineering and microscopic metallurgy. S/G/A

BIBLIOGRAPHY

Brandt, Daniel A. and J. C. Warner. Metallurgy Fundamentals. Tinley Park, IL: The Goodheart-Willcox Company, Inc., 1999.
Eberhart, Mark E. Why Things Break: Understanding the World by the Way It Comes Apart. New York: Harmony Books, 2003.
Kapp, Leon, Hiroko Kapp, and Yoshindo Yoshihara. The Craft of the Japanese Sword. Tokyo, Japan: Kodansha International Ltd., 1987.
Olin, Harold B. Construction Principles, Materials & Methods. 4th ed. Chicago: The Institute of Financial Education, 1980.
Schulitz, Helmut C., Werner Sobek, and Karl J. Habermann. Steel Construction Manual. Basel, Switzerland: Birkhäuser Publishers, 2000.
Smith, Cyril Stanley. A History of Metallography: The Development of Ideas on the Structure of Metals before 1890. Chicago: The University of Chicago Press, 1960.
Wertime, Theodore A. The Coming of the Age of Steel. Chicago: The University of Chicago Press, 1962.

1.57 Samurai sword blades show the microscopic distribution of carbon through their color. The harder material with less carbon is lighter in color and used at the leading edge of the blade. A gradual color transition from front to back is visible evidence of the material manipulation. Distinctive meandering lines on the blades reveal the crafts-man's refinement of technique and mastery of steel which is achieved though controlled heating and quenching.

CONCEPT FOR SITE TRANSITION TOWARD ENVIRONMENTAL REGENERATION

One hundred and thirty acres of Lake Michigan wetlands—a type of ecosystem on the verge of complete extinction—exist on this site. Over the years, the filling and rechanneling of the river, fly dumping, and the introduction of invasive species have damaged the site. The sequence of site activities provides a road map to restoring its health and developing the community's ecosystem ethic.

1.58 1932: OLD CALUMET RIVER COURSE

1.59 2004: START WITH WHAT IS THERE: PHYTOREMEDIATE
● Lead ● Chromium ● Arsenic ● Benzine
Emergent Industrial Marsh: cottonwood, phragmites, atta

1.60 YEARS 1–6: MAGNIFY THE SITE
Construct environmental center and canoe launch.
Celebrate industry. Reuse the rail. Reuse the slag.

1.61 YEARS 6–12: CULTIVATE, NEST, PERCH, FORAGE
Construct marsh overlook perch.

KEY: LANDSCAPE TYPOLOGIES

1 RIVERBED sedge meadow: carex sp., switchgrass, bluejoint grass, blue lobelia, shadbush, winterberry, sweetflag
2 COTTONWOOD COPSE to remain
3 PINE GROVE white pine at south & east buffers site from highway
4 FUELWOOD PLANTING black locust – 'nurse crop' for black walnut
5 PHYTODETOXIFICATION LAYER: 5a yellow poplar; 5b fern; 5c cordgrass, indian mustard
6 SUMAC THICKET smooth sumac, staghorn sumac

7 MAPLE SWAMP red maple, silver maple, black cherry, nannyberry, arrowwood
8 PIONEER OLD FIELDS eastern red cedar, little bluestem, side-oats grama, prairie dropseed, indian grass, goldenrod
9 OAK STAND quercus bicolor, q. rubra, q. imbricaria, q. rubra, spicebush, sassafras understory
10 HICKORY MIX bitternut, shagbark, dogwood, hawthorn, viburnums, vitis sp.
11 MARSH LAND reconnect with river

Site plans and succession images courtesy of Kate Orff / SCAPE

1.62 YEARS 18-24: CULTIVATE AN ECOSYSTEM ETHIC
Observe, participate in, and celebrate community and environmental regeneration.

FOREST SUCCESSION: A PROCESS OF PATTERENED RE-GROWTH AND CHANGE OVER TIME

1.63 Plant and tree species grow in cleared areas in a certain ordered progression leading up to the development of a mature and climatic forest. This proposal speeds up the progression through human intervention.

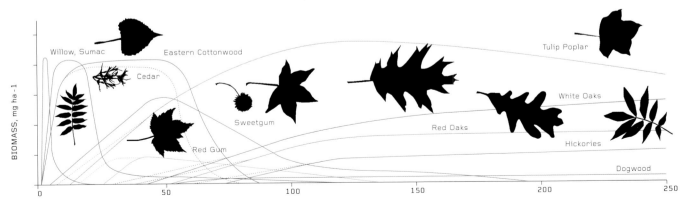

AGE OF STAND INDICATED IN YEARS
Dashed line represents adjusted time line through intervention.

PROJECT / FORD CALUMET ENVIRONMENTAL CENTER

CURRENT BIODIVERSITY AT HEGEWISCH MARSH

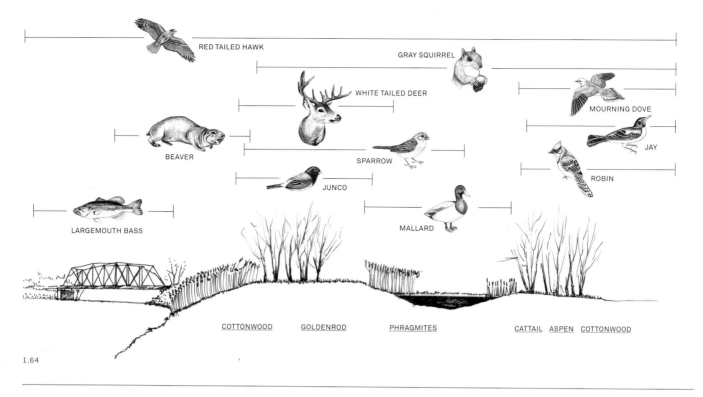

RED TAILED HAWK

GRAY SQUIRREL

WHITE TAILED DEER

MOURNING DOVE

JAY

BEAVER

SPARROW

ROBIN

JUNCO

LARGEMOUTH BASS

MALLARD

COTTONWOOD   GOLDENROD   PHRAGMITES   CATTAIL ASPEN COTTONWOOD

1.64

PROJECTED ADDITIONS TO BIODIVERSITY AT HEGEWISCH MARSH

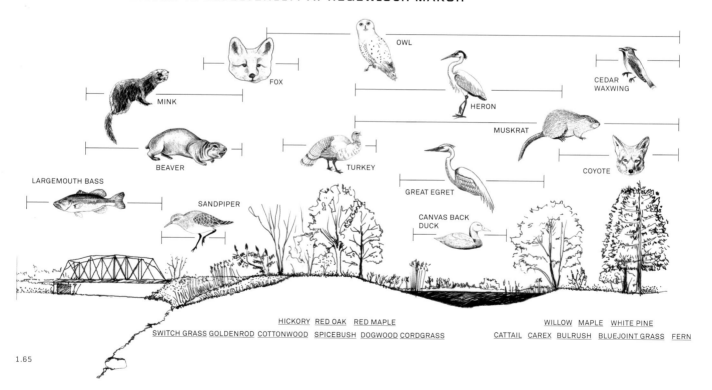

OWL

FOX

CEDAR WAXWING

MINK

HERON

MUSKRAT

BEAVER

TURKEY

COYOTE

LARGEMOUTH BASS

GREAT EGRET

SANDPIPER

CANVAS BACK DUCK

HICKORY RED OAK RED MAPLE

WILLOW MAPLE WHITE PINE

SWITCH GRASS GOLDENROD COTTONWOOD SPICEBUSH DOGWOOD CORDGRASS   CATTAIL CAREX BULRUSH BLUEJOINT GRASS FERN

1.65

1.64, 1.65 Along with the restoration of the site and succession of its plant species, a host of new animal species will be able to survive due to the more diverse food and habitat available.

1.66 View toward the railroad bridge from the western edge of the site

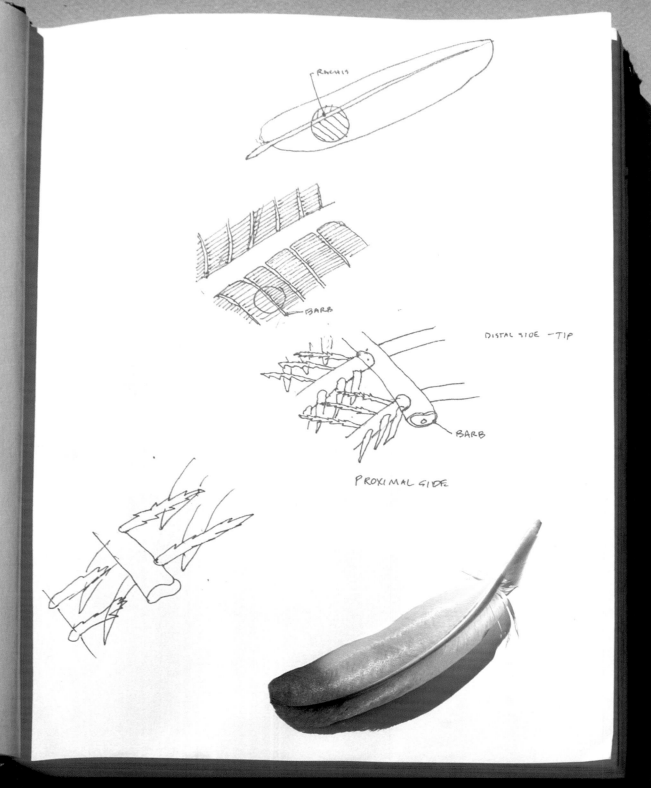

RACHIS

BARB

DISTAL SIDE —TIP

BARB

PROXIMAL SIDE

Sketch of feather at close scale

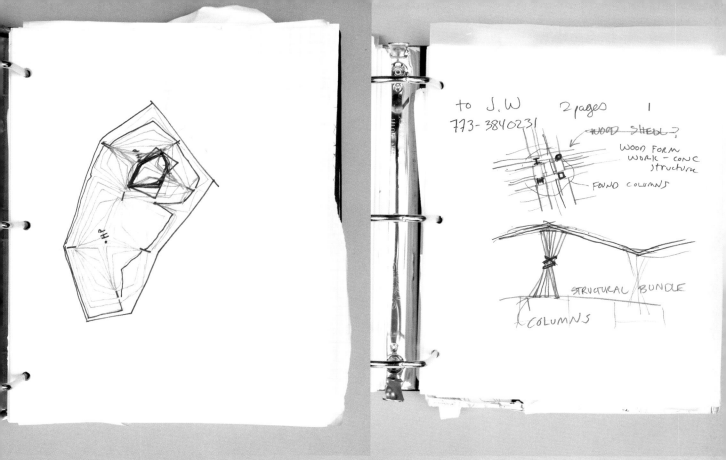

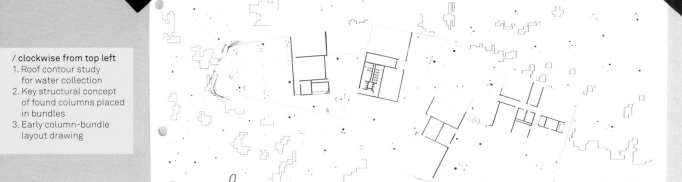

/ clockwise from top left
1. Roof contour study
   for water collection
2. Key structural concept
   of found columns placed
   in bundles
3. Early column-bundle
   layout drawing

EXTEA-R

PROJECT / FORD CALUMET ENVIRONMENTAL CENTER

STRUCTURE

Mark

From:	Lynda Dossey ▓▓▓▓▓▓▓▓▓
Sent:	Wednesday, March 17, 2004 10:13 AM
To:	Thorsten Johann; Jay Hoffman; Jeanne Gang; Mark
Subject:	FW: Calumet

-----Original Message-----
From: Ehsan, Faz [mailto:▓▓▓▓▓▓▓▓▓▓▓▓▓▓]
Sent: Saturday, March 13, 2004 7:02 PM
To: '▓▓▓▓▓▓▓▓▓▓▓▓▓'
Cc: Burns, Joseph
Subject: RE: Calumet

Hi Lynda:
Please see below for some comments. I will be out of the office on Monday and Tuesday -
back on Wednesday. Thanks Faz

> -----Original Message-----
> From: Lynda Dossey [SMTP:▓▓▓▓▓▓▓▓▓▓▓▓▓▓]
> Sent: Wednesday, March 10, 2004 9:28 AM
> To: Faz Ehsan
> Subject: Calumet
>
> Good Morning Faz!
>
> A brand new day: Brand new questions.
>
> 7-b. In reference to your 8" roof slab, is that based on max 25'-0"
> spacing between bundled column centerlines or 25'-0" Max spacing
> between column connection points to the roof slab? I realize I should
> have clarified the distinction in the original question, my apologies.
> [FEhsan] For single columns, the 25' span would be the distance to
> column centerlines. However, in the case of bundled columns as
> envisioned in your scheme, we are creating a virtual column capital
> (those inverted cone shapes you see near the top of columns at parking
> garages, for instance). In this case we should be able to go upto
> about 28 ft to the center of the column bundle with an 8 inch slab.
> However, we may have to come up with some stiffening elements for the
> green roof loads. Do you know how thick the soil needs to be, or are
> you planning to use a product such as Greengrid (I think)?
>
> Bird Mesh; We are thinking of having two layers of rebar screen with a
> gap of 4" between the rebar centerlines. They would connect at the
> top to the Roof slab and at the base to the Wood deck. The Vertical
> height spans range between 9'-0" and 16'-0" 12. Can we embed angles
> into the edge of the roof slab and then tack weld the rebar to the
> angles; will it be enough surface area for welding a structural
> connection? the idea is that we never see the edge of the roof
> slab. [FEhsan]   (pls see below)
> 13. Will we need to push-pull the rebar layers together and weld at
> strategic points along their length to help reinforce the mesh
> structurally? What is the best way to make the net stable? [FEhsan]   I
> think we may want to use something called "welded wire fabric". This
> stuff comes in pre-assembled sheets, woven together and spot welded.
> We can specify the spacing between the bars (they come spaced anywhere
> from 2 to 12-inches in one-inch increments - you can mix and match to
> provide some variation). Also, you have the option of using plain
> (smooth) or deformed (bumpy) wires or rebar, perhaps even galvanized
> or painted. The net will be flexible, which is OK. However, we have
> to recognize that the net will be too tempting for kids to resist -
> they will be climbing all over it. Hence it might be a better idea
> for the net to wrap over the top of the slab and get positively
> anchored into the slab from the top.
>
> Looking forward to these and other responses.
>
>
> Sincerely,
>
> Lynda A Dossey, AIA
>

28'-0"

NOT WELDED WIRE FABRIC

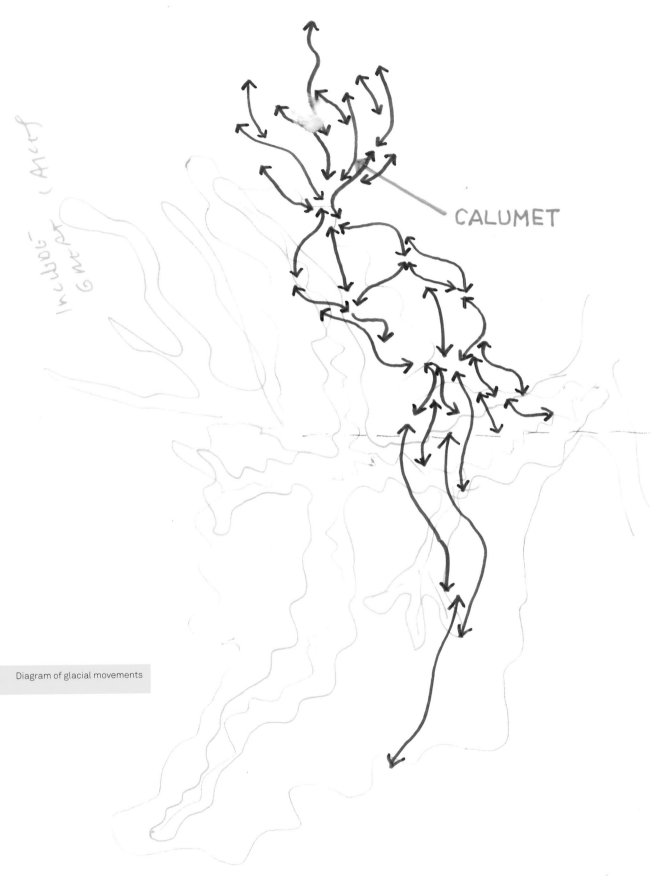

CALUMET

Diagram of glacial movements

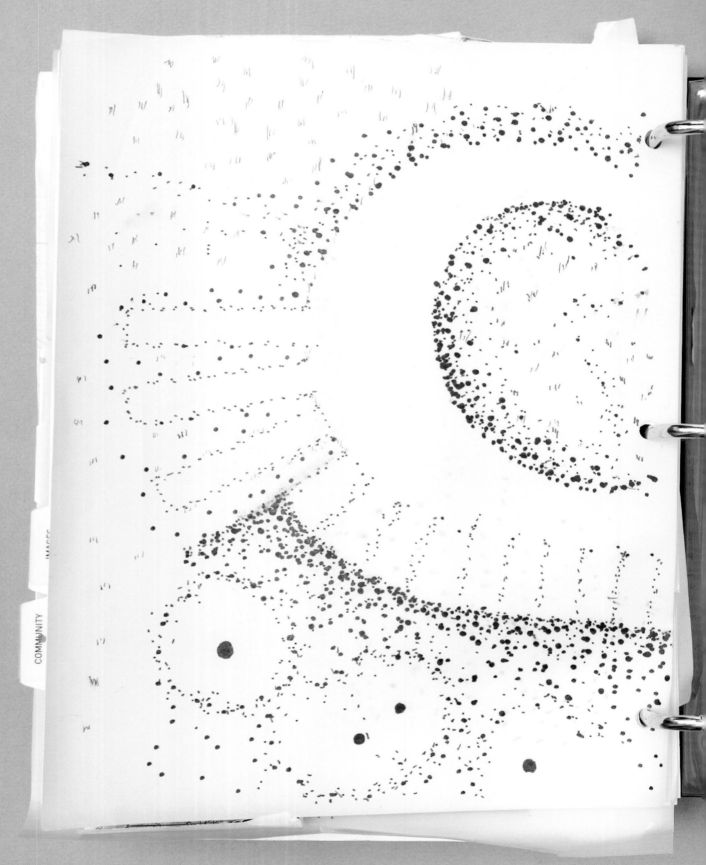

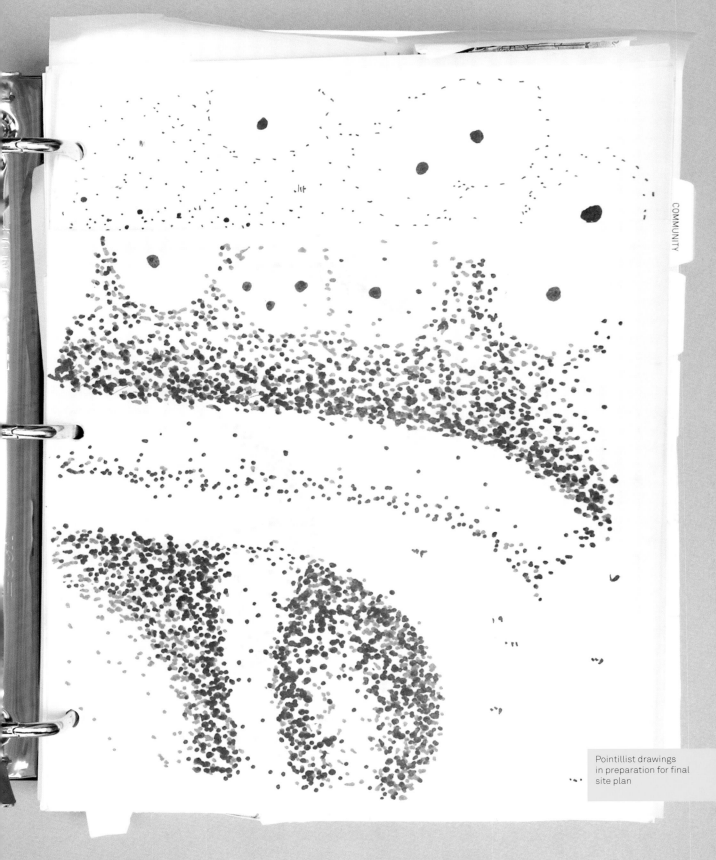

Pointillist drawings
in preparation for final
site plan

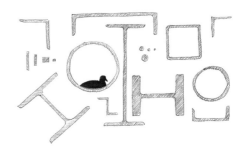

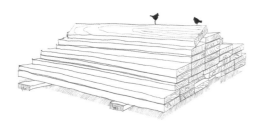

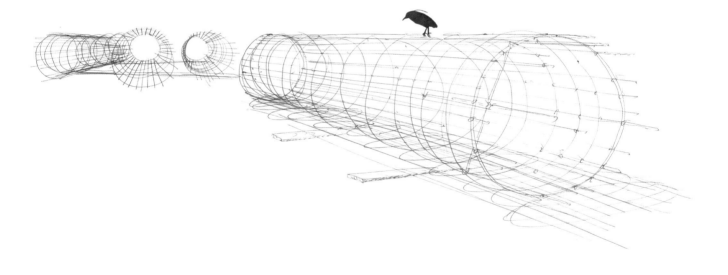

An effort to match words with site concepts

MAGNIFY
(EXISTING)
DIVERSITY

FOR THE SAKE OF

WHOLE ECOSYSTEM

POINTILLIST
(GENTLE, SELECTIVE)

TREE HARVESTING
(COTTON WOODS)

AND

RE-PLANTING
(VARIETY OF NATIVES)

MAGNIFY
LANDSCAPE
TYPES

PROJECT / FORD CALUMET ENVIRONMENTAL CENTER

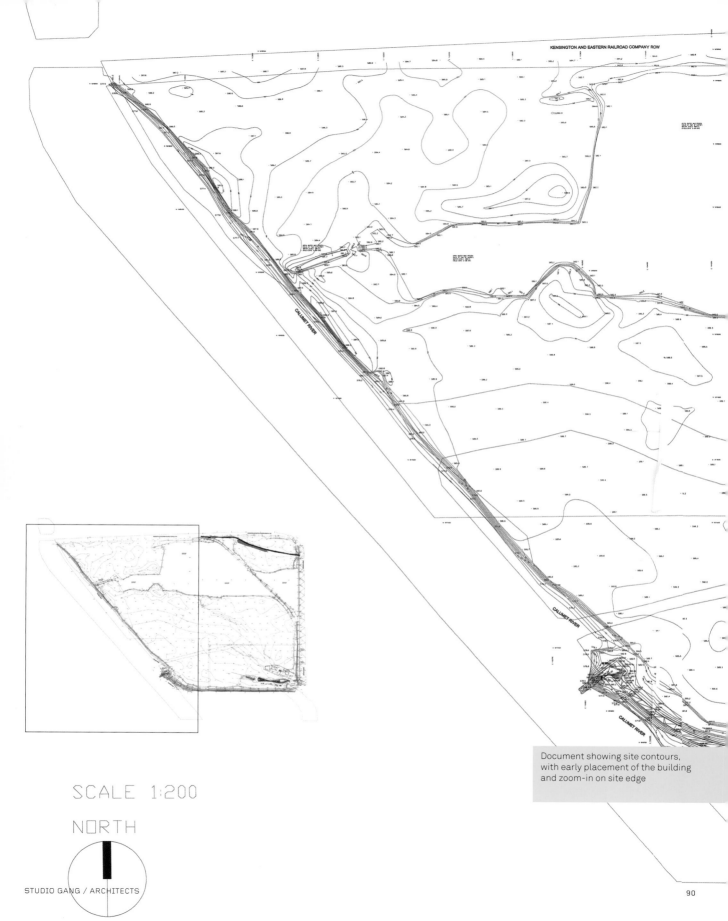

KENSINGTON AND EASTERN RAILROAD COMPANY ROW

CALUMET RIVER

CALUMET RIVER

CALUMET RIVER

Document showing site contours,
with early placement of the building
and zoom-in on site edge

SCALE 1:200

NORTH

STUDIO GANG / ARCHITECTS

90

Sw 83

SWAMP LAND ACT # 1849/1860

→ flood control
→ replenish shallow aquifers
→ H₂O purification → good but toxins
   left behind are bad for fish/animals

ARTICLE 1 SECTION 8 US CONSTITUTION
   interstate commerce act.
   migratory birds
   waterways & adjacent wetlands

WETLAND: ① SATURATION OR PERIODIC INUNDATION
legal   ② PRESENCE OF HYDRIC SOILS
definition ③ WETLAND VEGETATION

marshes, sedge meadows, bogs, fens, swamps

Lake Calumet river used to have tons of yellow lotus plants

Purple Loosestrife → exotic, European, since early 1800s

one stalk 300 K seeds → 24 billion seeds/acre
           80 K stalks/acre

Natural predators Galerucella calmariensis + G. pusilla adult
                  + Hylobius transversus. Hata are both adult + larva
                                                   feed on purple loosestrife

Started in 1994, to 96

Zebra Mussels → exotic, black/caspian seas. Since 1986

first in lake Erie in 1989, within 2 yrs all through + down to base of lake
  1 ♀ → 1 million eggs

COMBAT
① Chlorine $5,000,000/yr in storage
② hot water (kills plants)

1. clearing water 3x ~ 1989 30 ft now
2. ↓ plankton, ↑ organic detritus in bottom

062303 CALUMET NATURE CENTER   HARDCOPIES
                      *
FIND ENVIRONMENTAL-ISH   ENVIRONMENTAC SCI
        PERSON   ECOLOGY
                         → WRITTEN/RSRCHD CALUMET

CALUMET
HISTORY   NATURAL/PEOPLE GEOLOGICAL
ECOLOGY   USDA
HARBORSIDE GOLF → WHO HOW WHY   US FOREST SVC.
PORT - DREDGING DEBATE   CHICAGO GREEN COM
SLAGS   URBAN NATURALIST
PRESS
FLORA/FAUNA → WHAT'S THERE?   WARDS!
   MIGRATORY BIRDS ETC.   PICTURES BIRDS
LAKE CALUMET   PLANTS
                                         NESTING
WOLF LAKE NATURE PRESERVE SANDY SWAMP   BLACK CROWNED NIGHT
                    PROF. JIM LANDING   HERON
                    LAKE CALUMET STUDY COMM   YELLOW HEADED BLACKBIRD

GEOGRAPHY
→ MAPS OF IT
→ FIND OR MAKE

INDIAN TRAILS → RR | ROADS
                ETC.

research notes
NIGEL CALDER ON GLACIERS

MIGRATORY BIRD MAP
   SPECIES | ENTIRE ROUTE
                              MORAINIC ISLAND
BOOK ONE: REVEAL / ... LIB.   BLUE ISLAND   LAKE
                              STONY ISLAND CHICAGO
                              WHAT, WHY?
                              NAME
                         WHY
                    STEEL LOSS   FORD PLANT
                    POLLUTION   LOCATION

I TURN OFF
COPY MACHINE
AC
LIGHTS
STOVE
LOCK DECK
DOOR
FIRE ESC
MAIN DOOR

CHECK FOR CONTENT RELEASE EVERY DAY
REDO SCALE W/ CONTRAST. MOVE SITE BOX AROUND
RIDGES MAP.
BIGGER MORAINE MAP

BC NH WHEN NEST

                              NORTH VILLAGE
                              PARK
                              ENVIRONMENTAL
                              CENTER
LAND TYPES structure, graphic.
   SAVANNAH
   GRASSLAND/PRARIE   TIME
   FOREST   EVA MILLER   ENVIRONMENTAL
                                  QUALITY
WHAT IS SLAG   MARSH GRASS
STEEL WASTE from ore   ROOTS
                                 PLANT STRUCTURES
                    HOW IS STEEL MONOCOT DICOT
                    MADE?   GRASSES
DOLOMITE
CaMg(CO₃)₂   BIRD FEATHER
LIMESTONE CaCO₃   KARA | STRUCTURE
                     DATE | -LAYERS, TYPES
                     CAN | - DEVELOPMENT
BIRD WINDOW STRIKES
LIGHTS, MIGRATIONS   MAMMALS

LABOR
ACTIVISM → ENVIRON.

                    Wetlands plants of the Calumet

                    Gerould Wilhelm 1982

Photograph head
drill

UMET 06 2703

BOOKS TO GET:
                                                            KEG
A NATURAL HISTORY OF THE CHICAGO REGION   QH105.13674 2002
   BY JOEL GREENBERG / U of C PRESS

FORTHCOMING [CALUMET BEGINNINGS : ANCIENT SHORELINES & SETTLEMENTS @ THE
              SOUTH END OF LAKE MICHIGAN.
              BY KENNETH J. SCHOON / INDIANA UNIV PRESS

THE NATURAL RESOURCES OF THE CALUMET. A REGION APART
   BY MARK RESHKIN 1986 INDIANA U. NORTHWEST
                                    HAROLD WASH LIB
                                    QK157. S93 1979
                                    QK157- S93 1994
062403

CHICAGO FOLIO
REG MAP COLLECTION, RM 370 F QE77.A3 no.84   M-F 12:00-
                                                      5:20
   microfilm too! → print @ kinkos?   64042, 1565 1977. B45
PLANTS OF CHI REGION   6409, C665 1958. 67
   CRERAR QK157.S930 1994   G4104, C665 1970. W54
KIERKEGAARD BOOK   G4104. C665 1932. B7
1045 1232 1392 807 332405834

                    DR. JAMES LANDING
                    RICHARD DUKELIUS
                    ROBERT KAY   CH SOC Schaf maps
                    SCOTT PRINTS   10-4:30 Tues Thurs Fri Sat
                    * MARIAN BYRNES 1-4:30 weds

                    MUSEUM Th-Sat 9:30-4:30   LSU
                                                Coll Library
                            Clark @ North Ave Douglass library 305
                                               M-F 10-5
                                               9501 Ivy Dr

(S)Eastside Museum
Calumet Park Field House
98th St @ Avenue G
1-4pm Thursday YOP!
First sunday 12-3:00p

Business office phone

Museum
Rod Sellers Info

Annenberg Env History Coll

Turning Basin No 5

Footbridge

BM 586

Water Tank

E 130TH

E 127TH

Gris Sch

BM 585 ST

A. Corbett

Thomas J O'Brien Lock and Dam

E 134TH ST

36

650

4 LANE

585

CHICAGO
CALUMET CITY

CORPORATE
CORP

Light

BOUNDARY
BURNHAM CORP

Reality Check: In spite of its cultural significance as a former steel producer and its ecological importance as a habitat, pollution and garbage-landfill remain inherent features and urgent problems for the Calumet region.

675

EXPRESSWAY

RIVER

Mile 325

Radio Towers

Superfund Sites in 60618

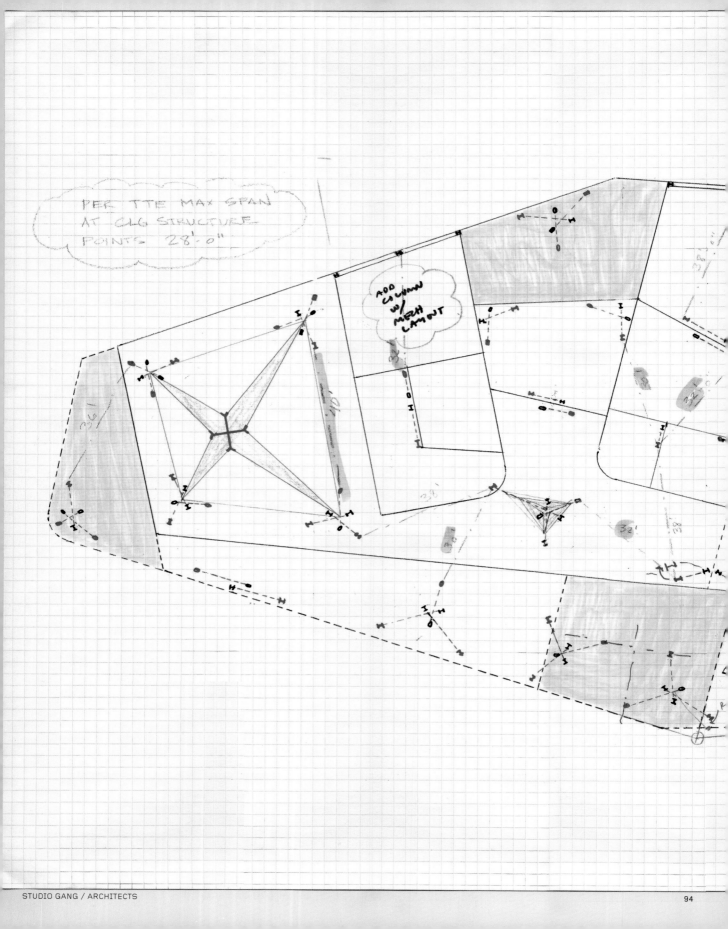

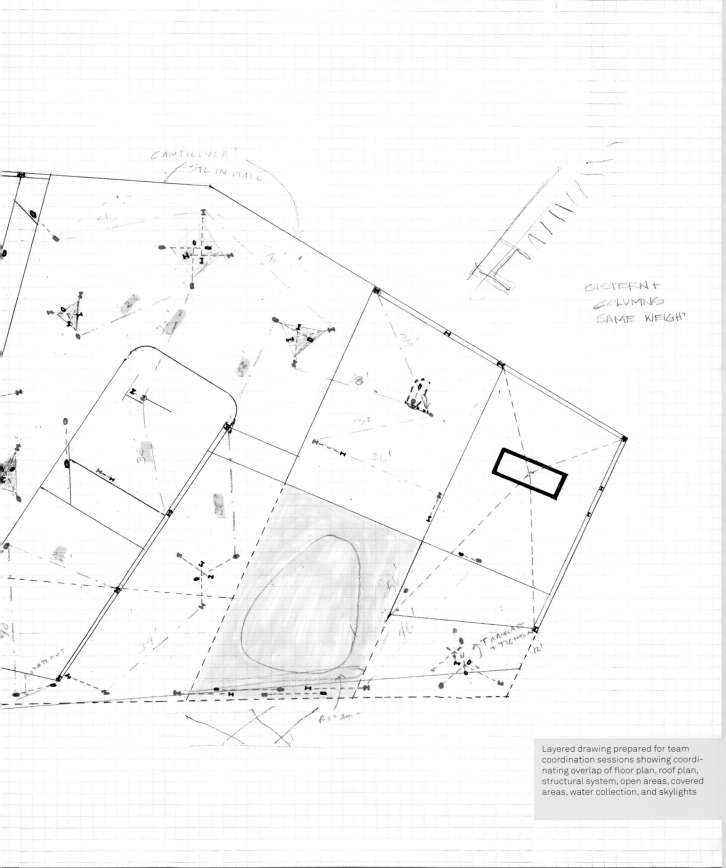

CANTILEVER?
STL IN WALL

CISTERN +
COLUMNS
SAME WEIGHT

Layered drawing prepared for team
coordination sessions showing coordi-
nating overlap of floor plan, roof plan,
structural system, open areas, covered
areas, water collection, and skylights

Press

As a leftover from the metal stamping process, the perforated plate (left) is typically considered waste. For the Ford Calumet project this salvaged material is to be incorporated into exterior fences and gates. Inspired by that found object, a refined version of stamped and bent metal (right) is employed in an apartment interior as a guardrail. Both elements exhibit steel's seductive malleability.

MAISONETTE

OWNER/OCCUPANT: Couple and two children

LOCATION: Chicago, USA

COMPLETION DATE: 2009

PROJECT / MAISONETTE

The Maisonette project transforms the ballroom space of a former hotel into a contemporary three-bedroom apartment in Chicago. New architecture takes the form of steel insertions that express their ductility. Glass bordered with bent metal bar forms the sides of the new floating platforms. Steel plates perforated with large holes create the guardrails for the passerelle, and plates with tiny holes wrap acoustic doors for storage areas.

A large void cut away from the second floor slab creates a dramatic vertical space in the center of the apartment. The void establishes visual connections between the living levels, dematerializing the traditional boundaries that characterize domestic space. Two ascending platforms linked by a narrow passerelle connect the high-ceiling space to the second floor.

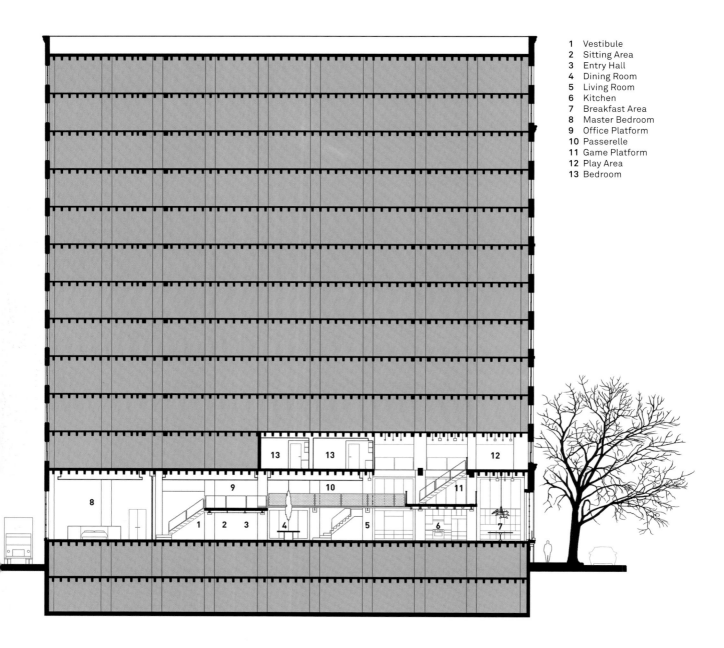

1 Vestibule
2 Sitting Area
3 Entry Hall
4 Dining Room
5 Living Room
6 Kitchen
7 Breakfast Area
8 Master Bedroom
9 Office Platform
10 Passerelle
11 Game Platform
12 Play Area
13 Bedroom

PROJECT / MAISONETTE

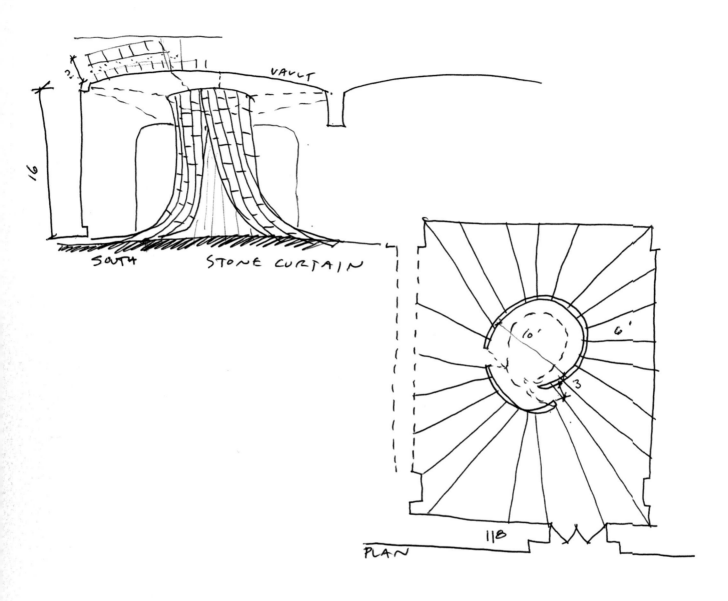

VAULT

SOUTH   STONE CURTAIN

PLAN

3.1 Constraints of the site: The floor structure of the National Building Museum can support little additional weight, but its ceiling is constructed of a strong masonry vault. This early sketch records a desire to hang a stone curtain from the ceiling.

THE MARBLE CURTAIN

Sponsored by the International Masonry Institute in conjunction with the National Building Museum, "Masonry Variations" was an installation demonstrating masonry design and craft skills. The exhibition sought to establish a renewed interest in the traditional building materials of stone, brick, lightweight concrete block, and terrazzo by engaging four architect-craftworker teams to design new applications. Exploring stone as its subject matter, the design of the Marble Curtain challenged conventional thinking about this age-old material.

SPONSOR: International Masonry Institute
GUEST CURATOR: Stanley Tigerman
LOCATION: The National Building Museum, Washington D.C., USA
EXHIBITION: Oct 18, 2003–April 4, 2004

PROJECT / THE MARBLE CURTAIN

HOW TO MAKE A MARBLE CURTAIN

Maybe it was the Marble Curtain's apparent fragility that tempted visitors to touch it. According to museum attendants who staffed the exhibit, visitors tried to push on the piece, gently probing its response to their applied force. It was as if those who encountered it were trying to decipher its secrets. But the big secret—that the stone was actually hanging in tension—was right in front of their eyes, there to be discovered by anyone who examined its shape and connections. Every aspect of the structure is a visual expression of this fact.

While the achievement may have been astonishingly clear to museum visitors, the story played out differently back in Chicago. A rumor circulated among local architects that the Marble Curtain had failed structurally. Obviously, it had not, yet how did such conjecture take hold? Maybe the idea of the Marble Curtain failing somehow relieved the discomfort of recognizing that an established order had been disrupted. Perhaps failure seemed a justifiable punishment for anyone who would so blasphemously hang stone in tension from the museum ceiling.

The story of the Marble Curtain, however, is less about the stir it caused during its short life as a museum exhibit, and more about a process of discovery that occurred between the collaborators who brought it to life. These are their stories.

3.2 (previous page) The Marble Curtain is composed of very thin, translucent stone tile cut into interlocking shapes that allow each stone to hang from the one above it.

Jeanne Gang: Matthew Redabaugh, the master craftworker who collaborated on the project and constructed the Marble Curtain, wanted to convince traditional stonemasons that the Marble Curtain should be considered a structural use of stone even though the stone was loaded in tension rather than in compression. He wrote the following description of the piece to his fellow members of the Stone Foundation.

Matthew Redabaugh: Last year I was involved with what proved to be a once-in-a-lifetime opportunity: an extremely unique project called "Masonry Variations." Sponsored by the International Union of Bricklayers and Allied Craftworkers (BAC) and the International Masonry Institute (IMI) in conjunction with the National Building Museum, "Masonry Variations" was an exhibit and demonstration of masonry design and craft skills—a challenge of traditional materials and how we use them. The opening of the exhibit coincided with BAC's first national apprentice contest in over fifty years, and a week-long celebration of masonry and the related craft skills.

Masonry Variations can be understood as a logical extension of IMI's Masonry Camp, which is a program where architectural students and apprentice masons are given the opportunity to work hand-in-glove for one week.

For this project, four architects and four masons were paired up and asked to create a masonry piece to be exhibited at the National Building Museum from one of four materials: stone, brick, terrazzo, and aerated autoclaved concrete. I worked with Jeanne Gang of Studio Gang in our assigned material, stone. The task, as presented by the curator, Stanley Tigerman, was to take the assigned masonry material and push it into the next millennium. The parameters of the challenge were quite loose: the teams needed to design and construct a structure with an inside and an outside, to give the masonry material a futuristic application, and to push the envelope. The project took almost a year.

Stone is a material that performs best when subjected to compressive loads, but Jeanne Gang took this timeless material and put it in tension, linking piece to piece in a series of chains to create a shell-like form: her Marble Curtain. The entire construction was 18' tall, made of 620 pieces, and weighed less than 2,000 pounds. It was hung stone-on-stone in tension from the ceiling, without any skeletal support or frame.

She chose a thin material, just 3/8" thick, because she wanted to exploit and explore the translucency of the material as part of pushing the envelope and enhancing her design. By the second meeting she had a complete design formulated, inspired by a dream she had. She envisioned a "marble curtain." The mechanics of the curtain were later designed like a jigsaw puzzle with individual interlocking elements.

A battery of tests was required to determine if we could actually hang stone in tension. Professor Sheldon Mostovoy, of the materials testing lab at the Illinois Institute of Technology (IIT), first insisted that we were wasting our time. According to him, stone in tension "would fail at 100 to 120 pounds." Push came to shove, or in this case to pull, and when we did pull the first stone it failed at seven hundred pounds, which was seven times stronger than predicted. That exceeded everyone's expectations and was in line with what the engineers were willing to accept for the structure. Word got out that we "were pulling stone apart," and students and faculty alike stopped by for a peek at our tests. No data existed on stone's strength in tension; until now, there was no need for such tests.

A marble from Turkey called Bianco Limone performed well in the tests. Bianco Limone, with its tightly formed internal structure, offered a resounding ring when struck with the knuckle, an age-old technique used by masons to sound the quality of stone.

As a built-in redundancy, and to create a safety net that was recommended by the engineers, we reinforced the backs of the pieces with epoxy resin and fiberglass, making them similar to laminated glass. This precaution would prevent the stone from falling on visitors if it were to break. However, since the architect wanted the stone to maintain a certain level of translucency, the fiberglass also needed to be clear. I was convinced that we could increase the amount of translucency if we were to hone the backs of the pieces first, bringing the surface to some level of consistency by reducing the size of the surface area. This would allow more light to penetrate the stone, instead of being refracted by the erratic and coarse sawn surface. A simple test using a light meter and a halogen lamp proved the point. Before and after honing readings proved that we were able to achieve 30 percent more light penetration, and translucency was now back in the mix.

We next needed to secure a transparent resin and fiberglass. We got both—it is amazing what you can achieve when you remain persistent. With a very transparent epoxy, a finely chopped fiberglass and the backs of the stone pieces honed, we still exceeded the translucency of the original stone before treatment.

The clock was ticking throughout this process. We were introduced to the project in late November 2002, with a scheduled opening date of October 16, 2003. The design challenge had so many uncertainties and the potential for failure. There were barely ten months to sort through all of the testing, make evaluations and changes, draw each piece for cutting, fabricate the pieces, build a centering, and hang the stone. Ten months seemed an impossibly short amount of time.

In the Middle Ages, a form of applied geometry that was specific to the cutting and shaping of building stones called stereotomy evolved. We had access to the modern equivalent of stereotomy through computer software. The architects used the computer to draw the intricate outlines of each piece, as well as the wooden shell centering.

Because of the complexities inherent to this project and the time constraints, I wanted to keep all fabricators close to the National Building Museum. We secured the stone from a distributor twenty miles east (ARC Stone, who donated nearly half of the material), the fiberglass and resin from a distributor fifty-six miles northeast (Fox Industries), and our water-jet cutter was not far from Baltimore (LAI International, Inc.). Given the potential for breakage and mis-cut stones (over 600 individual pieces), we needed to be able to replace any pieces immediately.

The structural form of the Marble Curtain is an arch-like shell, and its construction required the use of a temporary wooden frame similar to the centering used in arch construction. Unlike the lines of the Marble Curtain, the centering would have to adhere to the dictates of a grid with level and plumb, yet still reflect the stone form exactly. The lines of the Marble Curtain were curving in three different directions: round as a bell, out in near catenary, and laterally. Lines completely devoid of level or plumb now had to be tamed by the temporary wooden form upon which we would construct the actual stone shell.

Sequence of events and methods used:

Quality Test: Each stone (16" x 16" x 3/8") pre-fabrication was sounded or "thump" tested to determine if there were any hidden cracks. Those that failed to resound with a definite ring were discarded. With over 600 pieces, we used a metal chisel, not a knuckle.

Sorting/Shuffling: The stones were held up inches away from a strong halogen lamp to determine translucency level and color. Some pieces had inclusions which were very opaque, and if the inclusions were more than 20 percent, the pieces were discarded. Stones that were 80 percent translucent were sorted by color; we had five distinct colors: blue, blue-green, white, yellowish, and beige. These color separations were then randomly shuffled to avoid the possibility of having any single color–based splotches or areas within the fabric of our curtain.

Honing: The stones were placed facedown on an area covered with wet gypsum boards. This provided a surface with suction that held the pieces to the ground. Then, using a Clark floor re-finisher with open-screen abrasive pads, the backs of the stones were ground to a honed finish.

Lamination: The stones were delivered to Fox Industries for fiberglass lamination. Due to time constraints, we had to keep communications clear and concise. With some alterations to their proposed method of lamination, we were able to cut their delivery time by three weeks, keeping us on schedule.

Centering: We began constructing shell-centering off-site. Drawings for the centering were developed by Studio Gang and were sent digitally to a print shop in DC where I could pick up the templates. These drawings were full-scale and were printed on 3' x 10' paper. The templates were adhered to 3/4" and 1 ¼" plywood, cut, and assembled.

Water-jet Cutting: The laminated stones were then delivered to LAI to be water-jet cut. Fabrication of stone, honing stone backs, lamination, and cutting took two months.

Installation Begins: The plan for the curtain was laid out on the exhibit hall floor. The nineteen attachment points were transferred to the ceiling with a laser plumb bob. Anchors consisting of 9" stainless bolts with ¾" eyelets were epoxied into holes drilled into the brick-vaulted ceiling.

Erect shell-centering in National Building Museum: Meanwhile, laminated, cut stone was delivered to the museum. Tube and knuckle scaffolding was built around the outside and inside of the shell-centering to create the form for a work platform. Construction of the centering took four weeks with a three-person crew.

Hanging: Because this construct was in tension, work started at the top of the piece, and not at the bottom. A stainless turnbuckle was affixed to each eyelet on the ceiling. The first course of puzzle pieces, made from ½" thick aluminum, was hung from the turnbuckle. From it, the second course made of marble was hung. This top course of stones carried the weight of all those below it. Since structural silicone distributes lateral loads to the stone, all joints were taped on the back or inside the shell to control the amount of silicone pumped into the joint. Therefore, access to both the front and back of each piece was critical to the installation process. Two to three courses could be set before applying the silicone.

Stone installation: The stone setting tools I've been trained to use were all rendered useless when faced with this resplendent stone beast. Without the usual consistencies of verticals or horizontals such as level and plumb, the rules had clearly changed.

Much of the work was based on an essential trust in the wooden shell-centering. Beyond that, we worked by feel and sight. The fact that the form turned on three planes presented the constant challenge of controlling the obvious and persistent lippage that occurred. This held constant throughout the entire fabric of the structure. During the installation, we were overtly confronted with such anomalies because of our close proximity to these errors. Yet when we stepped back and examined the piece as a whole, the lippage melded into the truly sensuous curves of the form. The installation of the stone took four weeks with a crew of three.

Show Time: With stone installation complete, the centering was cut out and removed. Even with all of our elaborate tests and computer structural analysis, we were still nervous to remove the centering. However, everything came off without a hitch. The piece was an incredible treat to have worked on. When all of the theater lights were illuminated, the colors of the stone were overwhelming. Certainly, we were aware of the wide range of interesting colors in the marble, but with the true white light, the colors exploded into something none of us recognized. It was wonderful to complete the project having clearly exceeded all our expectations. The stone curtain was on display for six months.

JG: Peter Heppel collaborated on the project by developing the structural principles. He specializes in the design of lightweight structures, including sails for racing boats. Lightness was a necessity for the project, and Heppel brings insight and clarity as he outlines below how the curtain became a structure.

Peter Heppel:

What the curtain has to do:

It has to hang in its design shape, yet deform to carry imposed load.

The panel joints have to carry tensile loads, yet provide sufficient flexibility in bending.

The panels should form a smooth surface.

The ensemble has to be buildable.

Safety factors have to be adequate.

No single free-form shape or tiling pattern can reconcile all of these needs. Some trade-offs had to be made.

The structural solution for the Curtain was conceived of as a set of vertical chains of tiles, stretched from top to bottom. Each chain was given a shape which was almost a pure catenary (the shape it would take up if it were hanging on its own). Therefore, it relied very little on its neighbors to support its own weight. Only small loads were transferred laterally between neighboring chains, and a simple silicone joint was enough to connect the pieces. In addition, extra support was not needed at the side edges of the Curtain.

Each chain of tiles was in tension, so the bed (horizontal) joints were keyed together like a jigsaw. However, the keyed joint was only needed on the top and bottom of each tile, not on its sides.

JG: Structural Engineers Faz Ehsan and Joseph Burns from Thornton Tomasetti Engineers were confident that the Marble Curtain could behave as a shell using only structural silicone at the head joints. In addition to designing the tests for the stone and silicone, they analyzed models of the structure to determine its behavior under different circumstances. Ehsan describes the evolution of the design below.

Faz Ehsan: The curtain was conceptualized as a series of "chains" formed from interlocking pieces of marble, each with a glass fiber backing. The chains were conceived of as taking a natural catenary shape suspended from the top. To transfer load laterally between chains, it was assumed at an early stage that the design of a mechanical connection would be needed.

As the design evolved, it became apparent that the entire curtain could behave as a shell if the structural silicone between the "chains" could be relied on to provide both strength and stiffness, i.e., to provide load-carrying capacity while keeping deformation to a minimum.

The standard application of a structural sealant is to hold a panel of glass or marble to the side of a building or window mullion. The panel is subjected to transient wind loads through the thickness of the sealant. In applications where the structural sealant is required to support the sustained weight of the panel, the sealant undergoes large deformations due to creep and molecular re-formation of the material. Sealants designed to take 20 pounds per square inch of transient loads are usually specified to take only 1 psi of a sustained load.

In the case of the Marble Curtain, we were interested in using the structural silicone around each marble panel to support the sustained load. In order to correctly model the structure, properties of the silicone loaded in tension, compression, shear, and flexure would be required. The properties would include both the strength and stiffness (deformation under load). Such information was not available from the technical specifications of the silicon and could not be provided by the manufacturers.

A series of tests were devised and executed at IIT to gather data that could be incorporated into the structural analysis models. The tests are shown in figure 3.20. This data was used in the analysis described in the following section.

Analysis Model

A three-dimensional analysis model was created to study the behavior of the stone curtain. Some simplifying assumptions were made in order to keep the analysis model and the results from the analysis manageable.

The overall theoretical shape of the curtain was a smooth shell. However, it was actually constructed out of discrete, flat pieces of marble of varying sizes. In addition, exact modeling of the interlocking shapes posed further geometric challenges. For these reasons, we decided to model the individual pieces of marble as quadrilateral plate elements. Each element was further divided into four parts, providing the opportunity for modeling connectivity between elements.

Nodes along each side of a conceptualized piece of marble were attached to the adjacent piece using springs. The springs were assigned tension, compression, and shear values based on the test results. Upon analysis, the forces in the springs were checked against actual load capacities achieved during testing.

Stress distributions from the analysis models indicated a general state of tension towards the top half of the model and compression in the lower half, due to the restraint at the bottom (figure 3.19). The compression in the lower half caused an interesting phenomenon towards the end of the exhibition: the faceting between the individual pieces in the lower half of the curtain gradually became more visible, as the sustained compression loads on the silicone joints possibly caused them to creep. The final shape began to resemble a more stable configuration of a folded plate near the base of the shell.

Additional modeling was done to study the effects of potential breakage and loss of a single piece from key locations—at the top, in the body of the curtain, and along the edge. The entire model behaved as a shell, and the loss of a single element from critical locations did not impact the overall behavior. The stresses redistributed to adjacent elements without causing large stress concentrations.

Attachment to Existing Structure:

The ceiling of the exhibit space is a brick dome structure formed from 9"-thick bricks. The dome supports a wood floor system above, and had sufficient capacity to carry the weight of the Marble Curtain, as long as the weight was distributed.

The Marble Curtain was attached to the ceiling using stainless steel turnbuckles from the top of the aluminum header piece connected to eyebolts that were drilled and grouted into the ceiling structure. The turnbuckles allowed for adjustment in the field. Eyebolts were precisely located after the formwork was installed (fig. 3.27).

The analysis indicated that the geometry of the curtain was causing the entire curtain to displace sideways under its own weight. Two turnbuckles, one at each end, were installed at angles determined from analysis to maintain the geometry of the curtain.

JG: Stanley Tigerman, FAIA, curator of the Masonry Variations exhibit for the National Building Museum, was responsible for the exhibit concept, selecting the participating architects and assigning each one a material, and creating content and interpretation for the show. He also ran a series of critiques for the architects and their craftworker partners throughout the design process. I asked him to reflect on the Marble Curtain in the year following the exhibit. He had this to say:

Stanley Tigerman: Before I comment, I want to supplement your quoting of Gottfried Semper, Isaac Ware, and Viollet-Le-Duc, by adding that Roland Barthes' revulsion at professional wrestling where (in Barthes' view) the appearance of pain is not always the truth in what is presented. Thus, Barthes seems to suggest that what appears must be consistent with the facts supporting the appearance. Furthermore (and to my way of thinking, far more important), the Torah (the Old Testament of the Bible) clearly states that materials must be used in their natural form since nature is a manifestation of God's divine invention (e.g. Exodus 20:25: "...for if thou lift up any tool upon it [stone], thou hast polluted it").

Thus, in your Marble Curtain project at the National Building Museum, you not only defy philosophers, historians, and theorists, but you also disregard theological precedent. For my purposes here, let me confine my remarks to the biblical issue. Frankly, it's the theological issue that is troubling and, in my view, requires addressing.

What interests me in your work is that it falls squarely into the unique Chicago tradition that is related entirely to the science, not the art, of architecture. It seems to me that science has gotten stunningly short shrift in the race to make architecture increasingly artful, might I say, at any cost. And that's where your work, and precious few others, is so critical in interpreting the nature of the architecture of our epoch (just, if I may be so bold, as Mies interpreted technology within his own epoch). Now certainly, the way that you challenged the nature of materials by testing their limits is important to our understanding the concept of working within the limits in the first instance. Perhaps, within the context of these few remarks, you'll understand why I would rather focus on the theological implications that might better place your architectural production in another light.

I'm not suggesting that biblical mandates necessarily limit the ways in which you (and by extension, others) challenge things that have been extant within recorded history, but I do believe that the pre-existing biblical precedent needs to be addressed. Perhaps, one way might simply be acknowledging precedent, yet finding reasons that you feel necessary to challenge them. Once enunciated, these issues demand attention lest your "approach avoidance" appears to be cavalier. **S/G/A**

A STEP BY STEP GUIDE TO MAKING A MARBLE CURTAIN

STEP 1: SELECT MATERIAL

STEP 2: THE INTERLOCK

STEP 3: REDUNDANCY

STEP 4: TESTING

STEP 5: SHAPE

STEP 6: GLUE

STEP 7: SPLICE

STEP 8: XYZ

STEP 9: COORDINATION

STEP 10: FALSEWORK & CONSTRUCTION

STEP 1: SELECT MATERIAL

Little data is available concerning stone's capacity in tension, but with new composites, tools, and testing techniques, could stone be capable of the unexpected? If so, what stone should be tested? Try marble, a metamorphic rock that is formed under heat and pressure. Its fluid structure makes it the best type of stone to carry load in tension. The marble must be devoid of crystals, which are weak points in the body of the material.

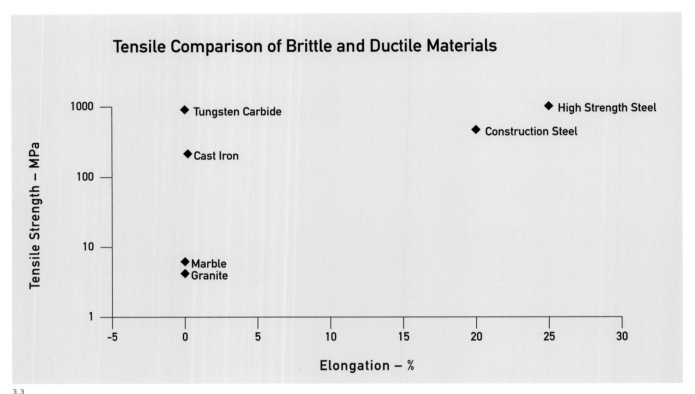

3.3

3.3 The graph compares relative tensile strength of brittle and ductile materials. Stone is considered a brittle material. In tension, marble and granite materials exhibit lower strength and do not elongate—they fail catastrophically—which is why most experts thought the marble curtain "couldn't be done." Source: N. H. Polakowski, <u>Strength and Structure of Engineering Materials</u> (London: Prentice Hall, 1966).

3.4 As a natural material, stone's structural capacity and fracture characteristics vary with its different compositions. In the images, fracture patterns revealed by an electron microscope tell a story about each material. Granite and onyx include quartz crystals that weaken the material with inconsistencies. Fractures originate at these points. Slate, a metamorphosed sedimentary rock, appears layered and sandy. Travertine, a sedimentary rock, is pitted with voids that cause weak points for cracks to propagate. We found that certain marbles have a more homogeneous composition and less quartz, making them better for resisting tension. Bianco Limone marble performed the best. This marble sample also produced a bell-like ring when thumped with a knuckle—the traditional mason's test for homogeneous material.

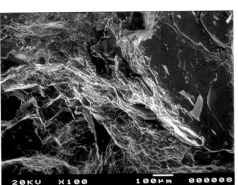

Granite

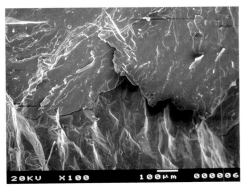

Onyx

Slate

Travertine

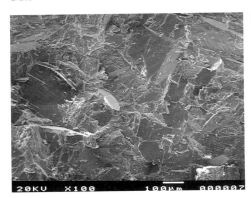

Marble– Pentelicon White

Marble– Bianco Limone

STEP 2: THE INTERLOCK

Hanging one material from another without additional hardware requires an interlocking geometry. Although a dovetail connection can work for material hung in tension, high stresses would build up at the sharp corners. For marble in tension, it is best to create a smooth geometry for the interlock by using rounded shapes, such as jigsaw puzzle pieces.

3.5

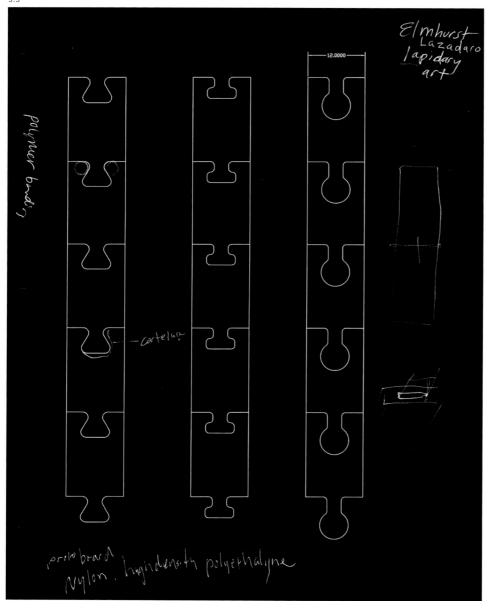

3.6

3.5 Sketch exploring various interlocking geometries

3.6 Small acrylic model made of individual laser cut puzzle pieces

STEP 3: REDUNDANCY

An installation hanging above visitors' heads must provide some redundancy in case of breakage. If one piece of stone were to break, the material would have to hold together and not fall to the ground. A layer of transparent adhesive plastic provides this redundancy in laminated glass; for marble, laminate a translucent layer of fiberglass to each piece of stone.

3.7 Various backing materials for the stone tiles were tested for both performance and appearance.

a) Fiber-tech, very strong, easy to apply, but not translucent

b) Honeycomb panel, good appearance, easy to apply, but not effective in tension

c) Six-ounce glass fabric to be applied professionally with epoxy-resin, strong, semi-translucent

d) Three-ounce glass fabric to be applied professionally with epoxy-resin, strong, very translucent

e) Fiberglass application with fire retardant additive in epoxy, too opaque

f) Final selection, three-ounce fiberglass application without additives

STEP 4: TESTING

Because of the lack of data available for stone in tension, the material needs testing. Create pairs of puzzle pieces and pull apart the assembly in a universal testing machine. The exact type and thickness of stone, geometry of the connection, and backing material must be employed in order to get accurate results. Pull the samples apart until they fail. Record the data needed for structural calculations.

3.8 Spreadsheet itemizing variables employed for the first battery of stone tension tests and their results

3.9 Data plot of all test results. Although stone was generally predicted to fail at approximately 150 pounds of tensile force, tests revealed that certain marbles could withstand up to 1,350 pounds. Stone with backing materials held together after the initial fracture, and withstood up to 1,750 pounds.

> 3.10 Most failures initiated at the upper left or right hand side of the puzzle "head."

3.11 Fixing a puzzle set into the universal testing machine

3.12 Various geometries and stone types ready for testing at the IIT materials testing lab

3.13 Fractured puzzle sets with tape securing the broken pieces are documented and stored for reference.

3.14 Drawing used to produce the testing combinations of stone material, puzzle geometry, and backing material.

March 6th 2003 stone Testing

Make-up Type	Geometry	Stone Type	No of Panels	No. of tests	No. of Tear Drops	Result: Load Test 1	Test 2	Test 3	Note:
Type 1 (No Tear Drops)	Puzzle Set A	Bianco Lemon	6	3	0	945	748	649.3	
3/8" stone no treatment	Puzzle Set B	Bianco Lemon	4	2	0	478.1	424.9		
	Puzzle Set A	Pentelicon white	6	3	0	332	133.6	571	
Type 2 (No Tear Drops)	Puzzle Set A	Bianco Lemon	6	3	0	698	646	848	
3/8" stone w/ akepox 1005	Puzzle Set A	Pentelicon white	0	0	0				
Type 3 (No Tear Drops)	Puzzle Set A	Bianco Lemon	4	3	0	690	1152		
3/8" stone w/FiberTech	Puzzle Set A	Pentelicon white	0	0	0				
Type 4 (No Tear Drops)	Puzzle Set A	Bianco Lemon	4	2	0	803	700		
3/8" stone w/ plastic honeycomb	Puzzle Set A	Pentelicon white	0	0	0				
Type 5(W/ Tear Drops)	Puzzle Set A	Bianco Lemon	2	1	1	1059			
3/8" stone w/FiberTech & tear dr	Puzzle Set B	Bianco Lemon	4	1	2	1758	1412		
	Puzzle Set A	Pentelicon white	0	0					
		Total:	36	18					

Not testing this time

3.8

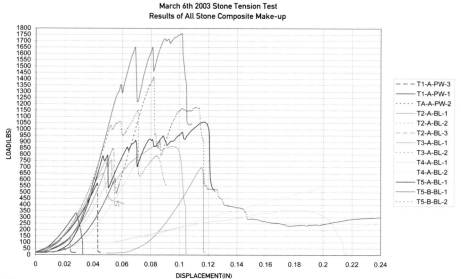

March 6th 2003 Stone Tension Test
Results of All Stone Composite Make-up

Legend:
- T1-A-PW-3
- T1-A-PW-1
- TA-A-PW-2
- T2-A-BL-1
- T2-A-BL-2
- T2-A-BL-3
- T3-A-BL-1
- T3-A-BL-2
- T4-A-BL-1
- T4-A-BL-2
- T5-A-BL-1
- T5-B-BL-1
- T5-B-BL-2

3.9

3.10

3.11

3.12

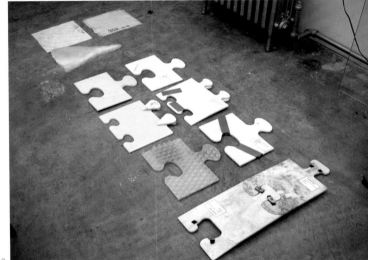

3.13

PANEL GEOMETRY

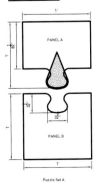

Puzzle Set A

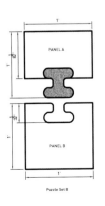

Puzzle Set B

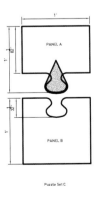

Puzzle Set C

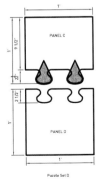

Puzzle Set D

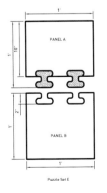

Puzzle Set E

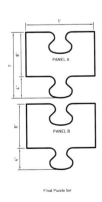

Final Puzzle Set

3.14

PROJECT / THE MARBLE CURTAIN

STEP 5: SHAPE

Pay attention to shape; it is important to the structure at several scales. At the smallest scale, the shape of each puzzle piece creates the interlocking connections and defines the bearing length necessary for one stone to hang from the next. On the middle scale, the shape of each geodesic chain forms a near-catenary curve in order to support its own weight in tension. Finally, the global structure of the Marble Curtain is a shell shape that resists lateral loads.

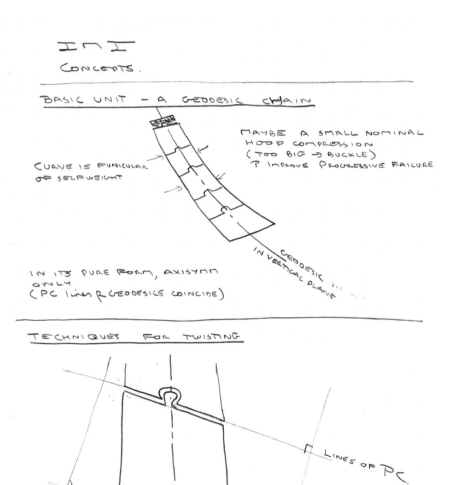

3.15 Engineer Peter Heppel's sketch describing the concept of the geodesic chains. The curve in the vertical plane is a function of the self-weight of the chain.

› **3.16** A layered drawing used by the water-jet cutting fabricator. The puzzle pieces are cut from 18" square stone tiles that have been pre-laminated with fiberglass. Each piece is cut with a unique number keying it into its final location in the Marble Curtain.

3.17 A script created to draw the appropriate shape of the puzzle heads.

3.18 The global shape of the structure is a shell that works to resist lateral loads potentially caused by visitors leaning on the installation.

3.19 The curve is made of flat pieces. To analyze and study its behavior structurally, the shape was modeled as quadrilateral plate elements.

3.15

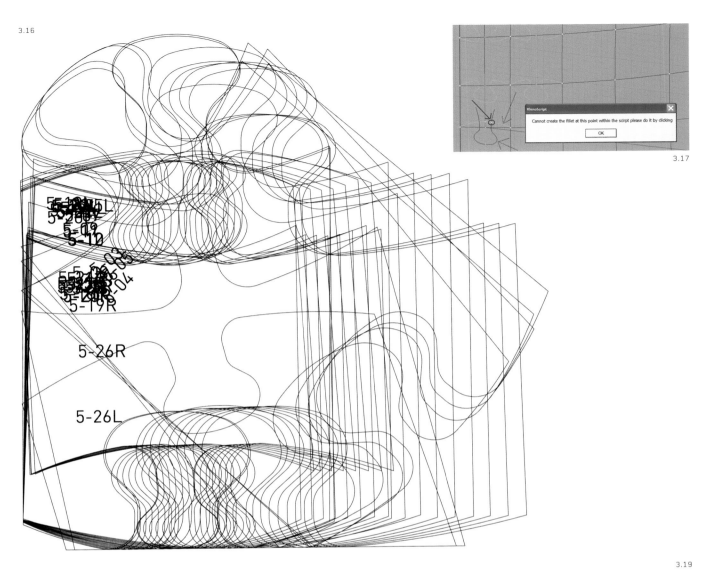

5-20H5L
5-20GV
5-10
5-10

5-6 03
5-34 -04
5-19R

5-26R

5-26L

RhinoScript

Cannot create the fillet at this point within the scirpt please do it by clicking

OK

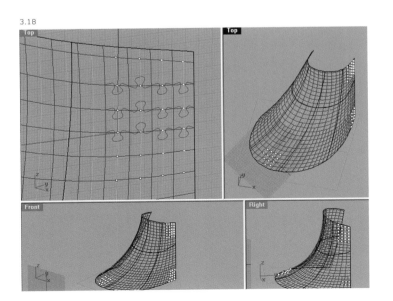

SAP2000   6/12/03 15:25:38

SAP2000 v7 44 - File:model4 -   Stress S11 Diagram   (SW) - Kip-in Units

-120.   -60.   0.   60.   120.   180.   240.   300.   360.   E-3

STEP 6: GLUE

Choose the right glue. Structural silicone transfers load laterally across vertical joints in the structure. These small load transfers are made possible by glue. The transparent structural silicone requires testing to determine its performance for the Marble Curtain's vertical joints. Adhesives have been and continue to be an important building material in architecture; there are many different types for different applications.

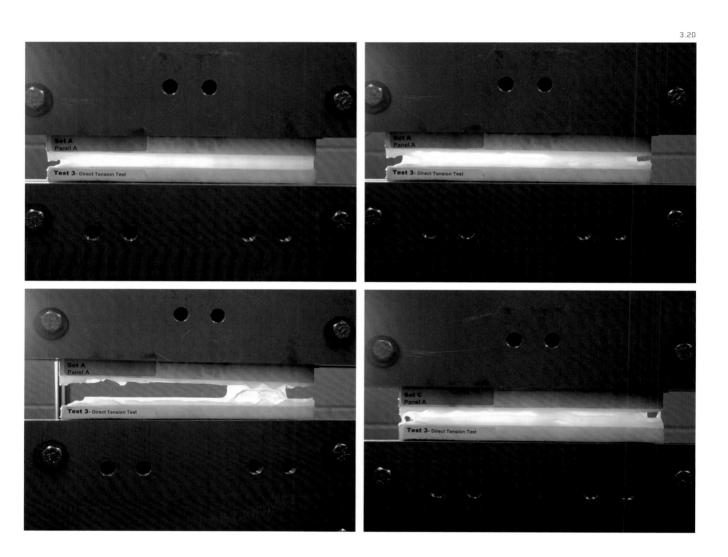

3.20 Structural silicone was also tested. A standard application of structural sealant is to hold glass to the side of a mullion with intermittent wind loads. The Marble Curtain is similar, but had to support a sustained load. To properly model the structure, the silicone had to be tested in tension, compression, shear and flexure.

STEP 7: SPLICE

Designed to be cut from thin marble tiles, the width of the curtain's geodesic chains depends on standard tile dimensions. Each piece is no more than 9" wide at the ceiling, flaring out to 24" wide at the floor. Some tiles, however, are not readily available in widths greater than 18". If no 24" tiles are available, create a splice to divide the chain into smaller widths. Pay attention to the bearing dimension in the geometry of the puzzle piece.

3.21 When it was discovered that the 24" tiles would not be shipped in time for the installation, a uniquely designed splice piece solved the puzzle. The splice divides the chains into two equal parts without changing the shape of the global form.

3.22 A graph showing the number of splice pieces substituted into the matrix

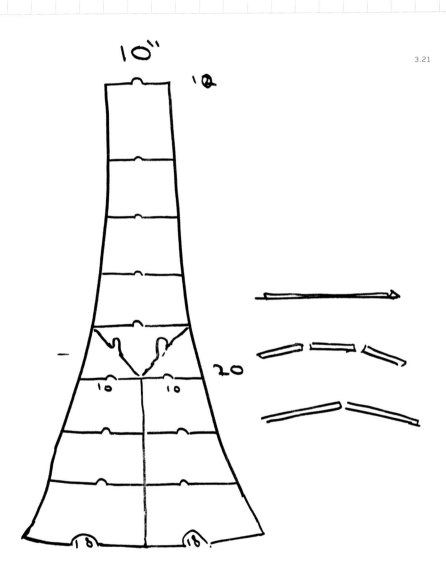

3.22

	1	2	3	4	5	6	7	8	9	10	11	12	13	14	15	16	17	18	19

STEP 8: XYZ

Because the structure curves in two directions, many drawing conventions prove useless. Designate the coordinates of the shape in three dimensions, since none of the lines will be parallel to the floor or walls. To set out the anchoring points in the room, a laser plumb bob can be used to find the "Z" dimension.

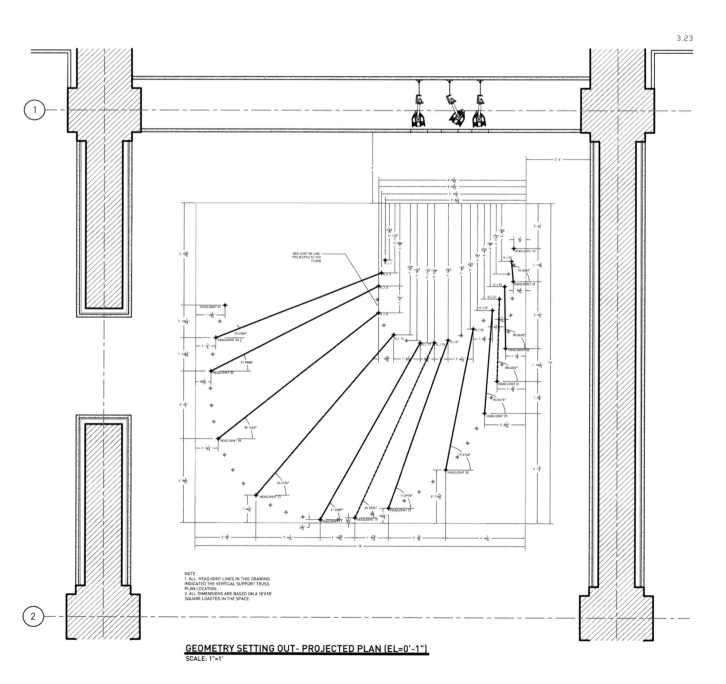

GEOMETRY SETTING OUT- PROJECTED PLAN (EL=0'-1")
SCALE: 1"=1'

NOTE:
1. ALL HEADJOINT LINES IN THIS DRAWING INDICATED THE VERTICAL SUPPORT TRUSS PLAN LOCATION.
2. ALL DIMENSIONS ARE BASED ON A 18'X18' SQUARE LOACTED IN THE SPACE.

‹ 3.23 A setting-out drawing dimensioning the footprint of the curtain on the floor contained within an 18' by 18' square. The connection to the ceiling is shown projected onto the floor.

3.24 This drawing indicates the curve of the Marble Curtain to be plotted full scale onto three long pieces of paper, which the mason would then use as a template in building the falsework.

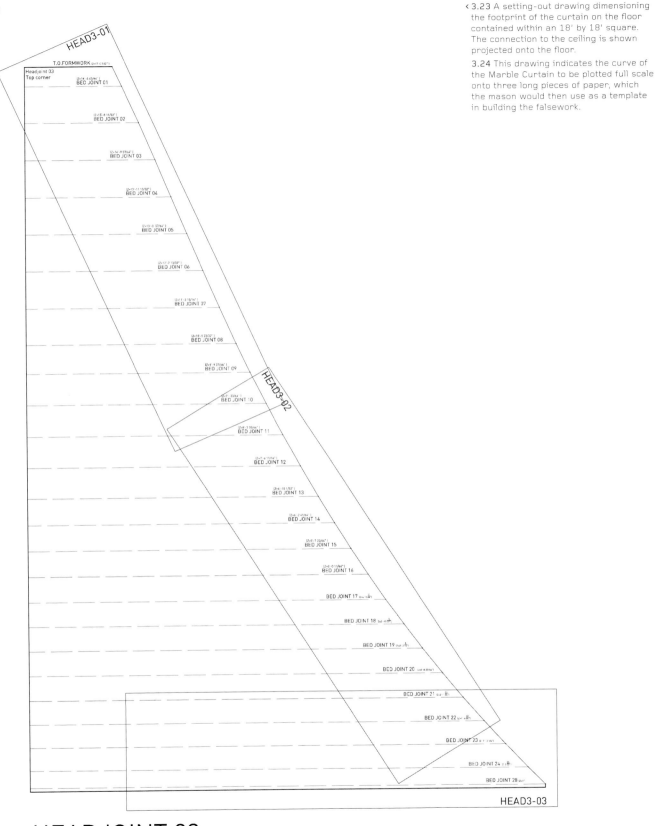

HEADJOINT 03

STEP 9: COORDINATION

Communicate frequently with all team members and make sure each member knows his or her responsibility. The many steps must all be coordinated. Stone tile must be ordered, honed, and visually inspected. Then the tiles must be laminated with fiberglass in a shop, sorted, and sent to the water-jet cutter. Every step is critical to stay on time.

STUDIO/ GANG /ARCHITECTS

07.16.2003

D. LAI to cut pieces by number which coordinate w...
Water jet cut number on polished face providing a perm...
marker number will be removed in water jet cutting pr...
preferences with Yu-ting Chen, Studio Gang. Test wate...
Studio Gang

6. Strategy and time constraints for replacement pie...
Extra laminated stone tiles to be stored at LAI for poss...
broken during installation. Turnaround time will be wit...

7. Lead times and schedule
Fox receive stones by August 1st (to be confirmed by Ar...
LAI receive stones by August 29th finished by Septembe...

8. Material Transportation
All materials to be hand delivered by IMI, dates to be o...

PLEASE NOTIFY J. GANG, STUDIO GANG FOR ANY COF...

Thank you

ARCHITECTURE
LANDSCAPE
URBAN DESIGN

1212 N. ASHLAND AVE.
STE 212
CHICAGO, IL 60622

T 773 384 1212
F 773 384 0231

STUDIO/ GANG /ARCHITECTS

07.16.2003

Meeting Minutes
Monday July 14th 2003
RE: Stone Curtain Coordination meeting
National Building Museum

Attendees:

Jeanne Gang, Studio Gang Architects
Maria Viteri, International Masonry Institute
Matthew Redabaugh, International Masonry Institute
Mike Simpson, Fox Industries
David Woodworth, LAI, Laser Applications, Ins
Thomas Sterner, LAI, Laser Applications, Ins

Distribution: above plus

Yu-ting Chen, Studio Gang Architects
Craig Duckworth, Arc Stone
    1. **URGENT: LEAD TIME needed:** Please confirm order that was made with Studio Gang when will stone arrive at Arc Stone. Sizes, quantities and honed

                                             C. Duckworth ARC STONE: CONFIRM

2. **FOX provide method spec, price and lead time** to Maria Viteri, IMI and Studio Gang. IMI to provide info needed for Purchase Order to Fox Industries. Confirmation of glass fiber and resin spec 3 (oz) was given prior to meeting. (lead time provided 7.16.03=4 weeks)

                                             M. Simpson, FOX, M. Viteri IMI

3. **Lamination Process** –no epoxy bleeding to polish side, Studio Gang observed some of this bleeding on several of the test samples. Mike Simpson to check with Fox on how to stop this and inform Studio Gang

                                             M. Simpson, FOX

4. **LAI provide pricing** -to include water jet mark on polished side of each piece. Price for each piece to be a unique cut. LAI Coordinate file preferences with Yu-ting Chen, Studio Gang to save time and reduce price. Studio Gang provide cad file for final pricing total length of cut.(sent 7.15.03) Test water jet number sizes on scrap stone prior to final coordinate with Studio Gang. IMI Provide info needed to set up PO with LAI

                                             D. Woodworth, LAI, M. Viteri, IMI

5. Method of color sorting to achieve random mix of various stone colors will be as follows.
    A. Stone will be shipped from ARC STONE to IMI training Center. Matt Redabaugh, IMI will arrange sorting by "thump-test" and color for final placement in the piece to achieve random mix. IMI will assigned number and edge mark stone per location in the final piece such as 01-15. This means chain number 01, 15th piece in the chain.
    B. Stone will be shipped by IMI to Fox Industries in boxes of 6-10 pieces per box, number up. Fox to laminate pieces and return to same boxes number side up in order. IMI ship to LAI

ARCHITECTURE
LANDSCAPE
URBAN DESIGN

1212 N. ASHLAND AVE.
STE 212
CHICAGO, IL 60622

T 773 384 1212
F 773 384 0231

∧ 3.25 Meeting minutes from the final summit for all participants prior to construction
› 3.26 Matrix showing all of the pieces and their location within the installation

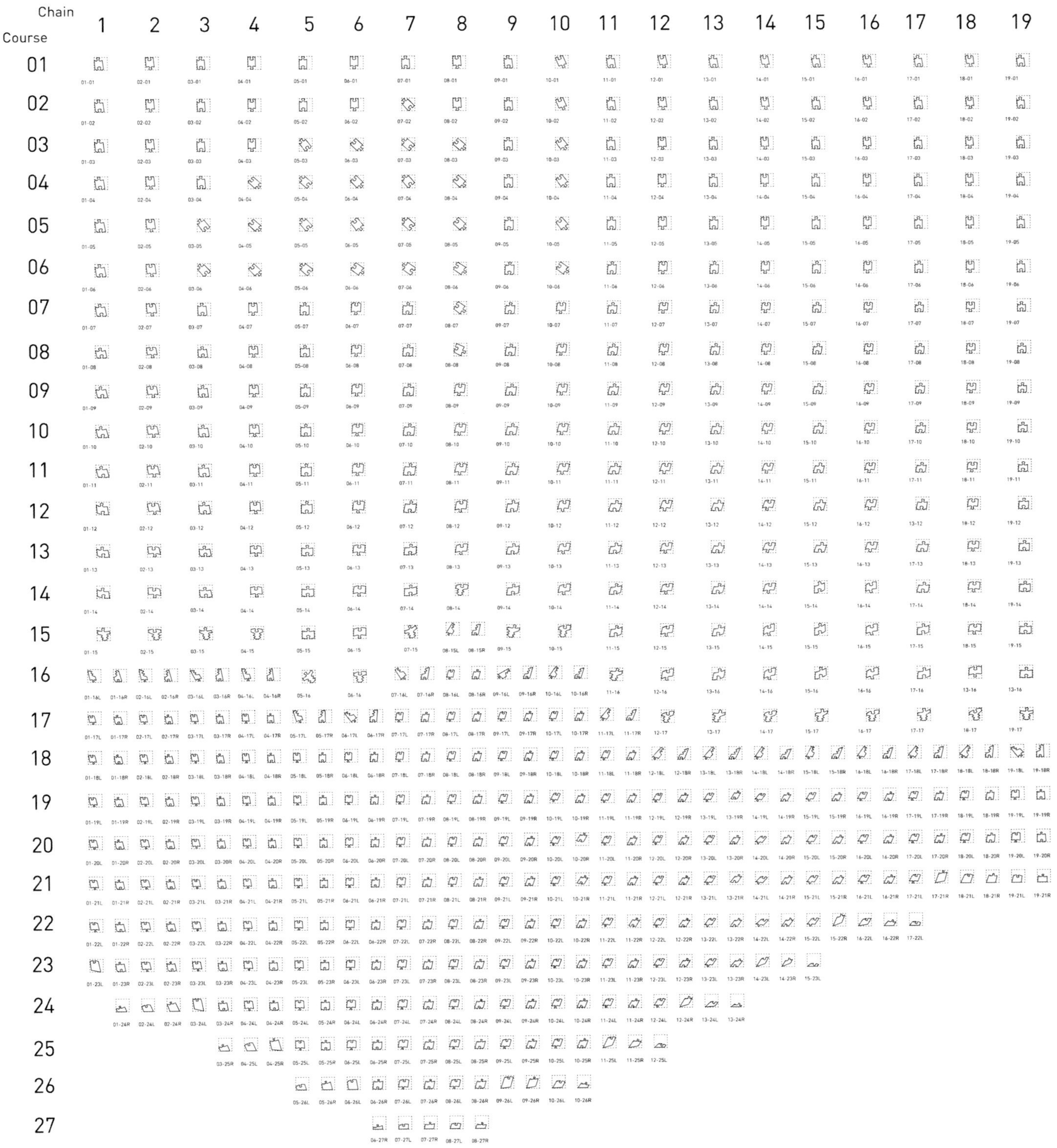

Chain

Course

	1	2	3	4	5	6	7	8	9	10	11	12	13	14	15	16	17	18	19

01
02
03
04
05
06
07
08
09
10
11
12
13
14
15
16
17
18
19
20
21
22
23
24
25
26
27

STEP 10: FALSEWORK

Construct plywood falsework to mimic the shape of the final form. It will be removed afterwards. Attach the first row of hardware to the ceiling with masonry anchors and epoxy. Set up the scaffolding and begin to hang the curtain from the top down. Use rubber spacers as bearing pads between the pieces. Silicone the head joints and the bed joints as the work moves downward. Fasten the bottom course to the floor. Let the silicon cure. Remove the falsework.

3.27 Falsework is mocked up off-site, dismantled, and then reinstalled inside the museum. The masonry anchors are installed in the ceiling and the first course of high-strength aluminum puzzle pieces are hung from them. The masons work to maintain the alignment of the courses and reduce the lippage between the pieces in the curving shape. When all is set, the plywood falsework can be removed.

& CONSTRUCTION

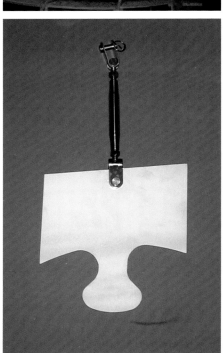

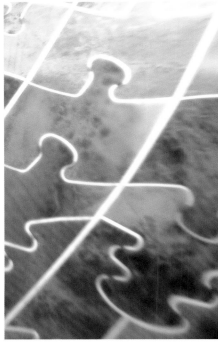

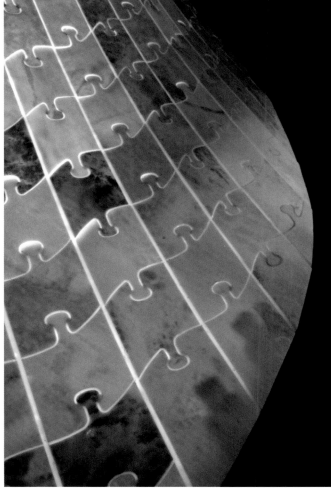

PROJECT / THE MARBLE CURTAIN

3.28 The Masonry Variations Exhibition conveyed the long history of masonry as a building medium and its extensive use throughout the world, highlighting some of the greatest masonry structures in history and many of the tools used to construct them. The Exhibition was not just a discussion of the past, however.

By asking architects and craftworkers (and ultimately engineers) to explore these traditional materials in light of new technologies, as well as societal and cultural changes, the Exhibition opened the door to future variations on a 5,000-year-old building practice. The other architect/craftworker teams included Carlos Jiménez and J. Keith Behrens with brick, Julie Eizenberg and Mike Menegazzi with terrazzo, and Winka Dubbeldam and Robert Mion Jr. with autoclaved aerated concrete.

3.29 A south elevation of Smeaton's Tower as it appeared in 1759, the year of its completion. This and other illustrations in this section originally appeared as plates in Smeaton's monograph on the lighthouse and its construction, which was first published in London in 1791.

Scale 6 Feet = 1 Inch.

South ELEVATION *of the* STONE LIGHTHOUSE *completed upon the* EDYSTONE *in 1759.*

Shewing the Prospect of the nearest Land, as it appears from the Rocks in a clear calm Day.

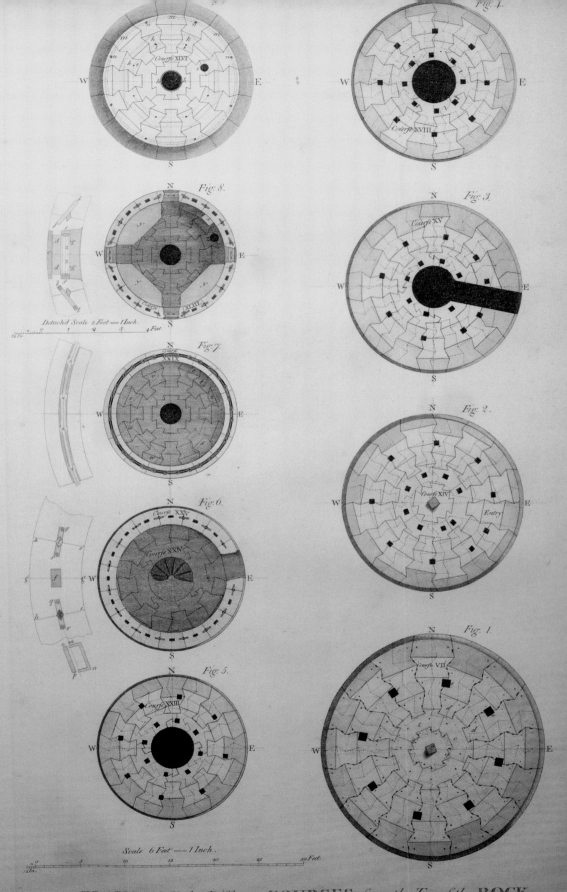

Fig: 4.

Course XVI

W — E

S

Course XVIII

W — E

S

Fig: 8.

N

W — E

Course XLIII

S

Detached Scale 2 Feet = 1 Inch.

Fig: 3.

N

Course XV

W — E

S

Fig: 7.

N

Course XXIX

W — E

S

Fig: 2.

N

Course XIV

W — E

Entry

S

Fig: 6.

N

Course XXIV

Course XXIV

W — E

S

Fig: 5.

N

Course XXIII

W — E

S

Fig: 1.

N

Course VII

W — E

S

Scale 6 Feet = 1 Inch.

PLANS *of all the Different* COURSES *from the Top of the* ROCK *to the Top of the* BALCONY FLOOR *inclusive.*

MATERIAL REPORT: GLUE
IT'S IN EVERYTHING

A pair of eyeballs carved from ivory, affixed to an idol in the ruins of a Babylonian tomb. The hull of a Roman ship, sealed watertight with tar and beeswax. The laminated bows and arrows used by the conquering armies of Genghis Khan. Though glue might initially seem invisible in the course of history, for 6,000 years it has been one of humankind's most tested and trusted materials, holding together a host of successive civilizations.

While glue is used extensively in building construction, its invisibility and lack of form make many architects disdain it. Instead of glorifying tectonic assembly, glue renders the connections between parts imperceptible—an almost mystical adherence that runs contrary to early Modernists' notions of clarity, honesty, and "truth" in construction. Visible (and sometimes exaggerated) hardware has been preferred in modern times: the gargantuan bolts on Otto Wagner's Postal Savings Bank; the repetitive rivets in Berlage's Stock Exchange. In contemporary buildings like airports, the desire for visible assemblage approaches fetish where turnbuckles, clevises, and pins are treated as a building's jewelry. Big steel couplings are of course more visually and conceptually obvious than the microscopic chemical workings of glue, but with current advances in adhesive technologies making glue stronger and more eco-friendly, its technical and conceptual potentials in architecture are worth exploring.

The first glues used by humans came directly from nature: the sap of trees and sticky plants, which satisfied the adhesive needs of early hunters and gatherers until approximately 200 BCE. At this time, humans discovered that glue made from boiled or ground animal bodies was stronger than vegetable-based adhesives. Various forms of animal-based glues then dominated human use for the next two thousand years, going out of favor only when the 1910 invention of phenol formaldehyde adhesives, compounded by further advances in the chemical and plastics industries during the 1930s, generated glues that were much more resistant to environmental failure. During World War II synthetic glue production accelerated and became cutting-edge, resulting in the invention of neoprenes, epoxies, and acrylonitriles. All these new glues were stronger and less overtly deadly for animals than their predecessors. They also came with a sticky consequence: many were made with carcinogenic chemicals—highly toxic pollutants that harm users and the environment.

This sudden technological transformation did little for glue's visibility, however, and despite its broad use it remained for the most part an overlooked material in the increasingly plastic postwar world. But its pervasiveness and unique fluid qualities did not escape the eye of certain artists—in particular the Minimalist Eva Hesse, who embraced its gooey formlessness in the 1960s. Rather than treating adhesives as materials whose invisibility could showcase or distinguish other materials, Hesse brought glue in the form of fiberglass, rubberized cheesecloth, and latex into the spotlight, revealing its fundamental characteristics, and subsequently, its potential in art. In pieces such as "Repetition Nineteen III" and many other sculptural works, she prominently featured glue itself as the primary or sole component, capturing its fluid nature while simultaneously highlighting the contradiction of using a highly synthetic substance to suggest intensely organic forms. (Hesse's art frequently evokes external and internal human body parts: fleshy tissue, skin, cartilage, bone marrow, hair, and genitals.) Like the organic matter they resemble, Hesse's fragile pieces were made to respond to the environment around them; they were often intended to change and decay, in order to trace their own lifespan and temporality. Her synthetic works therefore reverse assumptions and norms about sculpture as permanent art while also elevating a material seen as amorphous into both structure and form at once. Through her work, Hesse revealed glue's paradoxical beauty as it dissolved the divide between art, structure, and material. Sadly, while her sculptures intrigue the mind and eyes using an often overlooked material, they also remind us of glue's history as a highly poisonous substance. It was the toxicity of the glue and resin with which Hesse worked that contributed to her death from brain cancer in 1970 at the young age of 34.

In the years since, science has made strides to produce healthier and more sustainable glues whose strength rivals those made of plastic and resin. Just as Hesse was inspired by the organic body, so have current adhesives researchers come to focus on the natural world as a paradigm. Stronger adhesives now work to chemically mimic those found in nature, from the byssus complex in oceanic mussels that can withstand underwater tidal pressures, to the sticky substance produced by geckos' feet. These glues can be used for a wide range of purposes, from plywood manufacturing to a tape powerful enough to replace sutures following surgeries. As these new, advanced, and increasingly sustainable glues become more widely available, it is time to reconsider and acknowledge glue as an effective, if not essential, connector to be added to architecture's arsenal of hardware. In doing so, it is essential to contemplate structures with invisible connections—a wealth of which already exist in nature—and to imagine how glue's qualities of fluidity, transparency, and chemistry might be revealed. S/G/A

3.33 Eva Hesse
Repetition Nineteen III, July 1968
Fiberglass, polyester resin
Installation variable, 19 units
Museum of Modern Art, New York, gift
of Anita and Charles Blatt, 1969 © The
Estate of Eva Hesse. Hauser & Wirth
photo: Abby Robinson, New York

BIBLIOGRAPHY

Bland, Eric. "New Glue Has Mussel Power." Discovery News, April 16, 2008. http://dsc.discovery.com/news/2008/04/16/mussel-glue.html.

"Feminist Art Base: Eva Hesse." Elizabeth A. Sackler Center for Feminist Art, Brooklyn Museum. http://www.brooklynmuseum.org/eascfa/feminist_art_base/gallery/eva_hesse.php.

"The Essence, the Soul, the Center: Eva Hesse's Stubbornly Original Work." Translated by Andrea Scrima. Deutsche Bank Art Magazine, September 2004. http://www.db-artmag.de/2004/9/e/1/295.php.

Fildes, Jonathan. "Gecko glue exploits mussel power." BBC News, July 18, 2007. http://news.bbc.co.uk/2/hi/science/nature/6904175.stm.

Glueck, Grace. "Bringing the Soul into Minimalism: Eva Hesse." New York Times, May 12, 2006. http://www.nytimes.com/2006/05/12/arts/design/12hess.htm

Keimel, Fred A. "Historical Development of Adhesives and Adhesive Bonding." In Handbook of Adhesive Technology. Edited by A. Pizzi and K. L. Mittal. New York: Marcel Dekker, Inc., 1994.

ScienceDaily. "Glue Goes Green." October 16, 2007. http://www.sciencedaily.com/releases/2007/10/071014193722.htm.

4.1 A topographic map of the Grand Teton Mountain Range delineates heights in small increments; each line represents an 80-foot vertical difference. In plan, one specific line creates an unbroken loop around the mountain. The loop-line changes as it follows a path, jaggedly tracing the ins and outs of a mountain's creases and smoothing out across its broad surfaces. Evenly and distantly spaced loops represent contours with smooth and shallow transitions between them, while tightly packed, irregular contours are steep slopes with deeply incised surfaces. A mountain's three-dimensional physical features are visible through this two-dimensional representation.

AQUA

Aqua is a mixed-use residential tower located at Lakeshore East, a development situated near Lake Michigan in downtown Chicago. Divided into a hotel, apartments, and condominiums, the tower rises 260 meters in height. Its two-story plinth includes retail, a hotel ballroom, commercial spaces, lobbies, and parking topped by a large roof garden. At street level the project connects pedestrians to a six-acre park with two large public stairs. Design for Aqua began in 2004.

OWNER/DEVELOPER: Magellan Development Group, NNP Residential LLC.

LOCATION: 225 N. Columbus Drive, Chicago, USA

SIZE: 1.9 million SF including parking

COMPLETION DATE: 2010

4.3

4.4

4.3 The Grand Tetons, seen from across a frozen lake, are a silhouette of peaks measured against the horizon. While the mountain range out-scales the height of a city skyline by orders of magnitude, both elicit a sense of wonder.

4.4 Tall buildings clustered in cities create the visual sensation of landscape. Together, buildings stand in for landscape, especially when there is a noticeable lack of one nearby. From afar, both cities and mountains beckon as destinations of promise and opportunity.

TOPOGRAPHIC TOWER

Aqua is one of the few tall buildings where people, perched on exterior terraces over the tower's full height, become a part of its facade, a part of its vertical community, and a part of the city simultaneously. It operates as a landscape— an inhabitable cliff. In its design we explored what other benefits topography had to offer the tall building typology.

Cities as Mountains

4.2 (previous page) Aqua explores what can be achieved by constantly varying the tower's most prevalent structural element: its floor slabs. Slabs extending beyond the interior provide a strong connection between inside and outside by creating large outdoor terraces for people to occupy. Oblique vistas of the building form a virtual surface across the slab edges.

As is often observed, the skyline of a city creates the visual impression of a landscape. When clustered together, tall buildings make a city appear deceptively large—even on the scale of a mountain range. The variegated heights of buildings merge when viewed from a distance, despite the fact that their high and low points are not physically connected. After all, the city is an assembly of individual inhabitable vessels while a mountain range is a flowing, continuous mass of solid, impenetrable rock. But these visual associations do indicate that the city might play the role of surrogate for those who have left beloved mountainous locales for gritty urban ones. For others, the city's buildings stand in for an imagined landscape, especially when there is a lack of three dimensions nearby. Cities in deserts (Vegas, Dubai), cities surrounded by water (Shanghai, Manhattan), and cities on plains (Chicago, Toronto) compensate for the environment's lack of variation with their own architectural diversity.

There is also a similarity in the way that cities and mountain ranges beckon, drawing people toward the prospect and potential they hold. Rising from a relentless horizontal, seemingly out of nowhere, the first sight of a city produces a thrilling sensation in much the same way as the first sight of a mountain range can. Both cities and mountains hold opportunity for incredible success or miserable failure. They represent destiny, as if the highs and lows of their peaks and valleys were a physical manifestation of life's fluctuations.

In addition to these shared visual and conceptual traits, both mountains and cities have in recent times become the sites of extreme physical adventure, with cities presenting challenges for high-risk recreation as fierce as those of the great outdoors (fig. 4.8). Parkour athletes test themselves by leaping between buildings and trains; urban adventurers scale cranes and unfinished towers, and crawl through tunnels. For many, the built environment has become so immense and mysterious that exploring it offers a physical, spiritual, and psychological reward equal to traversing the remote, craggy rock formations of natural terrains.

> There is a known phenomenon among the urban adventure culture that the unsought-for places are usually the best. Popping open a random manhole for no real reason can lead one to an unexpected—and usually spectacular—find. So it was on this night. We had bailed on two prior endeavors and were heading back to the car when we passed over a hatch which was sort of in the middle of nowhere. As it rattled under our feet, Snail decided to go back and open it up. He went down and we closed the hatch above him and kept watch. A few seconds later he came back up and told us to come on down: it was a massive steam tunnel.
>
> (Anonymous post, Nopromiseofsafety.com, April 21, 2010)

Topography in architecture can potentially heighten experience and excitement for all city dwellers, including those less intrepid than the urban adventure set. For the inhabitants of towers, it is the altitudinal view of the city that provides the thrill. Unencumbered views (also a feature of landscape) are the desire, but this wish can be at odds with the increasingly constructed urban center, where towers without neighbors are somewhat rare or short-lived. More typically, new towers must negotiate views between many existing buildings.

This held true for Aqua. Its site was located amid a cluster of existing buildings within the large, mixed-use development of Lakeshore East. Considering that views are a primary criterion for a residential high-rise, we took them as

4.5 A 1:20 physical model demonstrates that interesting views are possible. Taut strings representing sightlines correlate with views between the cracks of neighboring buildings and through the caverns of adjacent streets. Sightline strings are lines of desire connecting living spaces in the "hills" on the facade to specific landmarks.

4.6 Named and rated navigable routes are desire-lines found on typical ski maps. Perspectival illustration of the slope is chosen over plan projection on ski maps in order to allow the detail of the paths to be shown simultaneously with the magnitude of the entire mountain range.

our starting point. It was clear that Aqua's height would allow for ample views at the upper floors, but with its site wedged between hotels, office towers, and other residential high-rises, capturing views for the mid and lower levels would prove more difficult. This difficulty would only increase once the master plan was completed, as made evident by a physical model at 1:20 that accounted for existing and planned buildings.

Nevertheless, sightlines extending from a digital city model demonstrated that interesting and particular views from Aqua were possible between the cracks of adjacent buildings and down the street corridors to specific landmarks. Taut strings connected to the physical model were used to focus the general sightlines toward landmarks, while detailed digital models lent greater geometric precision to the experiment.

It was soon discovered that three-dimensional sculpting on all four sides of the tower yielded better view connections—giving Aqua, with its topographic surface turned upright, hill-like curves that offer unexpected sights around corners and through gaps, just as they do on land. The individual hills in early modeling were positioned strategically on the form to exploit this phenomenon. Rather than opting for generalized panoramas, it was instead preferred to create a specific response to the city, providing a set of determined links between the building and its site.

Translation

As with topographic maps that translate physical conditions into two-dimensional abstractions, the initial study models of the building were converted into two-dimensional, map-like drawings. Hills became articulated as contour lines: unbroken loops describing areas of similar projection. Abstracting dimensional information from the models into drawings gave an understanding of the continuity of the surface, where small, one-foot increments of change could be communicated. Mapping also revealed the connections between the building's hills and valleys, and the steepness of these transitions (fig. 4.7). Four unique elevational maps emerged. Each drawing represents a different orientation: north, south, east, and west.

The next translation was made from the topographic elevation drawing to a new, three-dimensional model. This time, contours yielded a different result: instead of lines, they were converted to slices passing through the mass to produce a series of plates with individual outlines. These slices were interpreted as a series of slabs like strata in rock (fig. 4.10). Given the tools that connect our digital drawings to the builder's lay-out tools, we knew that varying the slabs would be viable from a construction standpoint. Re-conceiving the tower as a form made up of many layers or strata created new rules for the design's development.

Specificity & Difference

Modulation is achieved through extremely slight adjustments of the floor plates over the height of the tower. The slab edges are constantly changing, and no two are alike. Far from just creating a surface effect, these layers are integral to the building's construction, as each slab is an essential part of the structure. Curved in plan, the slabs cantilever away from the face and outer column line of the building. Each cantilever is dependent on its own back-span and precise column location. With the cantilevers presenting the most difficult structural challenge (some extend up to 12 feet), certain parameters were put in place to determine their proper location and maximum size (fig. 4.14). In addition to views, solar-shading, apartment size, form and structure, accessibility, cost, and construction methods all played a role in their final design: seemingly ordinary criteria that came to life when applied to the slabs of Aqua, providing a set of variables that contributed to its overall shape.

> *page 151*

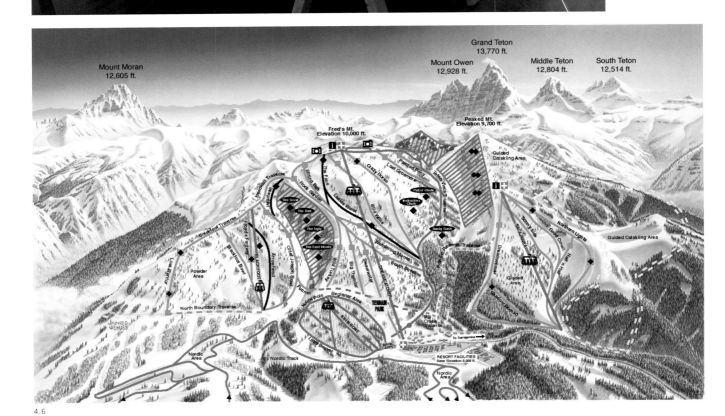

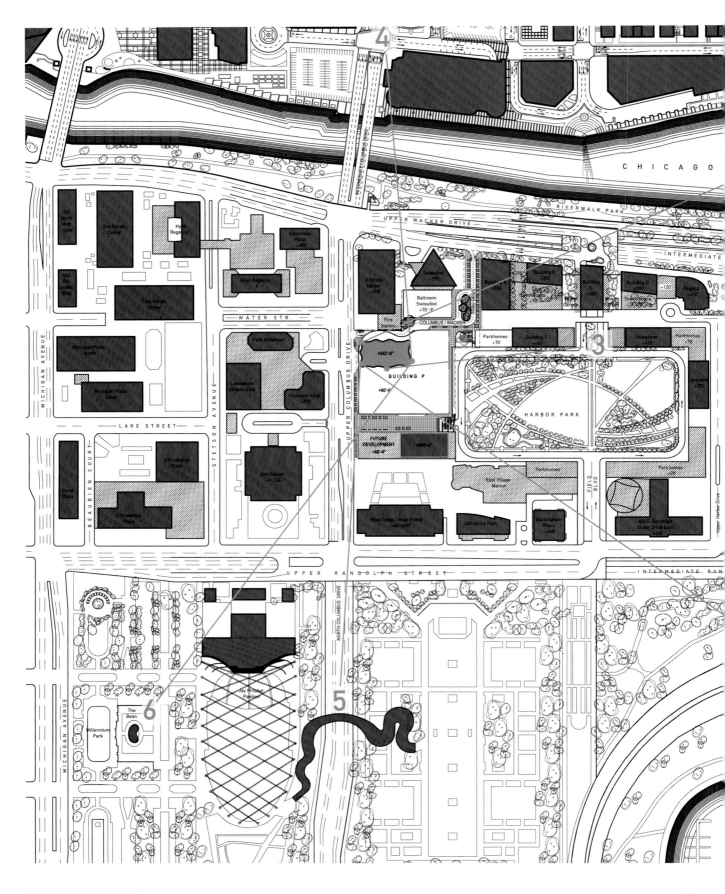

333
North
Michigan

One Illinois Center

Hyatt
Regency I

Columbus
Plaza
+495'

Old Re-
public
Bldg

Hyatt Regency
II

3 Illinois
Center
+390'

Swissôtel
+375'

Building A
+550'

Building B
+290'

Building C
+640'

Building D
+290'

Regatta
+410'

+120'

Two Illinois
Center

WATER STR.

Ballroom
Swissôtel
+70'-9"

COLUMBUS / WACKER

Fire
Station

Michigan Plaza
North

Park Millenium

Parkhomes
+70'

Building F
+640'

Shoreham
+410'

Parkhomes
+70'

Michigan Plaza
South

Lakeshore
Athletic Club

Fairmont Hotel
+375'

+942'-6"

BUILDING P
+90'-6"

HARBOR PARK

Lancaster
+290'

LAKE STREET

FUTURE
DEVELOPMENT
+88'-4"

+880'-4"

Parkhomes

2 Prudential
Plaza

Doral
Plaza

1 Prudential
Plaza

Aon Center
+1,136'

Blue Cross / Blue Shield
+660'/600'

East Village
Market

Parkhomes

Parkhomes
+70'

360 on the Park

Buckingham
Plaza
+440'

400 E. Randolph
(Outer Drive East)
+425'

UPPER RANDOLPH STREET

Jay Pritzker
Pavilion

The
Bean

Millennium
Park

STUDIO GANG / ARCHITECTS

148

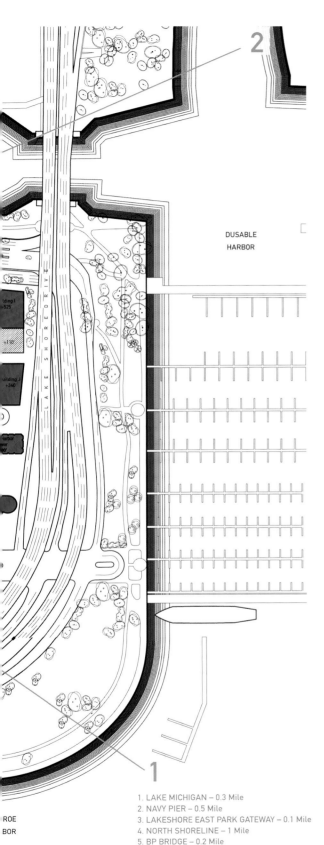

AQUA SITE PLAN

The site plan shows the existing and proposed buildings at Lakeshore East and the position of Building P (now Aqua) along Upper Columbus Drive. When all of the buildings are completed, a denser city fabric will surround the park, and change access to views for the mid and lower levels of the tower. Strategically positioning hills, which extend out from the facade at different heights, enables views of surrounding Chicago landmarks between other buildings. A hill located on the tower's east side, for example, yields a view of the landmark sculpture Cloud Gate by Anish Kapoor, even though the sculpture is located to the southwest of the tower. Around the corner and between two neighbors, Aqua connects to Cloud Gate along view line #6 in the drawing. Rather than general panoramas, the hills create visually navigable routes that identify a specific city and cement a relationship between the building, its site, and a moment in time represented by the contemporary surroundings.

DUSABLE
HARBOR

LAKE SHORE DRIVE

1. LAKE MICHIGAN – 0.3 Mile
2. NAVY PIER – 0.5 Mile
3. LAKESHORE EAST PARK GATEWAY – 0.1 Mile
4. NORTH SHORELINE – 1 Mile
5. BP BRIDGE – 0.2 Mile
6. CLOUD GATE - 0.2 Mile

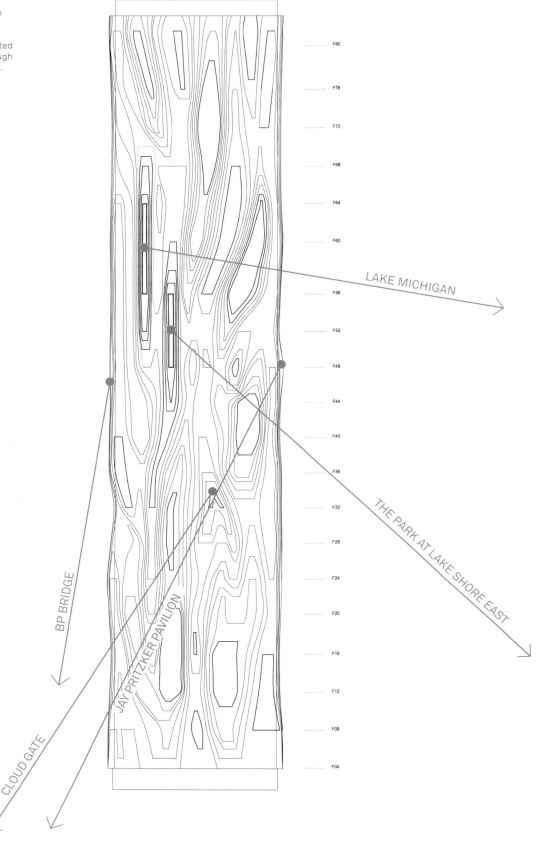

4.7 Specific connections to landmarks are achieved through sculpting the building's facade. "Hills" created on the building's vertical surfaces allow unexpected views around corners and through gaps between existing buildings.

F80
F76
F72
F68
F64
F60
F56
F52
F48
F44
F40
F36
F32
F28
F24
F20
F16
F12
F08
F04

LAKE MICHIGAN

THE PARK AT LAKE SHORE EAST

BP BRIDGE

JAY PRITZKER PAVILION

CLOUD GATE

4.8 Urban adventurers exploring (clockwise from top left): a tunnel; the Greco-Roman temple atop 360 N. Michigan Avenue; and Aqua's roof. Photos courtesy of Nopromiseofsafety.com

The design process exploited the opportunities presented by constantly varying the slabs. One of the greatest benefits of this approach are the large, unique outdoor terraces for people to occupy, from which oblique vistas across the building's exterior are possible. Parties, cook-outs, sunbathing, and reading on the terraces give vertical neighbors a chance to see and meet each other in a more comfortable situation than the elevator. Aqua's hilly surface gives residents outdoor access, while dually facilitating a relationship between occupants.

As extensions of the interior spaces, the slabs provide solar shading for the window wall, so that clear, low-e glass could be used for much of the building. But the variation also meant that some areas would be shaded more fully than others. Fine tuning the glazing to mitigate solar exposure was achieved through the introduction of reflective "pools": places on the facade where high-performance glass is introduced locally (fig. 4.15). Generated using sun angles, the figure of the pools is visible in the final design.

For pedestrians at street level, Aqua is a topographic tower that constantly changes as one moves around it. The form is sculptural when seen obliquely, from below, and resolves into a slender rectangle from further away. Its vertical landscape can be experienced from the public space at its base, from neighboring towers, and from its own terraces. Because it is not a two-dimensional elevation, or an immediately recognizable, cartoon-iconic shape (drill bit, Möbius strip, pagoda), it cannot be fully comprehended in an instant, thereby resisting any singular reading. The building aims to inspire exploration and asks if architecture can be more than shelter, inviting us to step out on its terraces and interact with the world around us. Its topography is formed with a great variety of peaks, valleys, and pools, resonating with landscape but redefining it by deploying it—for the first time—vertically.

S/G/A

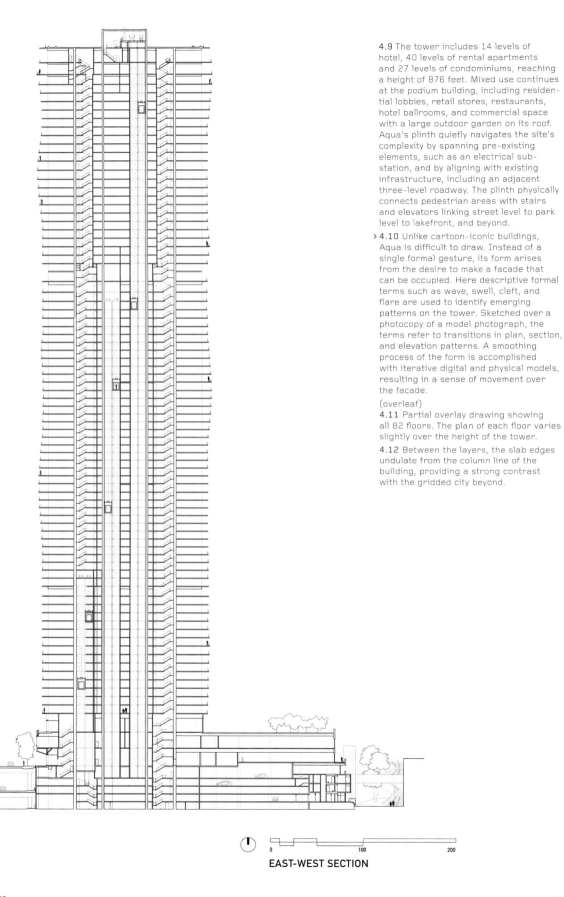

4.9 The tower includes 14 levels of hotel, 40 levels of rental apartments and 27 levels of condominiums, reaching a height of 876 feet. Mixed use continues at the podium building, including residential lobbies, retail stores, restaurants, hotel ballrooms, and commercial space with a large outdoor garden on its roof. Aqua's plinth quietly navigates the site's complexity by spanning pre-existing elements, such as an electrical substation, and by aligning with existing infrastructure, including an adjacent three-level roadway. The plinth physically connects pedestrian areas with stairs and elevators linking street level to park level to lakefront, and beyond.

> **4.10** Unlike cartoon-iconic buildings, Aqua is difficult to draw. Instead of a single formal gesture, its form arises from the desire to make a facade that can be occupied. Here descriptive formal terms such as wave, swell, cleft, and flare are used to identify emerging patterns on the tower. Sketched over a photocopy of a model photograph, the terms refer to transitions in plan, section, and elevation patterns. A smoothing process of the form is accomplished with iterative digital and physical models, resulting in a sense of movement over the facade.

(overleaf)

4.11 Partial overlay drawing showing all 82 floors. The plan of each floor varies slightly over the height of the tower.

4.12 Between the layers, the slab edges undulate from the column line of the building, providing a strong contrast with the gridded city beyond.

0   100   200

EAST-WEST SECTION

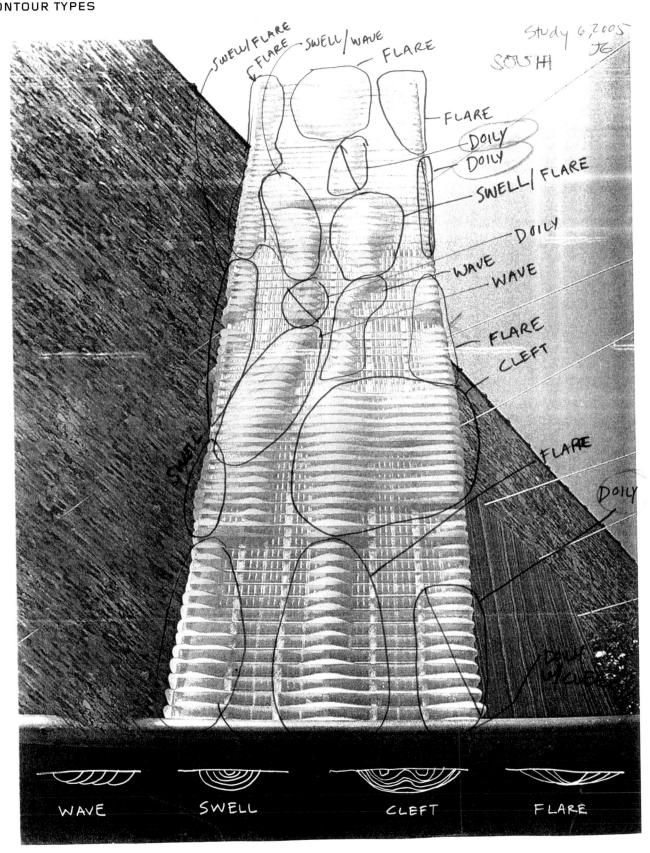

SWELL/FLARE
& FLARE
SWELL/WAVE
FLARE
Study 6, 2005
JG
SOUTH
FLARE
DOILY
DOILY
SWELL/FLARE
DOILY
WAVE
WAVE
FLARE
CLEFT
FLARE
DOILY

WAVE   SWELL   CLEFT   FLARE

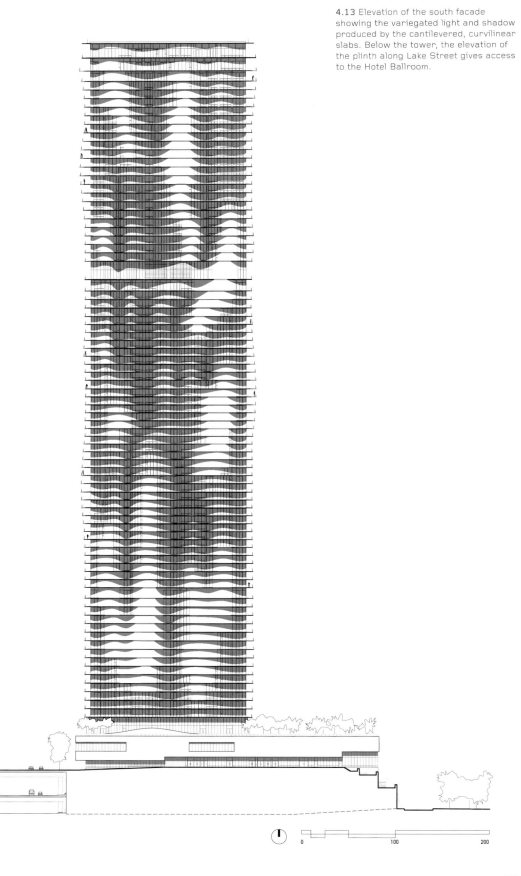

4.13 Elevation of the south facade showing the variegated light and shadow produced by the cantilevered, curvilinear slabs. Below the tower, the elevation of the plinth along Lake Street gives access to the Hotel Ballroom.

0   100   200

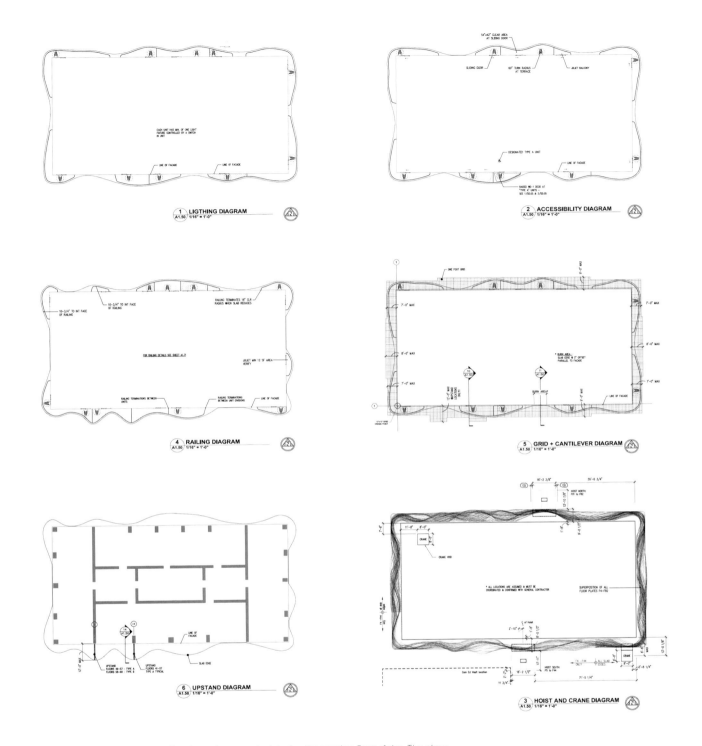

4.14 Structure and construction planning set up constraints for the varying floor slabs. The structural diagram outlines the location of the deepest and shallowest cantilevers allowable, while the
construction diagram indicates crane and hoist locations to be accommodated. The unique floor
slabs, in turn, parametrically cause variation in many other building elements. Handrails are particular to each slab, as are locations of sliding glass doors from living rooms to terraces. Door locations
adjust in every apartment to coordinate with terrace size, living room furnishings, and accessibility.

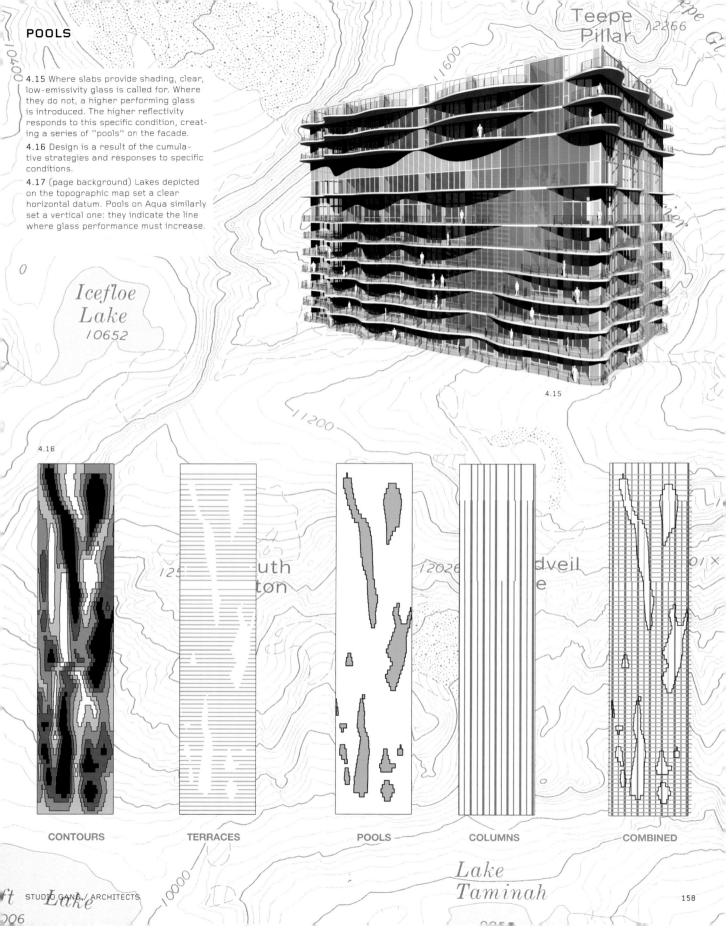

POOLS

4.15 Where slabs provide shading, clear, low-emissivity glass is called for. Where they do not, a higher performing glass is introduced. The higher reflectivity responds to this specific condition, creating a series of "pools" on the facade.

4.16 Design is a result of the cumulative strategies and responses to specific conditions.

4.17 (page background) Lakes depicted on the topographic map set a clear horizontal datum. Pools on Aqua similarly set a vertical one: they indicate the line where glass performance must increase.

4.15

4.16

| CONTOURS | TERRACES | POOLS | COLUMNS | COMBINED |

4.18 A sun study of the south elevation recording hours per day of solar radiation. Highlighted zones receive more than four hours of direct sunlight.

MARCH 21: VERNAL EQUINOX

Sun is: 32 degrees above the horizon at 9:00 am
49 degrees above the horizon at noon

March 21 average temperature: 42 F

Average high in March 21: 52 F
Possibility of sunshine: 50%

Probability of April 21 at 65F or above: 20%

Highest record temperature: 77 F

1 hr

2 hr

3 hr

4 hr

5 hr

6 hr

7 hr

8 hr

9 hr

10 hr

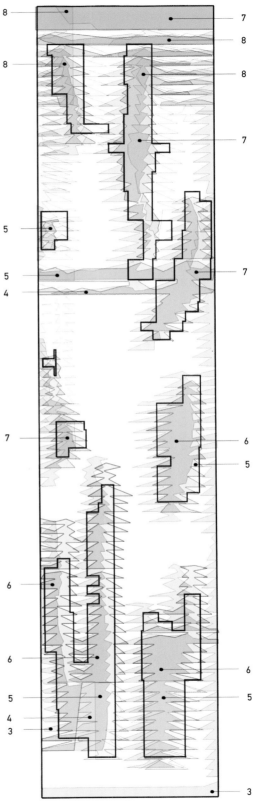

SOUTH ELEVATION MARCH 21 ALL DAY SUN STUDY

PROJECT / AQUA

Lynn Becker's writings on architecture have appeared in the Chicago Reader, Harvard Design Magazine, Long Island Newsday, Metropolis Magazine, and on his daily blog, Architecture Chicago Plus. Becker interviewed Aqua's developer and Architect of Record, Jim Loewenberg, during construction on the tower; Jim had this to say:

Jim Loewenberg: I've only had one job in my life, really. My father and my uncle were architects and engineers. When I graduated from MIT in 1957, I came to work for them. In 1980, I took over.

In my father's day—in the 1920s—they would do 12-story buildings. Those were huge buildings. I've been joking for the last few months that my 20-story building used to be a big building. Now, we're doing Aqua. Aqua is 87 stories when you count the five stories below street level.

Aqua is part of the Lakeshore East development, the genesis of which is that my partner, Joel Carlins, and I decided that we wanted to build over at Superior Place, and we partnered with Charles E. Smith and Company out of Washington, very large residential developers who specialize in in-town locations and high-rise buildings. They were looking to expand their national footprint and Chicago was one of their targets.

They said, "We really like Chicago. It's been very good to us. And we like you guys. Let's do some more business together." I said, "There's a huge piece of property that's been sitting vacant, the remnants of the old Illinois Central yard." Smith's success in Washington was that they bought a railroad yard between the Pentagon and the White House. They built a development called Crystal City over this old railroad yard. It was tremendously successful.

The parallels between Lakeshore East and Crystal City were very apparent to me, and so we approached Smith. Then we started to try and buy the large piece of land. It took us quite a while because the owner, Metropolitan Structures, was totally a rudderless ship. The land was owned by Metropolitan and the remnants of the old Illinois Central Railroad Company, which had become PepsiAmerica. It was a totally misplaced asset on their balance sheet and nobody was looking at it.

So we got the land, and now we had to figure out what to do with it. It was designated as an office building PUD (Planned Urban Development). But we didn't want to build 14 million sf of offices and the city didn't want to build 14 million sf of offices. We wanted to do residential. That was our forte.

The plan had included a deck to bring the whole thing up to the level of upper Columbus. It would have cost $100 million to build—totally uneconomical. We had Skidmore, Owings & Merrill come in and redesign the site plan. We put the park down on natural grade—a great idea and it reduced the infrastructure cost from $100 million to $17 million. It made it a buildable project.

Nobody can really sit and predict the market ten years in advance, and so as a part of the master plan, there were buildings of all sizes and scopes. The idea was to give us flexibility. The basic parameters were that it would be a mixed-use community, because it offered us a variety of product. We didn't want to be competing with ourselves with multiples of the same type of building. That's always been our mantra.

4.19 Glossy "splash" pages of the Aqua sales brochure

So we did a 207-unit condominium, and we did a 550-unit rental building, and two others. Then we came to the Aqua site, which is huge. The floor area ratio would allow us to build out to 1,200,000 sf. So now we violate all our rules. You don't want to build condominiums—it's too many. You don't want to build a rental, because now you're talking about one thousand apartments in a single building.

We decided to try something that's never been done here. We'll build a single building that's got multiple housing uses. We think this is a great hotel site, close to Millennium Park, close to the Loop and all the attractions here.

Economies of scale become magnified in apartments, so the bigger you can build them, the better. The next thing we know is who rents. I've been doing rental apartments for fifty years. I can sit here and put a shovel in the ground for a building and tell you pretty much what the demographics will be. Two-thirds of the people are going to be young adults, between 20–25, first job. Of that, 65 percent are going to be single, and 65 percent are going to be female, working in a Loop professional services firm. Sarbanes-Oxley was the greatest thing that ever happened to the rental market, because it's forced all these accounting firms to double and triple their staff. We get a lot of lawyers, young kids coming out of law school. They get relatively high pay, so they're high-income earners. They're single. They want to live close to work.

So we design our products to meet those people. We're very heavy on one-bedroom and studio apartments. We know we can get all the features in, and average around 820 sf across all units, about 1,000 sf grossed up. We know that our master bedroom, we like to go between 11 and 12 feet wide, so our sweet spot is 11½ feet wide. Why is it 11½ feet wide? Well, the bed is 6 feet. You got a dresser over here that's 24 inches, and that leaves you three feet between the bed and the dresser. If it gets much smaller than that, it gets too cramped.

The length of the bedroom we can go as low as 14 feet, but we like to go 16 feet. And how do you get to that? Well, you always work off of a king-sized bed. If you can get that in, you can get any bed in. A king-sized bed is about 6' x 6', maybe 72" x 75". Then you want to put a little nightstand on either side. That's 18", and you'd like 2' clearance. Also, you have to remember: two steps to daylight. That's a favorite saying of mine. From the door, to the time you can look out a window, in any room—I don't care what room it is—if you have to take much more than two steps, it's bad. Because the pop or "wow factor" is putting in a window and having them look out the window. They forget the size of the room. It opens it up. I have always maintained that the average renter in a high-rise building never looks above the third floor. He sees the building at street level. He doesn't look at the details above the third floor. It's more important that the apartment is a livable space. Critics hate me, but I have always said the inside is much more important to him than the outside. And the fact of the matter is that some of my ugliest buildings, in the critics' minds, are some of the most successful buildings.

The view is very important. That's marketing. We sell it. I'm a proponent of balconies, don't get me wrong, but balconies are the most useless thing. They're expensive to do, probably about $2,500 to $3,000 each. Why do people want a balcony? Well, he or she pictures him- or herself coming home from work. The partner of their choice hands them a martini, and they go and sit on the balcony. It's a concept that sells. But the guy who fantasizes about his balcony, what does he do? He winds up putting his $3,000 bicycle on the balcony because he doesn't want to leave it in the storage room down in the basement where it will get stolen .

Anything over 12 stories is too high, okay? Somewhere around 10, 12 stories you can still relate to the ground. You can see what's going on in Millennium Park. You're part of the action. After that, you don't really see the ground unless you walk up to the window and look straight down. Anything over that is ego. Height sells, but there isn't a hell of a lot of difference between the 40th floor and the 70th floor.

I decided early on that I would do a couple of buildings at Lakeshore East, to get it started, and then we would start bringing in the top architects to try different things, different housing techniques. I was looking for architects that would give me a wow factor, and I brought Jeanne in. We paid something extra for good design and it was worth it. It brings identification in the marketplace.

In Jeanne's design for Aqua, the slabs move in and out, and I bought into it immediately. I thought it was a great idea. But the thing that made it really great is the way she did it. I was able to convince myself, and then eventually the contractors, that this is not something you have to worry about. It's going to be really a basic, simple building. It may take you one man-day extra per floor to do it, to make the curves work, but once we got past that point in discussing that with the contractor, we were able to bring them on board and do it, relatively speaking, as an economical building.

I always like the general contractor to be the guy who pours the concrete, because the guy who pours concrete on a job sets the pace. And we like to have the same mechanical guys, the same electrical guys. We want them to understand what we need and the way we need it done and we don't want to have to listen to their tale of woe about how they didn't anticipate something. We want them to know going in what they have to deliver, to control costs, and control productivity. We buy tough, but the guys know that they're going to get a fair shake from us.

We start on the marketing as soon as we have a firm-enough handle on costs. The last thing you want to do is go out and sell something you can't afford to build. The banks say they won't open a loan with less than 50 percent of the units sold. We say we don't want to open a loan with less than 75 percent sold. When we opened the construction loan for Aqua, we were 87–88 percent sold. You run scared all the time. And you should, until it's completely sold.

How does a project wind down? With a condominium, when we deliver the last unit and turn over the board to the homeowners, we're totally out of it. We're gone. With rentals, we have a management company that comes in to run it. We always keep the point at which we want to sell in the back of our minds. There are guys in the office building market that buy a building, hold it for six months, eight months, and then flip it. We like to hold them somewhere around eight years. We're building a portfolio.

I'm a great believer in the master architect theory. The architect is really a functionary of a building process and really shouldn't—he does not manage—the process. He's just another consultant on a long list of consultants. And the architect in his traditional role has abdicated his responsibility. Go back to the time of the Middle Ages, and the guy who designed Chartres Cathedral, he told the bricklayer where to put the damn stone, you know? He told this guy to do that. He was responsible. S/G/A

PROJECT / AQUA

ENGINEERING AQUA

RON KLEMENCIC, Structural Engineer, Magnusson Klemencic Associates, Seattle, WA

Undulating Slabs

The most visible aspect of architecture merged with structure is found in Aqua's undulating slab edges. Maximizing views while providing unique balcony conditions for each unit requires the floor slab to cantilever as much as 12 feet, compared to the typical 6-foot standard balcony found on most tall buildings. To accomplish this gravity-defying feat, the structural design combined a unique column arrangement and state-of-the-art analysis techniques with requirements for a specific construction methodology.

Typical floor slabs in high-rise residential towers span 20 to 24 feet, with cantilever balconies of 6 feet. The thickness of these floor slabs is traditionally targeted at L/35, or 8" (22 ft x 12" per ft/35). Aqua capitalizes on a larger column spacing of 28 feet. Combining the larger bay sizes with the increased support offered by the larger columns (30" x 50" on average) required to support the 80 floors of weight allowed the slabs to cantilever 12 feet with a skinny 9-inch-thick slab. State-of-the-art finite-element computer modeling was employed to analyze and design the more than 70 unique floor slab conditions.

Pivotal to the design of the floor slabs is the forming method used to construct them. Typical construction methods utilize wood formwork supported by multiple levels of shoring below to temporarily carry the weight of the wet concrete. These construction loads can be greater than any loading the slabs will experience throughout the life of the building.

For Aqua, a unique formwork system was utilized which supports the weight of the wet concrete on steel trusses, which are in turn supported directly from the building columns. As such, the weight of the wet concrete is transferred directly into the vertical supports, eliminating the heaviest loading condition for the floor slabs. This direct transfer of loading enabled a slab design considered more aggressive than normal.

Bracing Against the Wind

Next to gravity, the most demanding effects considered in the design of tall buildings are those associated with wind forces. For most buildings, providing enough strength to resist these forces is relatively simple. Of greater concern is the sway of a tower and the resulting impact on occupant comfort.

Aqua combines traditional concrete shear walls with outrigger and belt walls strategically located throughout the tower's height to effectively manage the building's motion. Two shear walls and a central concrete core extend from the tower's foundation to the roof. Outrigger walls are provided at Levels 55 through 58 and 81 through 82, with supplementary belt walls between Levels 57 and 58. The purpose of the outriggers and belt walls is to activate all of the columns in the tower in resisting sway, thus effectively and efficiently distributing the wind loads. Similar to outriggers on a canoe or the support ski poles offer a skier, the outrigger and belt walls effectively broaden the "stance" of the building, improving overall stability.

Detailed wind tunnel studies were completed to confirm the performance of the structure under high winds. During the testing, it was discovered that the undulating slab edges disrupted or "confused" the flow of wind around the tower, effectively reducing the wind demands. Initially, it was thought that a supplemental tuned mass damping system might be required to appropriately manage the effects of the wind. The detailed wind tunnel studies confirmed the effectiveness of the structural design, and a supplemental damping system was not required.

Foundations

Unseen but critical to the support of the tower are the foundations. The enormous concentration of loading from the 88 supported floor slabs over the tower's relatively small footprint required a unique foundation design which tested the limits of any previously constructed in Chicago.

Typically, high-rise buildings in Chicago are supported on belled caissons bearing on Chicago's hard pan, which is located some 70 feet below grade. Average bearing pressures of 40 to 50 ksf are considered normal. Applying these "norms" to Aqua resulted in an overlapping geometry of caisson bells, yielding these standard construction techniques implausible.

Instead, 100-foot-deep rock caissons were designed with average bearing pressures of 500 ksf (ten times normal). The caissons varied in diameter from 5 to 10 feet, were constructed using 9,000-psi concrete, and were firmly socketed 6 feet into solid underlying bedrock. The load-carrying capacity of the rock caissons was confirmed using an Osterberg Load Cell Test, which proved that more-than-adequate safety margins exist in the tower's foundation design.

The commercial objectives of building a tower combined with the physical forces of gravity and wind have a great influence on building, but the most memorable tall buildings are the result of a thoughtful, sometimes poetic, duet played by the architect and structural engineer. **S/G/A**

MEASURES OF DENSITY

4.20 Urban dwellers benefit from density. A greater number of residents in proximity to employment brings cultural, recreational, educational, and mobility options within walking distance. Aqua Tower at Lake Shore East situates 738 new households minutes from the activities of everyday life, reducing reliance on driving.

4.21 In the city center, walking, taking a subway ride, or a minimal drive is all that is necessary to connect people to a high concentration of jobs. A compact city that locates residential dwellings near job density minimizes travel distances and commuting time, and thus reduces consumption of fossil fuels.

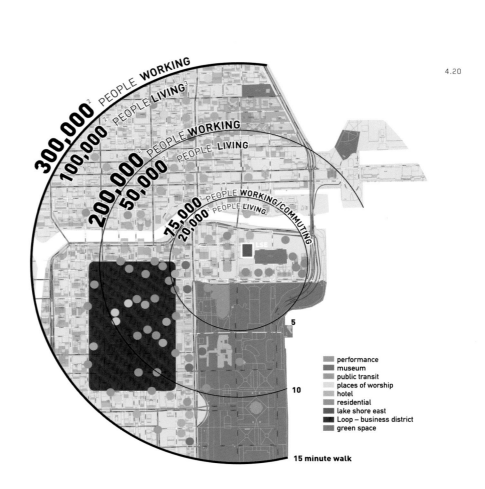

300,000² PEOPLE WORKING
100,000² PEOPLE LIVING³
200,000² PEOPLE WORKING
50,000² PEOPLE LIVING
75,000³ PEOPLE WORKING/COMMUTING
20,000³ PEOPLE LIVING

performance
museum
public transit
places of worship
hotel
residential
lake shore east
Loop – business district
green space

15 minute walk

4.21

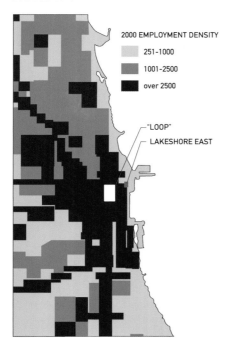

JOB DENSITY

2000 EMPLOYMENT DENSITY
251-1000
1001-2500
over 2500

"LOOP"
LAKESHORE EAST

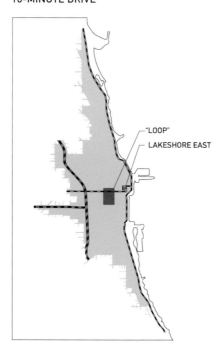

10-MINUTE DRIVE

"LOOP"
LAKESHORE EAST

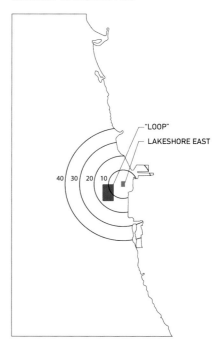

WALKING TIME (MINUTES)

"LOOP"
LAKESHORE EAST

40 30 20 10

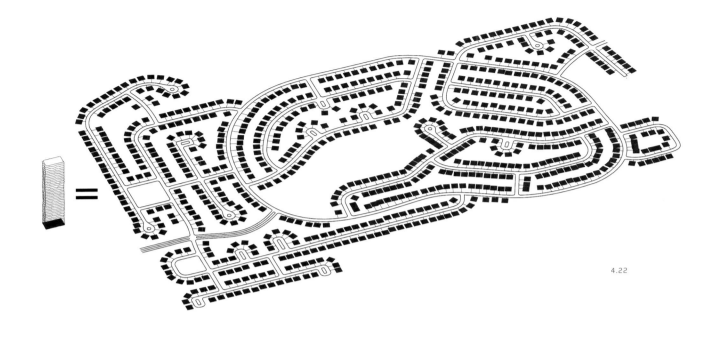

4.22

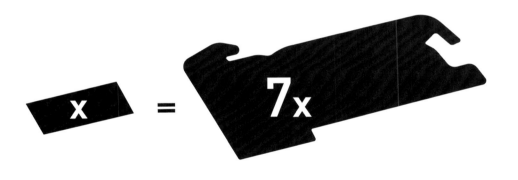

4.23

4.22 Land-use Comparison: Density can be measured in households per acre. Aqua holds 738 households on .32 acres yielding a density measure of 2,036 households per acre. A typical suburb would need 333 acres to accommodate the same number of households: approximately one thousand times more land.

4.23 Carbon Comparison: The metric tonnage of CO_2 produced by a household is directly related to the density of the settlement in which the household is located. For example, a typical household located in Aqua would produce 1.9 tons of carbon per year. A typical household in the suburb above would produce 14 tons of carbon per year. At seven times the size, the suburb leaves a Sasquatch-sized carbon footprint. Source: Center for Neighborhood Technology.

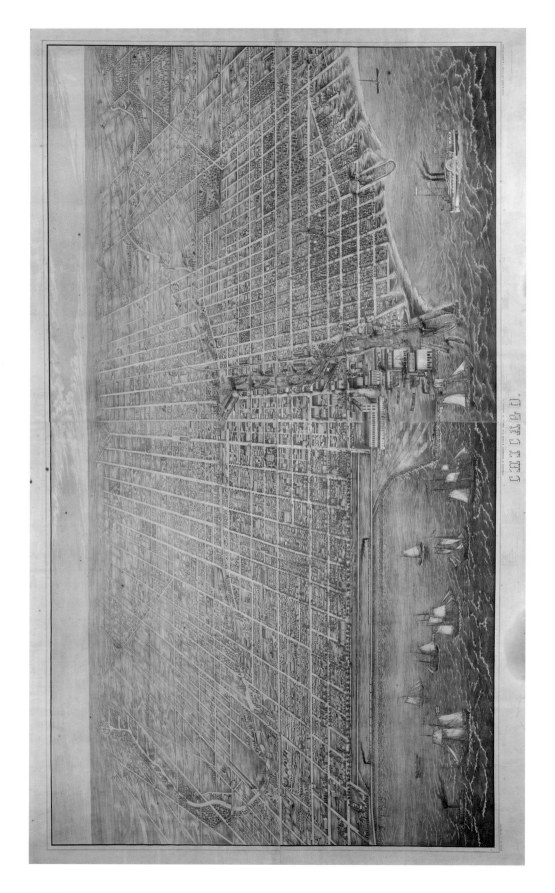

CHICAGO.

4.24 In 1857, a pre-fire "Birds-Eye View of Chicago" shows the Illinois Central Railroad along the lakefront. Its trestles define the shore solely as a railway corridor. The stretch of water between the city and the trestle would later be filled to become Grant Park. Reproduced by permission of the Chicago History Museum. ICHi-05658.

A LIFE *of* HARD TIMES: THE BOULDER'S STORY

DISCOVERED BY A BACKHOE DURING WORK ON FOUNDATIONS FOR THE AQUA TOWER, THE BOULDER'S EPIC JOURNEY WAS ABOUT TO COME TO AN ABRUPT AND DEFINITIVE END.

RIPPED AWAY FROM ITS STABLE BEDROCK IN CANADA, THE BOULDER WAS SENT ON A FORCED ROLL TO THE UNITED STATES 15,000 YEARS AGO.

BOULDERS IN THE NEWS 1904: The excavated glacial "Guthrie Boulder" (above) is prepared to be moved to Jackson Park as a monument. 2008: the submerged "Graffiti Boulder" (below) became the center of a border dispute between Kentucky and Ohio when it was removed from the Ohio River.

The boulder arrived via the Laurentide Glacier express, which moved approximately one to two feet per year on a trip that lasted over 10,000 years. After riding this head of ice as far south as Indiana, it reversed direction and moved north as the Laurentide receded.

On its way back to Canada on this harrowing journey, it happened upon Chicago. Its first indignity upon entering the city was to arrive on the muddy bottom side of a giant melting sheet of ice. It experienced not only dirt, but excruciating forces as the weight of the ice ground the boulder against hard earth. New scratches were added to its already scarred visage, a testament to its origin and to the long trip this rock had endured.

Unfortunately, the boulder never made it back to Canada. It was left behind as the glacier melted and receded to form Lake Michigan. At least it was not alone. It was deserted in Chicago along with many other chunks of Wisconsin and Minnesota. In fact, so many rocks were stranded in the Midwest that the area became nicknamed the "boulder belt."

Time, though, was good to the boulder's intactness and general state of being. It did what boulders do best for years and years: absolutely nothing. Enveloped by earth and dust, it remained buried fairly close to the earth's surface. It had no need or inclination to move. Others were not as lucky. When they were encountered by farmer's plows in the 1800s, they were frequently dug up and broken down to serve as fences, land markers, or even as part of a dam. Things were quiet for the Canadian boulder, however, even during the devastating fire of 1871. Located at the intersection of Michigan and Monroe Avenues, in the center of the fire's destruction, the rock's igneous composition was oblivious to what was, compared to its own life experience, a minor level of heat.

It was during the aftermath of the fire when all hell broke loose for the boulder. By 1870, the city's population exploded to ten times its size only two decades earlier. Chicago embarked on a massive building campaign that utterly transformed its surface, its shoreline and everything below grade. A new type of foundation system called grillage developed in 1881 that made tall buildings possible despite the mucky soil underfoot. Boulders were dug up and moved aside to make way for architecture.

There were several success stories such as that of the so-called "Guthrie boulder" that made it big after being discovered along the shore of Lake Michigan. In 1912, the Guthrie boulder was the center of a parade through the streets of Chicago as it was transported to a new home in Washington Park on the South Side. To this day, it has been able to sit contentedly doing nothing, while monumentalizing Samuel Guthrie, the inventor of chloroform.

Not many stories end happily for these ancient rocks. The Canadian boulder was unearthed to make way for an encyclopedia company's new building. Wrenched from the earth by a crew of fifty men digging by hand, it was levered onto a skid and nudged north across the street to what would become Grant Park. From this precarious position, exposed and potentially obstructing the park's progress, it was clear that the boulder's fate was in play. The city ordered the encyclopedia company to remove the boulder from its land.

In 1921, the boulder was rolled north along Michigan Avenue to the western edge of a railroad terminus. This site was slightly more secure because buildings were unlikely to be constructed along the railroad's gritty edges. Grime-covered and surrounded by a swirl of activity, the boulder

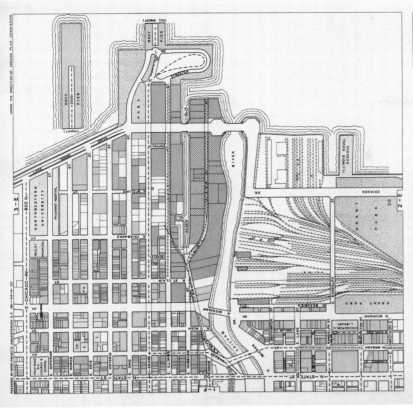

sat still for a brief forty years. As train transport was replaced by truck transport in the 1950s, railroads ceased operations, sold their land, and pulled up track. The land's availability led to the 1960 construction of a new commercial development on the site. The boulder's storied past was irrelevant to the men who were assigned to clear the site for construction for the Illinois Center project. To them, the boulder was simply an obstruction to be removed. Unlike the Guthrie boulder, which was elevated to "monument" status, the Canadian boulder was essentially banished. The contractors tried rolling it into the lake, but after the first few hundred feet of rolling, they simply abandoned the effort and left it for dead east of Columbus Drive.

There were humiliations at this location to be sure; curiously, the rock became an attractive pissoir for drunks, as the multilevel roadway built up around it gave the space the qualities of an underpass. One highlight, however, was the giant yellow peace sign tattooed on its surface in 1964.

In 1977, while making way for their new substation, a utility company was ordered by city officials to dispose of the boulder. After analyzing the cost of removal, the utility company decided to dig a hole and bury the rock underground next door.

Safely out of sight and out of mind, it wasn't until 2005, during site preparation for a new mixed-use residential tower called Aqua, that the boulder was rediscovered. Its remaining days were numbered, as it was sitting squarely on the future location of one of Aqua's largest caissons. Among other things dug up from alongside the Canadian boulder were some wood piles from a former lake edge pier, shoring from the former lake edge and strands of iron rail track. All of this detritus had to come out to make way for foundations.

In the future, perhaps someone will value a rock like this one more highly. They might try to save an old rock as a memorial to geologic history. They might think to place it in a museum, in a park, or on a podium in the city. One day, people might even consider it holy and come to worship near it. On this day, though, the end came quickly and unceremoniously. With the help of jackhammers and bull-dozers, the aged boulder that had traveled so far on a river of ice was converted to an ordinary pile of gravel and dust to fill the sub-surface of a mundane driveway.

4.25 (page 171, on fold) A view of the Illinois Central Railroad terminus and yard shows its prime real estate on Chicago's lakefront circa 1915. The Peristyle at Grant Park's northern edge is visible in the lower left-hand corner and the future Aqua site is in the center of the photograph.

4.26 (page 172, below fold) A 1904 photograph shows a man standing next to the Guthrie Boulder on Michigan Avenue. The boulder was found during building excavation work and later converted to a monument for a physician who discovered chloroform, Samuel Guthrie. It was paraded down the major street to its new home in Jackson Park. Photograph by the Chicago Daily News reproduced by permission of the Chicago History Museum. DN-0003261.

4.27 (page 172, lower) A boulder that has long been present in local lore was rolled into Kentucky's portion of the Ohio River over a hundred years ago. In 2008 Steve Schaffer, an Ohio historian, removed the "Graffiti Boulder" from the river and brought it to a Portsmouth, Ohio, garage, sparking a border dispute between the two states over its rightful owner.

> 4.28 A 1935 Works Progress Administration (WPA) map showing the relationship between the Illinois Central Railroad terminus and the Chicago River to the north and Lake Michigan to the east. When the Railroad ceased operations, many of the tracks and other detritus were simply buried below grade. Reproduced by permission of the Chicago History Museum. ICHi-38518.

MATERIAL REPORT: MAPS
REVEALING INVISIBLE STRATA

We tend to think of maps as ultimate authorities: as unimpeachable references that give us the answers and settle debates. The best maps are those which deliver information straightforwardly, without unnecessary additions or flourishes. These achieve a seamless graphic elegance—almost an omniscience—that allows their users to grasp concepts without noticing their communication.

But however easy it is to think of maps as infallible, they are often commissioned by people with an agenda, and as such are the result of multiple subjective choices regarding content and medium. The making of maps for political advantage, for example, is an age-old game of chess in which natural resources or constituent voters are the pawns. Perhaps the most famously manipulated voting district map dates from 1812. Redistricted to benefit Elbridge Gerry, the incumbent governor of Massachusetts, this map of Essex County inspired a political cartoonist to redraw it as a clawed, lizard-like creature and title it "The Gerry-Mander" (after Governor Gerry + salamander). The name inexplicably stuck, and today "gerrymandering" continues to be a common concept in world politics—for mapmaking continues to be recognized as an important tool in political power play.

Some maps, however, are so powerful they can transcend the sometimes narrow motives of their commissioners. William Smith's Great Strata-Map of 1815 is one of these. More than a factual regurgitation, it is a work of personal observations, bold imagination, a strong aesthetic sense, and—once in a while—a wild guess. Now known as the first geologic map of Great Britain ever drawn, the map began as a passionate side project for Smith, who traveled throughout early nineteenth-century Britain as a surveyor and drainage engineer financed by various coal mine owners. While inspecting mines and charting the best courses for coal canals, Smith (who had since childhood been fascinated by all things geologic) took the opportunity to observe cross sections of the earth like no one else before him. Here he recognized distinct layers of different types of soil and rock, and came to hypothesize that they had somehow been "set down," one on top of the other. More importantly, he came to realize that these layers, which he chose to term "strata," were arranged in the same way all across Britain. By paying attention to what was previously underground and unseen, he had discovered a larger pattern.

It was in making the decision to map this pattern that Smith's observations took on their greatest importance. Looking for the clearest way to differentiate between strata too similar in color and other qualities to be recognized by their rock and soil makeup, he discovered that fossils—which he had collected since he was a boy—were the key to distinguishing which strata were which. Those fossils abundant in one layer, Smith found, could be completely absent from the next. Additionally, each stratum contained its own unique fossil combination

which remained its identifying characteristic throughout the whole country. These careful observations led him to posit an idea previously unthinkable in its heresy: that the creation and seemingly random location of fossils were not in fact the product of Noah's flood—that instead their whereabouts were regular and corresponded with other geologic phenomena. The world was much, much older than previously imagined.

Smith's 1815 map of "England and Wales with part of Scotland" makes the reality of these rock and fossil patterns, as well as their greater implications for science (and, eventually, for turning the Christian worldview on its head), beautifully clear. Originally printed in fifteen sections to total a size of more than eight feet by six feet, the map is hand-colored in twenty-two different shades of ochre, umber, rust, gray, blue, and green, each corresponding to a unique, age-defined stratum. It is startlingly accurate: a fact that is all the more surprising when it's considered that Smith was never formally trained in cartography. Instead he developed his graphic techniques through a long and painstaking process of trial and error, eventually settling on the medium and methods that most effectively enabled him to communicate the invisible complexity of the underworld. Displayed in such a masterful way, his observations have since profoundly changed the way humans understand the history of the earth and our place within it—most famously, in its use by Charles Darwin as part of his theory of natural selection, as well as in the realms of continental drift and climate change.

The story of Smith's map has great relevance for the realm of architecture, too, where maps, diagrams, and plans are key tools for conveying information. As in any other kind of mapmaking, the creation of these architectural drawings involves many subjective choices about what to include or leave out—choices that may relate to the client's specific economic or political intentions for a project. As Smith proved with his work for the coal mine owners, however, faithfully fulfilling a client's needs and exploring one's own interests and convictions are not mutually exclusive. Part of the role of the professional is to deploy all of one's skill, previous experiences, and powers of observation toward an issue, while still maintaining an open mind. When observing, researching, and intelligently synthesizing visual information in this way, architects have the power to elevate data above purely pragmatic purposes, opening the door for discoveries on a grander scale and beyond the confines of professional boundaries. S/G/A

BIBLIOGRAPHY

Griffith, Elmer C. The Rise and Development of the Gerrymander. 1907. Reprint, New York: Arno Press, 1974.
Winchester, Simon. The Map That Changed the World: William Smith and the Birth of Modern Geology. New York: HarperCollins, 2001.

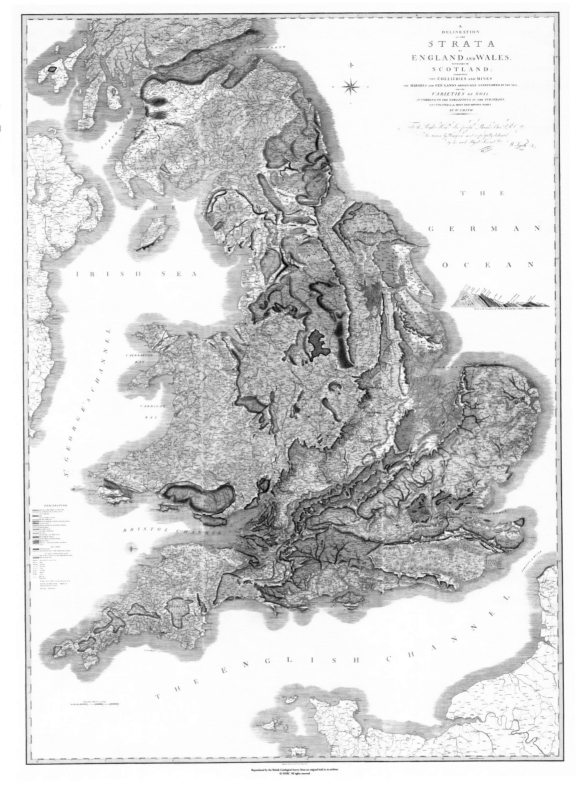

4.29 William Smith's revolutionary map, formally titled "William Smith's delineation of the strata of England and Wales with part of Scotland; exhibiting the collieries and mines, the marshes and fen lands originally overflowed by the sea, and the varieties of soil according to the variations in the substrata, illustrated by the most descriptive names."
© NERC 2008

PROJECT / AQUA

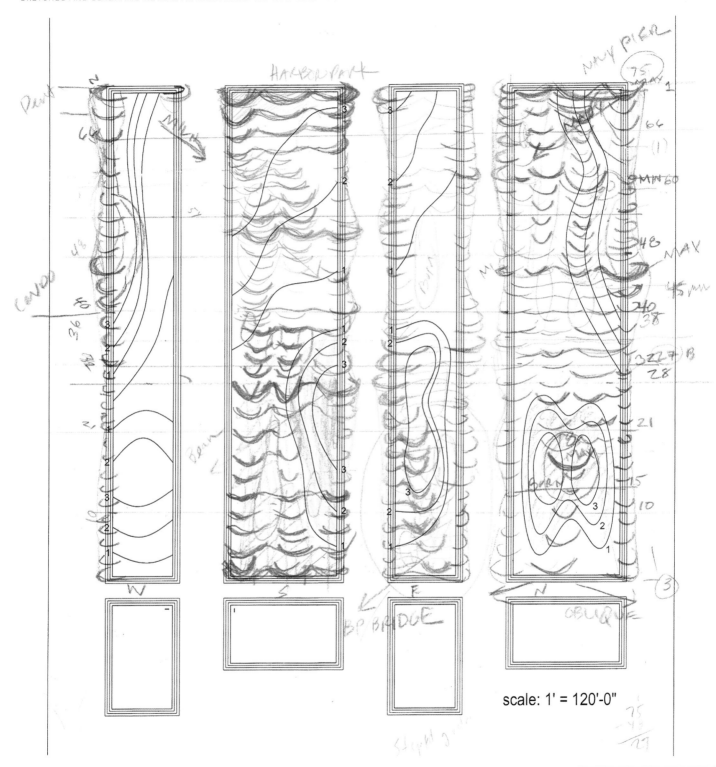

scale: 1' = 120'-0"

Overlay drawing studying the
convergence of view targets w
slab delineation

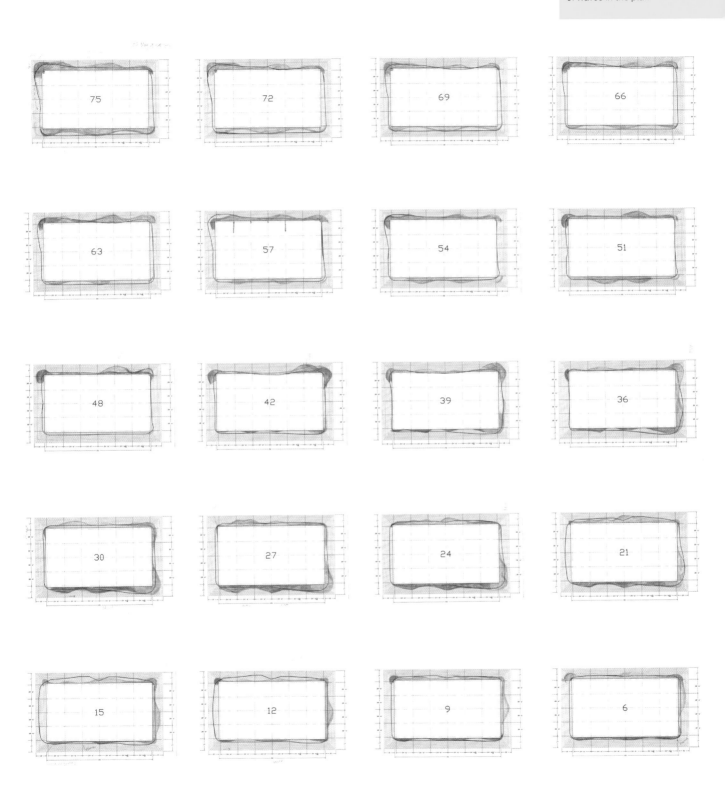

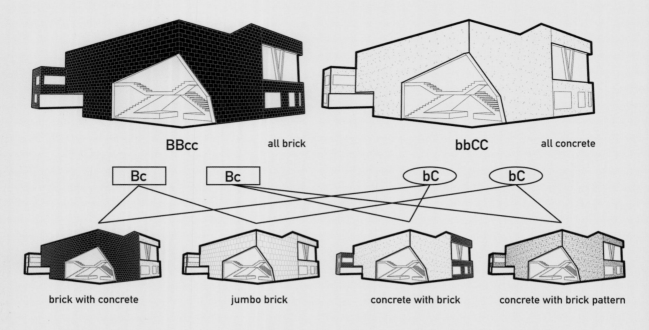

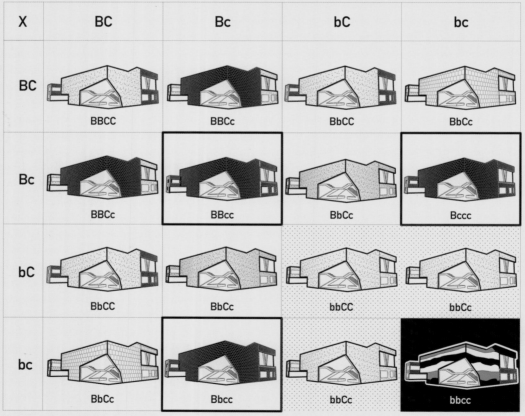

5.1 Inheritance: value engineering together with the procurement of material donations produces a range of potential outcomes for the building's exterior envelope. Efforts to reduce cost often result in hybrid designs as opposed to "pure" tectonic expressions. Occasionally, the combination yields something unexpected and new. This diagram shows two traits arrayed in a matrix (masonry and concrete, small units and large units) and their combinations. The unexpected solution is a combination generated from inherited materials.

SOS CHILDREN'S VILLAGES
LAVEZZORIO COMMUNITY CENTER

SOS is an international social service organization that was founded
after World War II to help orphaned children reunite with siblings who
were separated by war. Today they continue to bring siblings together
into a common foster care family, train foster care parents, and provide
housing and other services. The Lavezzorio Community Center is the hub
of activities and social services for the greater SOS Children's Village
Chicago, a residential neighborhood housing 20 foster care families
mixed with affordable single family homes, completed in Chicago in 2005.
It is the first urban village of its kind in the United States. The City of
Chicago donated the site, a former mattress factory, on the city's South
Side in the Auburn Gresham neighborhood.

OWNER: SOS Children's Villages Illinois
LOCATION: 7600 South Parnell Avenue, Chicago, USA
SIZE: 16,000 SF
COMPLETION DATE: 2007

PROJECT / SOS CHILDREN'S VILLAGES

SOCIAL EXPENDITURE TRENDS

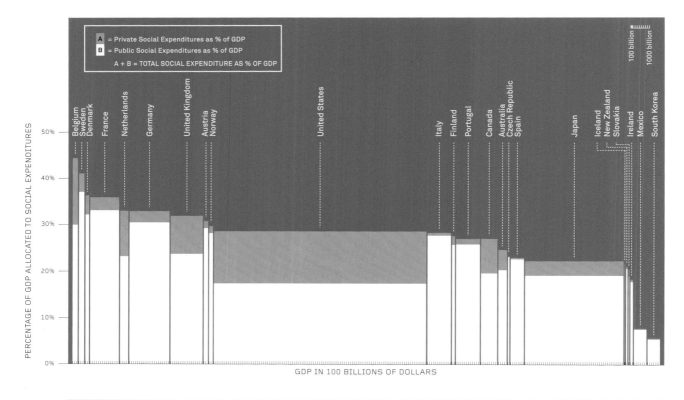

A = Private Social Expenditures as % of GDP
B = Public Social Expenditures as % of GDP
A + B = TOTAL SOCIAL EXPENDITURE AS % OF GDP

PERCENTAGE OF GDP ALLOCATED TO SOCIAL EXPENDITURES

GDP IN 100 BILLIONS OF DOLLARS

100 billion
1000 billion

BELGIUM
GDP **$239,600,000,000**
PUBLIC **30%** ($71,880,000,000)
PRIVATE **14.4%** ($34,502,400,000)

SWEDEN
GDP **$253,700,000,000**
PUBLIC **37.1%** ($94,122,700,000)
PRIVATE **4.0%** ($10,148,000,000)

DENMARK
GDP **$162,600,000,000**
PUBLIC **32.2%** ($52,357,200,000)
PRIVATE **4.1%** ($6,666,600,000)

FRANCE
GDP **$1,381,300,000,000**
PUBLIC **33.1%** ($457,210,300,000)
PRIVATE **2.8%** ($38,676,400,000)

NETHERLANDS
GDP **$394,100,000,000**
PUBLIC **23.2%** ($91,431,200,000)
PRIVATE **9.8%** ($38,621,800,000)

GERMANY
GDP **$1,920,200,000,000**
PUBLIC **30.5%** ($585,661,000,000)
PRIVATE **2.4%** ($46,084,800,000)

UNITED KINGDOM
GDP **$1,546,700,000,000**
PUBLIC **23.7%** ($366,567,900,000)
PRIVATE **8.2%** ($126,829,400,000)

AUSTRIA
GDP **$199,300,000,000**
PUBLIC **29.3%** ($58,394,900,000)
PRIVATE **1.5%** ($2,989,500,000)

NORWAY
GDP **$176,000,000,000**
PUBLIC **28.2%** ($49,632,000,000)
PRIVATE **1.5%** ($2,640,000,000)

UNITED STATES
GDP **$10,249,800,000,000**
PUBLIC **17.4%** ($1,783,465,200,000)
PRIVATE **11.2%** ($1,147,977,600,000)

ITALY
GDP **$1,121,300,000,000**
PUBLIC **27.7%** ($310,600,100,000)
PRIVATE **0.6%** ($6,727,800,000)

FINLAND
GDP **$129,400,000,000**
PUBLIC **25.7%** ($33,255,800,000)
PRIVATE **1.9%** ($2,458,600,000)

PORTUGAL
GDP **$1,149,900,000,000**
PUBLIC **25.8%** ($296,674,200,000)
PRIVATE **1.2%** ($13,798,800,000)

CANADA
GDP **$773,400,000,000**
PUBLIC **19.6%** ($151,586,400,000)
PRIVATE **7.4%** ($57,231,600,000)

AUSTRALIA
GDP **$399,600,000,000**
PUBLIC **20.3%** ($81,118,800,000)
PRIVATE **4.3%** ($17,182,800,000)

CZECH REPUBLIC
GDP **$61,300,000,000**
PUBLIC **23.1%** ($14,160,300,000)
PRIVATE **0.1%** ($61,300,000)

SPAIN
GDP **$637,000,000,000**
PUBLIC **22.6%** ($143,962,000,000)
PRIVATE **0.3%** ($1,911,000,000)

JAPAN
GDP **$4,754,600,000,000**
PUBLIC **19.1%** ($908,128,600,000)
PRIVATE **3.1%** ($147,392,600,000)

ICELAND
GDP **$9,200,000,000**
PUBLIC **21.7%** ($1,996,400,000)
PRIVATE **0.0%** ($0)

NEW ZEALAND
GDP **$59,000,000,000**
PUBLIC **20.6%** ($12,154,000,000)
PRIVATE **0.5%** ($295,000,000)

SLOVAKIA
GDP **$22,900,000,000**
PUBLIC **19.0%%** ($4,351,000,000)
PRIVATE **1.4%** ($320,600,000)

IRELAND
GDP **$112,800,000,000**
PUBLIC **17.8%** ($20,078,400,000)
PRIVATE **0.5%** ($564,000,000)

MEXICO
GDP **$593,200,000,000**
PUBLIC **7.6%** ($45,083,200,000)
PRIVATE **0.2%** ($1,186,400,000)

SOUTH KOREA
GDP **$585,900,000,000**
PUBLIC **6.5%** ($38,083,500,000)
PRIVATE **0.2%** ($1,171,800,000)

ARCHITECTURE DESERT

Process greatly shaped the design of the SOS Community Center. Designing for a social service agency in the United States requires a different mode of practice because there is so often a lack of sufficient funding. Design for SOS began in the aftermath of Hurricane Katrina, with the increased demand for construction supplies resulting in extraordinary price escalation. To combat the difficult timing, SOS decided to secure as many in-kind donations as possible for the building. Materials, products, and services were courted from the building industry. Donations included anything builders had on hand or in surplus. But what does a strategy like this mean for architecture? Is design possible with whatever leftover materials happen to be pitched in? For the SOS project, the design team needed much more than design skills; it needed a coping mechanism.

5.2 (previous page) Concrete's liquidity is expressed through horizontal layering, creating an effect similar to that of strata below the earth's surface.

‹ 5.3 In the graph, the bar heights compare nations' social spending as a percentage of Gross Domestic Product (GDP). Each bar is sub-divided into amounts contributed by the public and private sectors. The width of the bars compare total GDP for each nation. The U.S. depends on a high percentage of private contributions for social spending. Source: Society at a Glance: OECD Social Indicators 2006. (Paris: Organization for Economic Co-Operation and Development, 2007).

Why must social service agencies rely so heavily on these donations in order to construct the buildings they need? The main reason is: public funding barely exists. Since the U.S. socio-economic system fails to provide for all of its citizens' needs, individuals try to make up for this lack of support with a system known as "giving back." For people grateful for their own good fortune, giving back is a chance to do something for others: they contribute to a charity and convince other people and corporations to join the cause. Social service agencies have come to rely heavily on these donations not only for their bricks and mortar, but also for providing basic services.

While private donations present the advantage of focusing on a specific issue, the donors choose who benefits from their generosity. Government must spread relief more thinly and evenly across the wide spectrum of needs, and is held accountable for ensuring a balanced distribution of relief. It seems fair to question the true effect of private and corporate sponsorship taking over the role of government-provided, crucial social service. Capitalism has succeeded in responding to what consumers want to buy, but the notion of giving back shows that democracy has had difficulty responding to what people want as citizens.[1] The lack of federal dollars toward social service is evident in comparisons of the U.S. to other developed countries. The United States' ratio of social spending to the nation's GDP is among the lowest in the first world. Philanthropy is so desperately needed that agencies must focus on courting the private sector rather than on searching for the causes of the shortfalls in the system.[2]

For architects, all of this means that designing the physical structures needed by social service agencies presents a complete departure from the typical design process. Though it is commendable that citizens and companies contribute to social service agencies, giving back actual building materials can affect the architecture in unexpected ways. Typically, a design becomes more definitive as the last details are specified. Designing buildings that rely on donations, however, requires parts to remain in flux until the end in order to make use of products and services as they materialize. A large donation might result in a change for a major building component, even if the donation is made during construction. At minimum, changes at this scale and this late in the building process can cause a monumental headache for the architect; worse yet, they can mean uncoordinated systems, substituted inferior products, loss of energy efficiency, and reduction of the building's quality and life cycle—essentially, the loss of design control.

At the same time, a potentially liberating paradigm for design resides within this circumstance. Like the Ford Calumet Environmental Center, which takes locally available material as a starting point, a design that relies on donations can also work with what is "given." Mining this process for opportunity presents an entirely new method for design.

› page 189

CENSUS MAP OF CHICAGO
(RACE) BY NEIGHBORHOOD

01 Rogers Park
02 West Ridge
03 Uptown
04 Lincoln Square
05 North Center
06 Lake View
07 Lincoln Park
08 Near North Side
09 Edison Park
10 Norwood Park
11 Jefferson Park
12 Forest Glen
13 North Park
14 Albany Park
15 Portage Park
16 Irving Park
17 Dunning
18 Montclare
19 Belmont Cragin
20 Hermosa
21 Avondale
22 Logan Square
23 Humboldt Park
24 West Town
25 Austin
26 West Garfield Park
27 East Garfield Park
28 Near West Side
29 North Lawndale
30 South Lawndale
31 Lower West Side
32 Loop
33 Near South Side
34 Armour Square
35 Douglas
36 Oakland
37 Fuller Park
38 Grand Boulevard
39 Kenwood
40 Washington Park
41 Hyde Park
42 Woodlawn
43 South Shore
44 Chatham
45 Avalon Park
46 South Chicago
47 Burnside
48 Calumet Heights
49 Roseland
50 Pullman
51 South Deering
52 East Side
53 West Pullman
54 Riverdale
55 Hegewisch
56 Garfield Ridge
57 Archer Heights
58 Brighton Park
59 McKinley Park
60 Bridgeport
61 New City
62 West Elsdon
63 Gage Park
64 Clearing
65 West Lawn
66 Chicago Lawn
67 West Englewood
68 Englewood
69 Greater Grand Crossing
70 Ashburn
71 Auburn Gresham
72 Beverly
73 Washington Heights
74 Mount Greenwood
75 Morgan Park
76 O'Hare
77 Edgewater

LEGEND

African-American
- 10-49%
- 50-89%
- 90-100%

Polish
- 10-24%
- 25-82%

Italian
- 10-24%
- 25-43%

Asian/Pacific
- 10-49%
- 50-89%
- 90-100%

Russian
- 10-22%

Hispanic
- 10-49%
- 50-89%
- 90-97%

Lithuanian
- 10-22%

Not in City

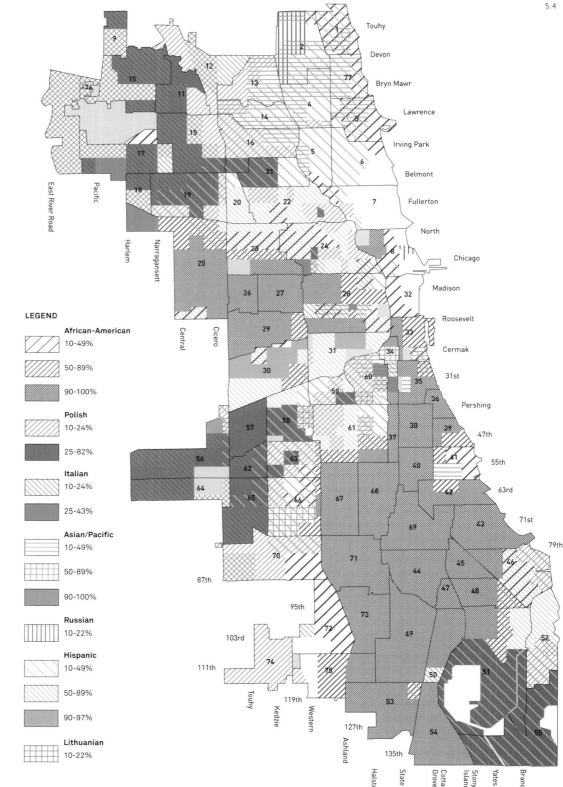

ARCHITECTURE DESERT

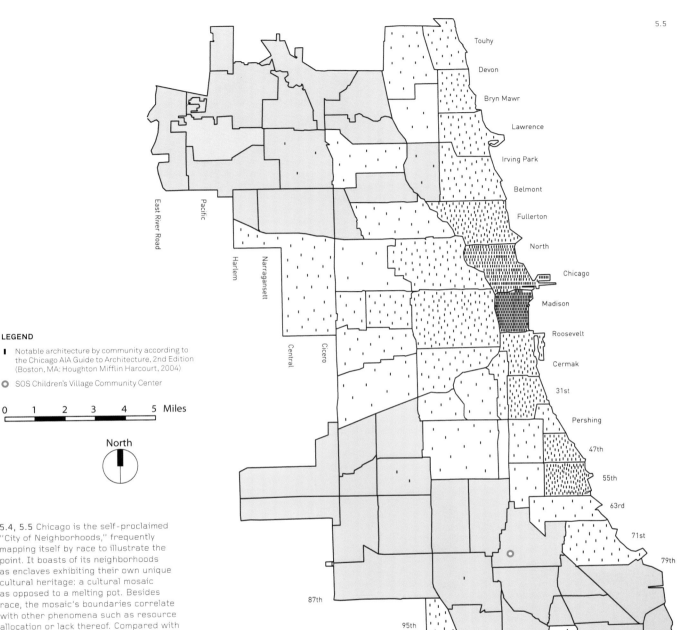

LEGEND

▌ Notable architecture by community according to
the Chicago AIA Guide to Architecture, 2nd Edition
(Boston, MA: Houghton Mifflin Harcourt, 2004)

◎ SOS Children's Village Community Center

0   1   2   3   4   5 Miles

North

5.4, 5.5 Chicago is the self-proclaimed
"City of Neighborhoods," frequently
mapping itself by race to illustrate the
point. It boasts of its neighborhoods
as enclaves exhibiting their own unique
cultural heritage: a cultural mosaic
as opposed to a melting pot. Besides
race, the mosaic's boundaries correlate
with other phenomena such as resource
allocation or lack thereof. Compared with
the map on the right, architecture, as
categorized by the AIA's list of noteworthy buildings in Chicago, is conspicuously
absent in certain neighborhoods. The
"architecture deserts" of Chicago
demonstrate the obvious: money, power,
and whiteness beget Architecture with
a capital A.

Sources: Boundary data from "City of
Chicago Community Areas," prepared
by Chicago Area Geographic Information
Study (CAGIS), Department of Geog-
raphy, University of Illinois at Chicago;
Race data from Chicago 1990 Census
Maps from the University of Chicago
Map Collection, http://www.lib.uchicago
.edu/e/su/maps/chimaps.html

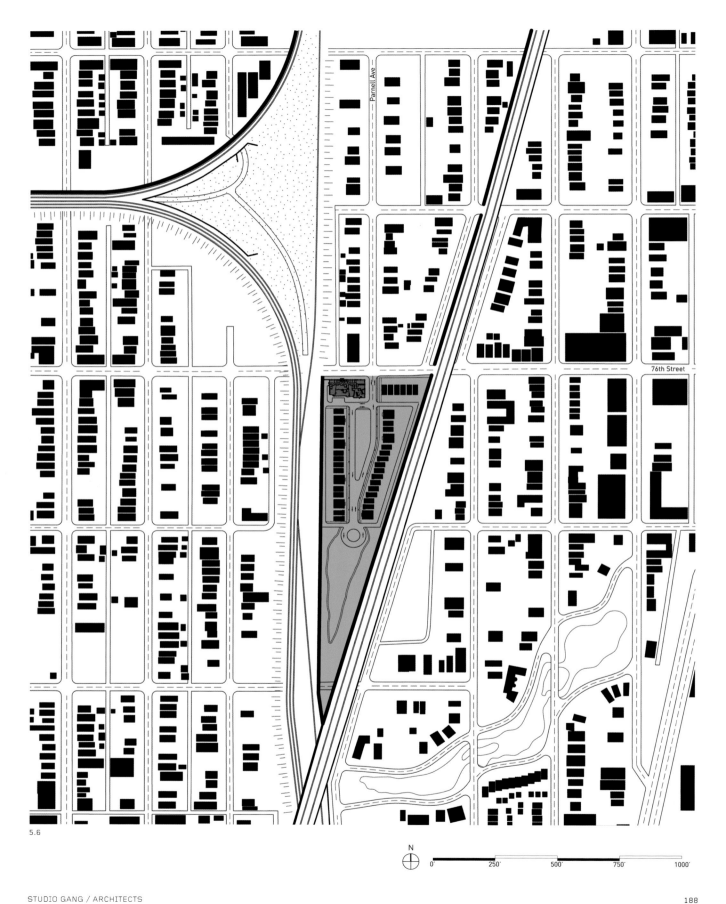

5.6

Parnell Ave

76th Street

N

0'   250'   500'   750'   1000'

5.7

5.8

5.9

< 5.6 SOS benefits from leftovers and contingencies. A sliver of land cut off by two elevated railroads and squeezed down to a point in a V shape presents an anomaly in the Chicago grid lacking the connections necessary for commercial development. Its configuration however, provided a cul-de-sac arrangement beneficial for this residential community. The community center at the northern open end of the V mediates between and opens to both the SOS residents and the rest of the neighborhood.

5.7 A large red and white radio tower like a giant tinker toy in the distance

5.8 Serendipitous entertainment provided by a view of the elevated railroad yard with constant train traffic

5.9 Donated Victorian street lamps at the southern tip present a curious juxtaposition with the viaducts of the railroads— rather than an urban soccer field for kids or something equally useful.

5.10 Large-scale apertures on the building's corners are positioned to address each of the urban approaches and the site's unique vistas.

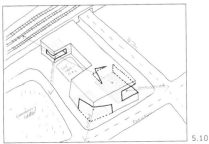

5.10

Given SOS's limited funding, a new method was worth pursuing. Refusing donations for the sake of the "original" design would have been counterproductive to the goal of achieving a building for a very needy cause. Instead of losing control, we invented a system to manage the flow of donations.

In this new system, the original design maintained a series of placeholder elements. Each element was treated as a variable that required re-shuffling and re-integrating once a donation of material was secured. A donated material was studied in relation to all of its immediately adjacent parts. The donation could therefore affect other elements or even suggest new donations to be sought. Each new combination of parts had to be analyzed, but because this has become easier to do than in the past (tools make it faster), understanding the repercussions and the potentials of new materials and combinations was possible like never before.

In one example, a donation of steel (a material donation) prompted a new configuration for a lobby stair that was originally intended to be concrete. Steel then produced a different and unexpected effect on the surrounding space. Although naturally much deeper in section, it offered the possibility of introducing a light cavity between its members. This positive aspect inspired the team to secure a donation for translucent polycarbonate panels to enclose the new light cavity. Later in the process, when a contractor donated concrete, it was directed toward the facade of the building rather than toward an attempt to recreate the "original" concrete stair. The re-shuffling produced something new and heterogenous through this non-linear process. Concrete as "given" for the facade led to our experimenting with the physical pouring process. In the meantime, the inherited steel for the lobby stair was retained. In essence, a material flip-flop had occurred, producing an unexpected formal relationship with a different expression.

Unlike value engineering, which eliminates or substitutes materials using less expensive alternatives, here specific windows, finishes, skylights, and plumbing fixtures were all variables. Mechanisms for coping with and anticipating change included keeping lists of confirmed donations, potential suppliers, and donor naming opportunities. All potential donations lived on a spreadsheet until they were integrated into the building. Incorporating a donation yielded surprising formal and material juxtapositions, which could never have been conceived from the beginning, and could never be repeated in exactly the same way.

With certain pieces of the building subject to change, the architect becomes an organizer of a set of chance circumstances. The design work is the creation of a system that facilitates change. It should allow for compelling discoveries, surprise juxtapositions, and hybrids given the somewhat arbitrary donations at somewhat random points in the process. Design in the age of giving back becomes less about the delineation of a set of definitive parts and more akin to a changing genetic model of inheritance. With the inheritance model, combinations of certain genes can produce more than one result. As with nature, the accidental may provide an advantage.

One of the biggest accidents that became advantageous for SOS was a donation of concrete that replaced brick on the primary facade, and led to an unprecedented use of the material. With so many condominium buildings under construction in downtown Chicago, the idea was to seek out donations of leftover concrete at the end of each construction day. Trucks could come and dump the remains of their load in the SOS wall. This would create a

> page 195

5.11

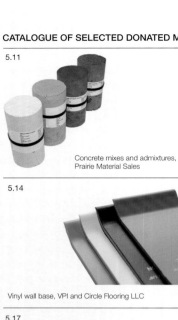

Concrete mixes and admixtures, Prairie Material Sales

5.12

Naturalite Skylights, Harmon, Inc.

5.13

Polycarbonate panels, Gallina USA LLC

5.14

Vinyl wall base, VPI and Circle Flooring LLC

5.15

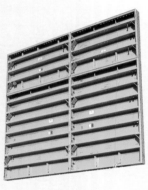

Cork tiles, Capri Cork and Circle Flooring LLC

5.16

Mohawk carpet, Circle Flooring LLC

5.17

EFCO steel formwork, Adjustable Forms, Inc.

5.18

Snaidero cabinetry systems, Studio Snaidero Chicago

5.19

Gypsum wallboard, RG Construction Services, Inc. and Drywall Supply Illinois, Inc.

5.20

Acoustical ceiling tile, Armstrong World Industries, Inc.

5.21

Street sweeping services, Elgin Street Sweeping

5.22

Polyisocyanurate rigid insulation, ALL Sealants, Inc.

5.23

Epoxy rebar, Gerdau Ameristeel

5.24

Vinyl composition tiles, Armstrong World Industries, Inc. and Circle Flooring LLC

5.25

Drinking fountains, S.K. Culver Sales and Thomas Litvin Plumbing

5.26

Grilles and diffusers, Hill Mechanical Corporation and Titus Inc.

5.27

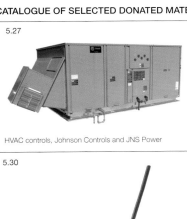

HVAC controls, Johnson Controls and JNS Power

5.28

Beto-film plywood, Adjustable Forms, Inc.

5.29

Scissor lift, Randall Industries

5.30

Final cleaning services, Vega Cleaning Services, Inc.

5.31

Painting services, All-Tech Decorating Inc.

5.32

Glazing systems, Harmon, Inc.

5.33

Endicott brick partially, Prairie Material Sales

5.34

Maple flooring, The Bahr Co. and Circle Flooring LLC

5.35

Paints, All-Tech Decorating Inc. and Sherwin Williams

5.36

Ceramic tile, Dal-Tile Corporation and Circle Flooring LLC

5.37

Tectum ceiling tiles, WNK & Associates
and Magellan Development LLC

5.38

Waste management services,
Allied Waste Management Services of Chicago

5.39

Granite countertops, Granite Innovations, Inc.

5.40

Revolving door, Crane Revolving Door Company

5.41

Concrete masonry units and mortar,
Garth/Larmco Joint Venture

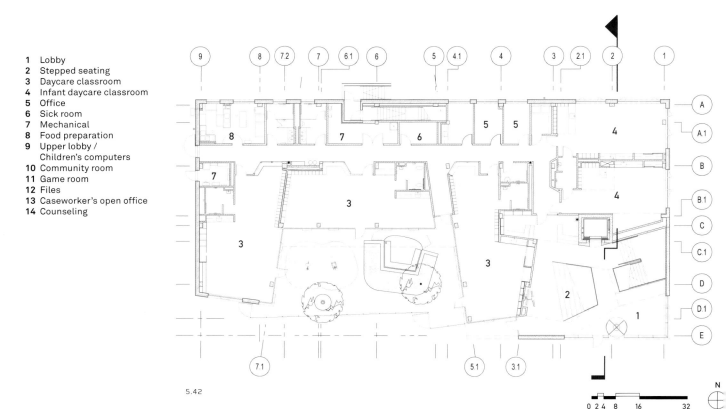

1 Lobby
2 Stepped seating
3 Daycare classroom
4 Infant daycare classroom
5 Office
6 Sick room
7 Mechanical
8 Food preparation
9 Upper lobby /
Children's computers
10 Community room
11 Game room
12 Files
13 Caseworker's open office
14 Counseling

5.42

N

0 2 4 8   16   32

5.43

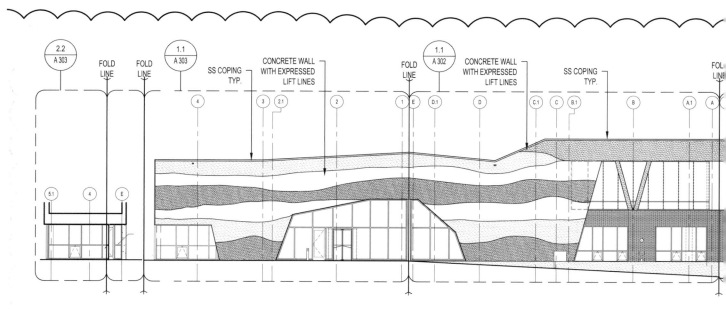

2.2 / A 303   FOLD LINE   FOLD LINE   1.1 / A 303   SS COPING TYP.   CONCRETE WALL WITH EXPRESSED LIFT LINES   FOLD LINE   1.1 / A 302   CONCRETE WALL WITH EXPRESSED LIFT LINES   SS COPING TYP.   FOLD LINE

2.1 UNFOLDED BUILDING ELEVATION @ NORTH, EAST + SOUTH ELEVATION
SCALE: 1/16"=1'-0"

5.42 Program includes daycare and early childhood daycare organized around a courtyard on the ground floor.

5.43 Partial unfolded elevation articulates apertures and transitions between materials.

5.44 Computer lab and large multipurpose community room on the second floor connect by means of two entwined stairs that crisscross the lobby. Their geometry and scale activate the space by setting up a giant three-dimensional play-mountain for children to navigate.

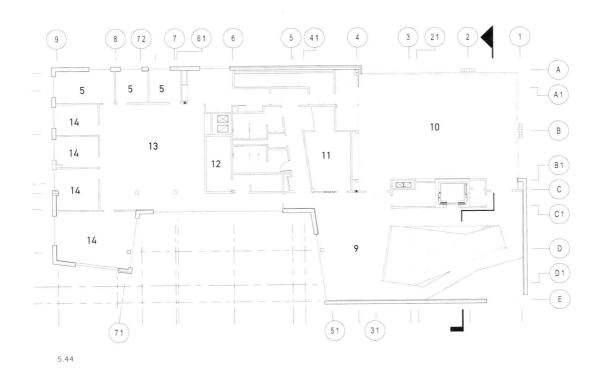

5.44

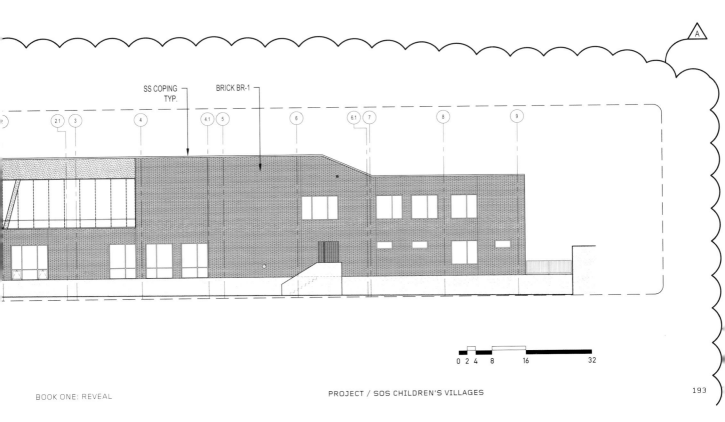

5.45 After formwork is removed, the banded concrete cantilever wall is exposed and the physics of the liquid state of the
concrete is visible.

5.46 (overleaf) From 76th Street the second floor community
room is a beacon to the neighborhood. Inside, occupants find
a perch above the car and street noise.

Notes
1 Robert Reich, Supercapitalism: The Transformation of Business,
Democracy, and Everyday Life (New York: Alfred A. Knopf, 2007).
2 Society at a Glance: OECD Social Indicators 2006 (Paris: Organization
for Economic Co-operation and Development, 2007).

5.45

horizontally banded structure made of varying gray tones of concrete as the different dona-tions literally came pouring in. Concrete, when wet, behaves like viscous lava. The intention was to coax the concrete to retain its interesting fluid character even after it cured. Through multi-ple pours that accentuate this hilly slump, the physics of its once-liquid state are revealed.

At its root, the project benefited from many leftovers, accidents, and contingencies. The site itself is a leftover sliver of land squeezed between two elevated train lines, one derelict, and the other an active freight and commuter rail. Donated by the City of Chicago and cleared and remediated with help from the state, SOS's isolated location between the railroads' retaining walls proved advantageous to promoting a community. Backed up to the retaining walls, the houses in the SOS village face inward to a central green space. The SOS community center is a connector between the SOS village to the south, and the rest of the Gresham and Englewood neighborhoods beyond. Large-scale openings in the building's exterior are posi-tioned to address each of the major urban approaches and views. Corner openings contribute to the oblique views from within the building. At the ground level, a corner opening creates the primary entrance on Parnell Avenue, affording safe access from the southeast. The northeast second floor corner window gives public presence and visual access to the community room from 76th Street.

The building's program includes daycare and early childhood daycare organized around a courtyard on the ground floor with caseworkers' offices, counseling areas, and a large multi-purpose community room on the second floor. Connecting the levels, two entwined stairs crisscross the lobby. Their geometry and scale activate the space by serving as a giant three-dimensional play-mountain for children to navigate. The intersection of the two stairs creates a structural arch that is passed under upon entering the building. Diagonal and oblique views across the two-story lobby space are choreographed by the position of the stairs, encouraging interaction and communication. One segment of risers morphs into bleachers for after-school classes, movies, and climbing. At the top of the stairs, the second-floor lobby doubles as a computer lab. Like the first-floor entry corner, the second-floor community room opens up to the corner under a cantilevered roof structure. Oblique views of the neighborhood and its street life, its townhouses with turrets, an orange and white broadcast tower, and the elevated rail beds are seen through the corner window.

A process is revealed in the final design. Unexpected relationships between materials and elements in the building are the physical result of the flow of donations that bring a social services building into being. Traditional design practice has no way of integrating unexpected and unspecified materials into the architectural object. Change in any form is usually consid-ered negative and counter to the originality of the design; but architecture must be able to use change or be ruled by it. The SOS project took the idea of change as a liberating opportunity and gained an original outcome. Some will surely contest the idea of designing a system of flow instead of a linear route to the final object—similar to biologists who contested the Mende-lian model of heredity because it implied that heredity was discontinuous and accidental. It is through understanding and later experimentation with systems present in the building process that it is possible to bring architecture closer to biological systems and make it more viable in a world where material is in short supply and must be re-used or redeployed in buildings. S/G/A

5.47 Daycare classrooms are organized around a south-facing courtyard.

5.48 The intersection of the two stairs creates a structural arch to both pass under and climb over. Diagonal and oblique views across the lobby space encourage interaction and communication.

5.49 The second floor community room opens up to the corner under a cantilevered roof structure. Oblique views of the neighborhood's masonry townhomes, red and white broadcast tower, and elevated rail beds are framed by the corner window.

5.50 The bleacher-stair is employed for educational programming, after-school activities, climbing, playing, and hanging out.

5.51 Twists and turns in the crisscross stair encourage movement and oblique views of the space.

> 5.52 Partial plan from second floor

5.53 Cross section delineating space under the bridge formed by the criss-cross stair

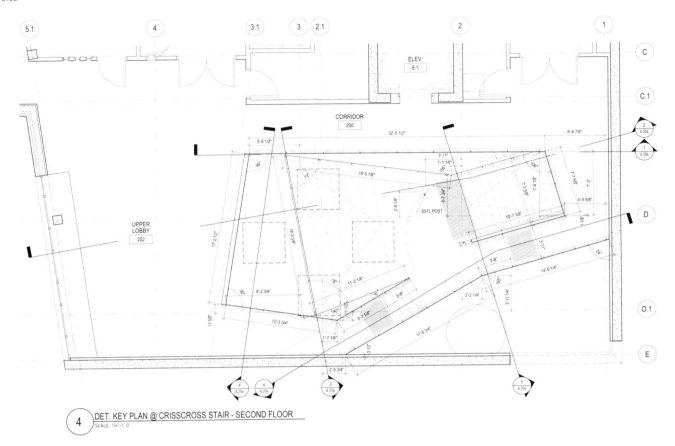

4 DET. KEY PLAN @ CRISSCROSS STAIR - SECOND FLOOR
SCALE: 1/4"=1'-0"

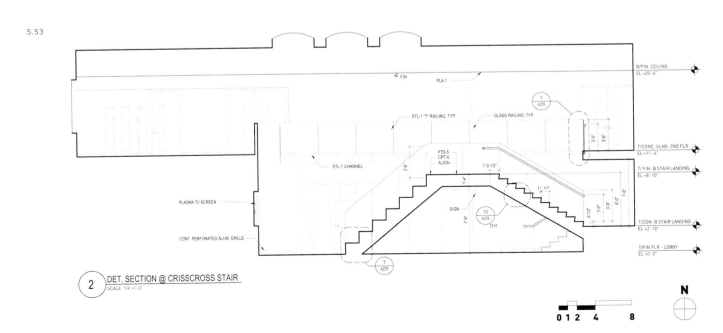

2 DET. SECTION @ CRISSCROSS STAIR
SCALE: 1/4"=1'-0"

N

0 1 2 4 8

Photos: Figures 5.54 & 5.56 reproduced by permission of the Chicago History Mu...

202

WHAT'S UP *on the* SECOND FLOOR?

IN THE GRAND PALACES OF THE RENAISSANCE, THE SECOND LEVEL OF THE BUILDING WAS OFTEN USED AS THE NOBLE RESIDENTS' PRIMARY LIVING AND ENTERTAINING SPACE.

Known in Italy as the piano nobile, or "noble floor," the second level maintained a physical and behavioral divide between the servants' quarters and the presiding nobility, and was treated with architectural significance on the exterior. This special architectural designation for the second floor transferred to typologically and programmatically very different buildings over time. At the turn of the century, the piano nobile usefully articulated the second floor space in tall buildings, accommodating everything from executives' offices to speakeasies and brothels. When high Modernism abandoned it as a remnant of all things classical, attention was refocused on the ground floor. Indeed, much of contemporary architecture remains invested in the lobby level as the primary place of architectural impact. But with changes in the way contemporary cities function, there is renewed architectural potential for the piano nobile.

Originally, the Renaissance-era piano nobile satisfied a patrician's desire for a route to bypass the ground floor entirely, as it was usually inhabited by servants. This was often achieved through an ornate exterior staircase that endowed the nobilities' passage with prestige and authority, and prevented their unnecessary exposure to any mundane household chores or business. The design of the piano nobile developed and flourished most notably in Venice, necessitated by the city's speci-

levels too damp to inhabit. Designed with a land entrance and a water entrance, the water-side of the building was always considered the principal facade. The first floor of a water-side facade would begin with an open loggia, with the piano nobile above it, and often a second piano nobile above that. Inside, these rooms were used primarily for entertaining guests, and lavish decoration and original artwork adorned the walls. Banks of arched windows stacked on top of each other made the different floors easily recognizable from the exterior. Further exterior distinction between floors was often provided by rusticated walls.

Italian aristocrats made the piano nobile into an essential architectural element for their living style. The first tall buildings in America, in contrast, simply copied this architectural element and applied it to completely new programmatic uses unrelated to its original intent. In the U.S., late nineteenth-century tall buildings were the residences of choice for wealthy people who had no desire for a large home with its upkeep, servants, and staff. Luxurious buildings like Chicago's Lexington Hotel provided residents with all the comforts and conveniences of a private mansion or palace on the upper floors of a ten-story steel and terra-cotta structure. The 1898 edition of the Chicago Blue Book listed 201 permanent residents of the Lexington Hotel, living like nobility in sumptuous private quarters.[1] In Chicago, the combination of a building boom in search of architectural élan and a restrictive liquor law requiring discretion for those who imbibed gave the piano nobile a new reason to exist. The elegant second floors in hotel-apartment buildings easily transitioned into suitable locales for illicit speakeasies.

Similar to a Venetian palace, the Lexington employed a plan with a central light court extending from the second floor to the tenth floor. Rooms and suites were arranged along the perimeter of this court, which was embellished with ample bay windows. The Lexington's first-floor lobby had a glazed ceiling, allowing light to filter through the piano nobile's large bank of windows. The piano nobile had a central porch supported by six columns on the entry facade. With the porch providing a screening element to the large glass windows behind, the space originally designed as a ballroom found new purpose as a convenient lookout with the arrival of prohibition in the 1920s. During the height of the Prohibition era, speakeasies filtered into many of the hotels on South Prairie Avenue. Up on the second floor with a view to the street, it was easier to serve liquor and avoid police raids. Conversely, only a glimpse of the ballroom's ornate ceiling was visible from the street.

The Lexington found its reputation further tarnished when the notorious gangster Al Capone took up a permanent residence there in 1928. Capone's block of suites in the Lexington provided the necessary armor to shield a crime empire that included gambling, prostitution, and a liquor racket. Even though the Lexington Hotel fell upon hard times, eventually became dilapidated, and was torn down, its colorful history represents the diversity of uses for a piano nobile and points to the potential of this special perch, in a completely different building type from the one where it originated.[2]

With the tall steel frame building finally being understood as a type unto itself and not simply as a receptacle for classical embellishments, Modernism rejected the classical architectural distinction of the second floor in favor of transparency at the ground level. This movement saw no relevance for the architectural element of the second floor porch in the age of the machine. In contrast to buildings like the Lexington, modern apartment buildings and corporate headquarters alike emphasized the lobby level and embraced the exterior repetitiveness of the floors above it. Transparency accomplished a visible extension of the ground plane into the lobby. But Modernism's once-radical transparency and emptiness at ground level is now a conventional approach in need of an update.

Cities have transformed, and additional uses at ground level make it more difficult and less desirable to maintain transparent lobbies devoid of programs. Cities are becoming denser. With more people living in the center, the retailers and grocers that serve them look to lease ground floor space that is convenient to pedestrians. Multi-use buildings now require multiple lobbies at grade for their independent entries and elevator banks. As cities fill in and ground floor spaces become charged with providing essential services, other important spaces are left with nowhere to go but up. New potential for public space quietly awaits up on the second floor.

Notes

1. Luciano Iorizzo, *Al Capone: A Biography* (Westport, CT: Greenwood Press, 2003).

2. It wasn't long after Capone's four-year stay at the Lexington that the hotel left behind its days hosting an aristocratic lifestyle. Following Capone's exit, the Lexington served as a bordello, then a briefly as the New Michigan Hotel, followed by several changes in ownership. Finally, before its demolition in 1995, it played host to a Geraldo Rivera ratings gimmick: the talk show host failed to find Capone's hidden vault of gold, but still got rich when 30 million viewers tuned in to see bits and pieces of the Lexington Hotel blasted away on live TV in the search for the mob boss's treasure.

THE LEXINGTON

5.58

HERE CAPONE'S FAMILY LIVED WHEN VISITING HIM

EXECUTIVE OFFICE OF AL CAPONE

CAPONE'S PRIVATE DINING ROOM SEATING 52 GUESTS

ORIGINAL MAIN HEADQUARTERS OF CAPONE

PRIVATE MOVIE THEATER FOR FIRST RUN FILMS

BALLROOM LEASED AS GYM FOR HIS MEN

NEW MICHIGAN HOTEL

TELEGRAPH OFFICE WHENCE MONEY WAS WIRED TO CAPONE

MAIN HOTEL ENTRANCE

TAILOR

5.59

5.60

5.61

5.54 (page 202) At Chicago's luxurious Palmer House hotel, formal dining for the wealthy residents took place on the second floor. The city's elite often lived on the upper floors of the hotel, while the business of operating the hotel was confined to the ground floor.

5.55 (page 203) The lagoon environment of Venice necessitated multistory buildings: the ground floor was often surrendered to the water and servants charged with running the homes of the wealthy.

5.56 (page 203, on fold) The nobile floor of the Drake Hotel in Chicago stood out with its colonnade, balcony, and ornate ceiling.

5.57 (page 204, below fold) The piano nobile of the Lexington Hotel is set apart from the rest of the building with balconies and exterior terra-cotta detail.

5.58 A postcard from 1915 shows the Lexington Hotel as a hub of activity for the upper class.

5.59 Exterior view locating Capone's suites before the Lexington Hotel became the New Michigan Hotel in the 1950s.

5.60 The Lexington Hotel's main entrance on Michigan Boulevard, now Michigan Avenue, featured a second-story balcony for the hotel's affluent guests.

5.61 Floor plan of Al Capone's suites on the sixth floor in the Lexington, which served as the clandestine headquarters for the mob boss and his gangsters.

Gangster's Room						Gangster's Room
Gangster's Room						Gangster's Room
Gangster's Room						Jack McGurn's Room
Gangster's Room						Capone's Bedroom
Kitchen where the mob's food was cooked	The mob's Dining Room	Gangster's Room	Gangster's Room	Frankie Rio's Room	Guard's Room	Capone's Living Room

CONCRETE UNPLUGGED

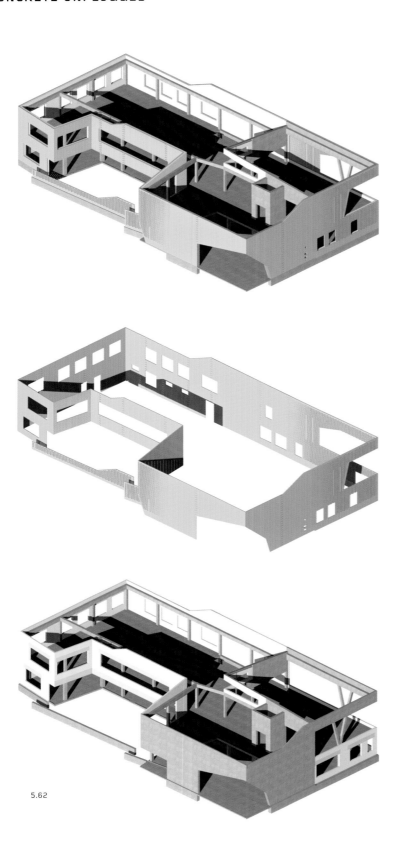

5.62

5.62 Conceived of as a masonry structure, the original project reveals the inherent void that is present in cavity wall construction. The design shows that the exterior layer of brick can be drastically perforated. Through its delineation as a screen, the exterior wall design calls attention to the highly representational role of brick in architecture, compared to that of the second surface, where the heavy work of waterproofing and insulation is carried out. Ironically, at the moment the brick screen design had poetically expressed this fact of construction, it became clear that it would be impossible to justify its cost. If it were not doing any work, it would have to come off.

Unveiling the building beneath by removing the screen presented another matter. Behind the brick mask waiting for its turn to be noticed stood the "ugly" second wall. With its gritty combination of block, concrete, and some miscellaneous steel, the second wall lays bare the blunt truth of the economics that drive construction. Rather than pure tectonic expressions of one material, second walls are ultra-hybridized products of global material availability, trade familiarity, and local market pressures. Perhaps if reconsidered, this under-layer, already tweaked for cost effectiveness, could produce something unexpected and new. The second wall was about to be given a chance to be seen.

Worries of client: Will it be too brutal for the context? Worries of design team: Without the brick screen, is it still architecture?

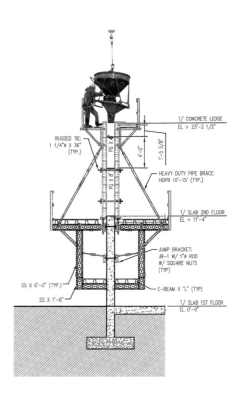

5.63 One of the first issues addressed was the problem of the cold joint in an exposed concrete wall. A wall of this height would need two separate pours that would leave a visible scar across its surface. Thinking of concrete as a poured fluid is what inspired efforts to investigate increased waviness of the cold joint rather than straightening or controlling this line of confluence between hard and soft material. Multiplying the number of cold joint lines further elevates the significance of the "casting" action in construction. By varying the mix design, an intense differentiation would be visible between the horizontal layers. Different strengths are different colors. In the strata-wall, the physics of a once-fluid material are preserved and visible in the final architecture. Structural advantages from the different characteristics of each mix combine to make the cantilevered entrance walls possible.

5.64 Sketch shows the various mixes and predicted variation in elevation between sequential pours as agreed upon with tradesmen.

5.65 A jump-form system was employed so tradesmen could see inside the form as they cast and vibrated the material.

5.63

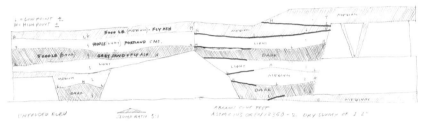

5.64

5.65

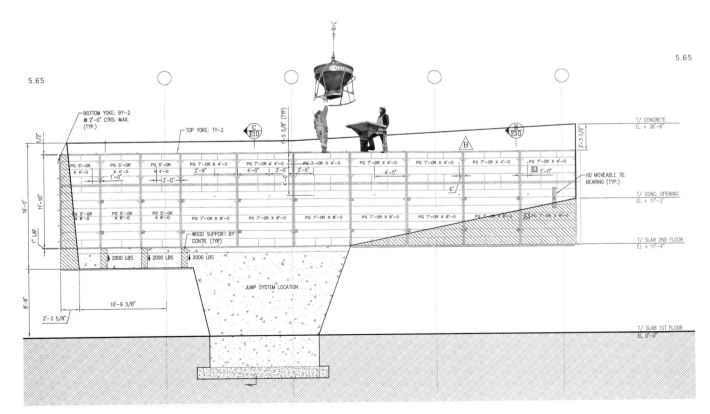

5.65

PROJECT / SOS CHILDREN'S VILLAGES

TALES OF THE TRADE: POURING WALLS AT SOS

SCOTT KENNEDY, Operations Manager for Adjustable Forms Inc.

"We utilized twelve-foot high steel wall forms supplied by EFCO from Des Moines, Iowa. Two roughly six-foot high pouring lifts were made each time the form was set. One lift was poured in the morning and one lift in the afternoon. The wait between pours in the process was around two and a half to three hours. Great care was taken to keep the sides of the steel forms clean after the morning pour.

"The architect's initial thought was to vary the fly-ash, slag, and cement ratios to achieve the varying shades. I disagreed, and thought a greater contrast would be necessary. We utilized three mixes that had a combined strength for the cantilever: The first was a durable 5,000 PSI mix to minimize shrinkage cracks and water infiltration. The second mix included the addition of a black color additive. For the third mix we substituted white Portland cement for standard gray cement.

"To get the waviness seen in the final wall, the slump of the concrete had to be kept extremely low, so that we could vary the finish elevation by at least two feet. I met with our superintendent, Michael Hrnciar, several times to convey the intent of the design team and general contractor. Michael and the skilled tradesmen understood the intent after several pre-task meetings and reduced the slump to a point where they could ensure consolidation, while achieving an average of half the height of the form panel. After the forms were removed, the wall needed to have a light sand-blast to remove minor imperfections.

"Most of the work that we do is structural concrete that gets covered up in pre-cast, glass curtain/window wall, drywall partition, or painted with an acrylic coating and is never seen. Architectural concrete is considered a luxury medium to our tradesmen. This project gave our workers the chance for their work to be visible long after completion. This building showcases their knowledge of their material to the extreme and shows a new way concrete can be utilized; they are all proud that their work can be showcased for such a good cause." **S/G/A**

Adjustable Forms Inc. performed the concrete work for the strata-wall.

> 5.66 Test of idea on the elevator shaft before construction begins on the final wall. Light sand blasting ensures water leakage could be removed.
> 5.67, 5.69, 5.71 For casting the wall, mix is transferred from the truck to a bucket to the top of the wall. The final placement depends on the tradesmen's judgment. An extremely low slump allows concrete to maintain its wavy form even after vibrating.
> 5.68 Plaster models indicate the design intent to the contractors.
> 5.70 Cantilevered wall is revealed when forms are removed.

5.86

STABLE FORMS

5.67

5.68

5.69

5.71

MATERIAL REPORT: CONCRETE
BUILDING ON THE LEGACY OF THE INDUSTRIAL REVOLUTION

If the English bricklayer Joseph Aspdin, who died in 1855, were somehow to rise from his West Yorkshire grave and walk among today's living, he would no doubt be overwhelmed by the state of our contemporary world. Amidst all of our social changes and strange new technologies, perhaps the only thing that could amaze Aspdin more would be a visit to a construction site where workers are mixing concrete. Here, printed on each bag of cement (the main binding ingredient of concrete), Aspdin would recognize the bold letters spelling out PORTLAND CEMENT, the very same name he had coined for his own patent in 1824—for Aspdin's formula and process are still commonly used around the world today.

Unfortunately, the enduring popularity of Portland cement is also shocking when the negative environmental impact of its use is considered—impossible to have foreseen in the early years of the Industrial Revolution. To make common cement, it is necessary to heat its raw ingredients (finely-ground limestone and a second material, usually clay) to a peak temperature of 1450° C within a cement kiln. As the temperature increases, a complex set of chemical reactions takes place. These reactions result both in the desired product—cement "clinker," fine particles comprised mostly of calcium silicates—and exhaust gases released into the atmosphere. Primary among the emissions is carbon dioxide (CO_2). Additional CO_2 is also released from the kiln as the fossil fuels used to heat the reaction are burned. High carbon fuels (such as coal, petroleum coke, and heavy fuel oil) are preferred heat sources for cement manufacture because they burn brighter and hotter than cleaner fuels, making them more efficient at the radiant heat transfer necessary to bringing the raw materials to their very high peak temperature.[1] Choosing to burn high carbon fuels, of course, also means generating even higher quantities of CO_2.

All told, the CO_2 emissions created during cement manufacture (60 percent of which are byproducts of the raw materials' chemical reactions, 40 percent of which are generated by burning fossil fuels) are staggering: for every ton of cement produced, approximately a ton of carbon dioxide is released into the atmosphere.[2] In the United States, this one-to-one ratio makes cement production the third largest source of greenhouse gas; worldwide, cement plants generate five percent of the world's total CO_2 emissions.[3] Cement manufacture, therefore, is a major culprit of global climate change. The facts are clear: contemporary global atmospheric concentrations of CO_2 are at least 35 percent higher than they were before the Industrial Revolution; the world that we know today is at least 1.2 to 1.4° F warmer than Joseph Aspdin's.[4] Why, then, is concrete so slow to change no matter how toxic?

Three short answers are its long evolutionary refinement, dependable structural performance, and absence of a replacement—but all of these would mean nothing without demand, for concrete has become synonymous with progress. As emerging states continue industrializing at an ever-increasing pace, cement is a central—if not the central—material element in the construction of modern infrastructure. Buildings, roads, bridges, dams, and a host of other concrete structures are all composed primarily of cement. It is also the central ingredient of mortar, stucco, and grout. When viewed in this light, it's not as surprising that 80 percent of cement is made and used in countries with emerging economies. China alone uses 45 percent of the world's output, and former Soviet republics like the Ukraine are doubling their production every four years.

Because the industry demand for cement and concrete is so high, there is currently little incentive to work toward inventing greener cements, or to invent concretes which use less or no cement. In fact, the majority of research in cement technology continues to be focused on tweaking mixes in order to build faster, including speeding up curing time and improving plasticity. Regulatory bodies have thus far done little to encourage research into greener cements; in the case of the European Union—whose policies are the most progressive in the world—regulatory measures are actually increasing the output of CO_2. Here's how: by giving companies financial incentives to retrofit their current plants with greener technologies, cleaner and more efficient plants are the result. Unfortunately, these more efficient plants now produce even more cement; thus total production, and total greenhouse gas emissions, continue to grow.

Despite all of this, however, there is still hope for a radical reinvention of cement to take place within our lifetimes. Improved research methods, which for years were based on trial-and-error testing, now make it possible to analyze the reduction of emissions in concrete manufacture. Computer-generated modeling now gives researchers the ability to design mixes digitally and calculate their structural and environmental properties virtually.[5] Some answers to greener cements are even beginning to be sought in nature. One company has recently patented a process that mimics the way corals take magnesium and calcium ions from seawater to produce the "marine cement" that bonds reefs, sequestering one half-ton of carbon per every ton of cement produced. While this process is yet to be proven, and its effects on the marine ecosystem require study, it is a hopeful example of the type of revolutionary materials innovation that is needed now. S/G/A

BIBLIOGRAPHY

Bullard, Jeffrey and Karthik Obla. "Virtual testing of Ready Mixed Concrete." Concrete InFocus 3, no.1 (2004): 38–41.

Francis, A. J. The Cement Industry 1796–1914: A History. Devon, UK: David & Charles Press, 1977.

Madrigal, Alexis. "Rethinking the Material World." Dwell (July–August 2008): 164–168.

5.72 Reef building corals found in tropical oceans secrete calcium carbonate to form a hard skeleton. This is done without heat. A new green cement might look to coral for inspiration. At the same time, coral reefs might end up relying on actual concrete as their savior. Coral reef specialists have recommended using concrete modules to help stabilize reefs impacted by ocean acidification.

Notes
1 Kurt E. Peray, The Rotary Cement Kiln (San Francisco: CHS Press, 1998). See chapter 4.
2 David Biello, "Cement from CO2: A Concrete Cure for Global Warming?" Scientific American, August 7, 2008. http://www.scientificamerican.com/article.cfm?id=cement-from-carbon-dioxide.
3 Elisabeth Rosenthal, "Cement Industry Is at Center of Climate Change Debate," New York Times, October 27, 2007. http://www.nytimes.com/2007/10/26/business/worldbusiness/26cement.html.
4 "Carbon Dioxide," United States Environmental Protection Agency, http://www.epa.gov/climatechange/emissions/co2.html.
5 Chiara F. Ferraris, "Measurement of the Rheological Properties of High Performance Concrete: State of the Art Report," Journal of Research of the National Institute of Standards and Technology 104, no.5 (1999): 461–78.

Two words recur in the design team's collective brain at the end of each not-for-profit project: NEVER AGAIN. The pain is due mostly to designs being value engineered beyond recognition, drawn and redrawn. Weeks of work and coordination are "bubbled" and deleted from the sets as if they were mere comic book character thought clouds.

As with child birth, all of the pain is somehow forgotten as the building starts to take shape. All of an architect's labor can be put into perspective by imagining the people who might be transformed by inhabiting a work of architecture. By the time the building opens and starts functioning, the pain is but a distant memory, and is replaced by fulfillment. Like nature's little trick, one might just consider doing it all again.

The people who run community organizations are committed, hardworking, and savvy. Why do they share the pain of fighting for ideas and design? Why not just build a shed? Here are some thoughts by devoted social service advocates who believe in design.

KATE STOHR
Co-Founder
Architecture for Humanity
Pine Cone House, post-Hurricane Katrina
Designed in 2006

Jeanne Gang [JG] Kate, you spend all of your time—your job—trying to bring good design to people who are economically challenged. Why do you think design is important for these people?

Kate Stohr I see design playing a larger role in tackling all sorts of systemic issues from housing to childcare to education. A broader range of people—policy experts, lenders, community leaders—are recognizing that investments in design translate into any number of tangible and intangible benefits—from cleaner water and energy savings, to a sense of empowerment and hope. Often these investments are made project by project, detail by detail. Nevertheless, they signal change.

More and more, we are beginning to understand that there is no one solution that can be replicated to fit every site. When it comes to investments in low-income communities, we get what we pay for. Structures that are poorly designed and built do not gain in value. Not only do they cheat the people who live and work in them, they rob the entire community of equity and future investment. Housing built for working families one hundred years ago is now some of the most prized real estate. It offered generations of families who bought and sold these homes an economic ladder. Will future generations be able to say the same about the houses we are building in low-income communities today?

For me, design represents thoughtfulness: thought for the people who live in a place, thought for the environment, thought for the community and thought for future generations. And to build without thought is tantamount to littering.

5.73 Pine Cone House, Biloxi, Mississippi
For Architecture for Humanity
5.74 SOS Children's Villages Lavezzorio
Community Center, rendering, Chicago
5.75 Chinese American Service League's
Kam L. Liu Building, Chicago

LYNN KILEY
Member of the Board of Directors
SOS Children's Villages Illinois
SOS Children's Village Chicago
Lavezzorio Community Center
Completed October 2007

BERNARDA WONG
President
Chinese American Service League
Chinese American Service League,
Kam L. Liu Building
Completed March 2004

JG How did you become involved with SOS?

Lynn Kiley [LK] SOS Children's Villages was founded in Austria following WWII, by a young medical student named Herman Gmeiner, to care for orphaned and abandoned children and has grown to 441 Villages in 131 countries today. It is a not-for-profit child welfare agency with a unique Sibling Program offering sibling groups permanency in a safe, stable, nurturing environment. SOS provides the opportunity for siblings to live together in a single home, within the Village, with a professional SOS parent.

In Chicago, an SOS Children's Village opened in August of 2004, becoming the first Urban Village in the world and only the third SOS Village in the U.S., with others located in Florida and Lockport, Illinois. It serves children in the foster care system by providing the original "Sibling" model and has introduced pilot programs to serve the needs of SOS children and their families. For example, the "Parenting Teens" program provides teens with the opportunity to complete their education, as well as learning prenatal, postnatal, and parenting skills. The "Fostering Families" program works to stabilize, educate, strengthen, and reunite biological families.

There are many organizations providing singular needs to children. SOS Children's Villages provide wrap-around services enabling children to become independent, self-reliable adults. I recognized that SOS Children's Villages addresses the whole of a child's needs: a safe, nurturing home, educational and spiritual growth opportunities, health, and emotional counseling, all in family, community environment.

JG Why is a designed environment important for SOS children?

LK Children respond to a positive environment; we all do—function and form make our lives productive and pleasant every day. The SOS Chicago Community Center is vitally important to the SOS Families as well as the surrounding community. The building needed to be the inviting, friendly catalyst that brings people together to feel welcome and secure, whether engaging in recreational, educational, or counseling activities. A well-designed environment is critical in providing a space that is multi-functional, non-intimidating, and non-institutional.

JG Bernie, many not-for-profits build non-descript structures, perhaps out of concerns for cost. You had a different idea about the Kam L. Liu Building, your community center. In retrospect, how has committing to design affected your organization?

Bernarda Wong In order for a social service agency to be successful, it must attract clients, and we have attracted more clients. Our building, with its titanium shell, fairly glitters in the sunshine. It is brilliantly different from the surrounding structures. Large windows on the ground level allow the passersby to look in and watch the busy activities against a background of soothing colors and clean, open interior lines.

The building shouts out modernity, cleanliness, and professionalism, appealing to younger people, but there are also subtle Chinese references which appeal to our older clients—the latticework in front of the great window of the Grand Hall, the "dragon scales" of the titanium cladding, and the gray-black coloration of the slate foyer floor.

The Kam L. Liu Building's design has attracted not only more clients, but the attention of the media, government officials, and donors. Our Grand Hall is always the venue of choice for press conferences and ceremonies, not only for CASL, but for other partnering organizations in the area. Shortly after we opened the new building, Tracy Butler of ABC7 News broadcast a weather report from the Kam L. Liu Building, literally putting CASL on the map. The Governor announced his Prescription Drug Plan in our Grand Hall while on a tour of the facility, and many other dignitaries have visited and been impressed by it. In short, the Kam L. Liu Building has raised CASL's profile and prestige considerably. The staff is proud to work in such an excellent facility, raising job satisfaction.

Of course, the building has made our work much easier by combining all our functions in one location. It has also made interdepartmental programs easier because of the close proximity of the departments, so the functional design helped our work.

The staff as much as the clients benefits from the feeling of brightness and spaciousness provided by the many windows and high ceilings. The openness of the design reflects the type of open management we try to maintain at CASL. It is a perfect match to our needs. **S/G/A**

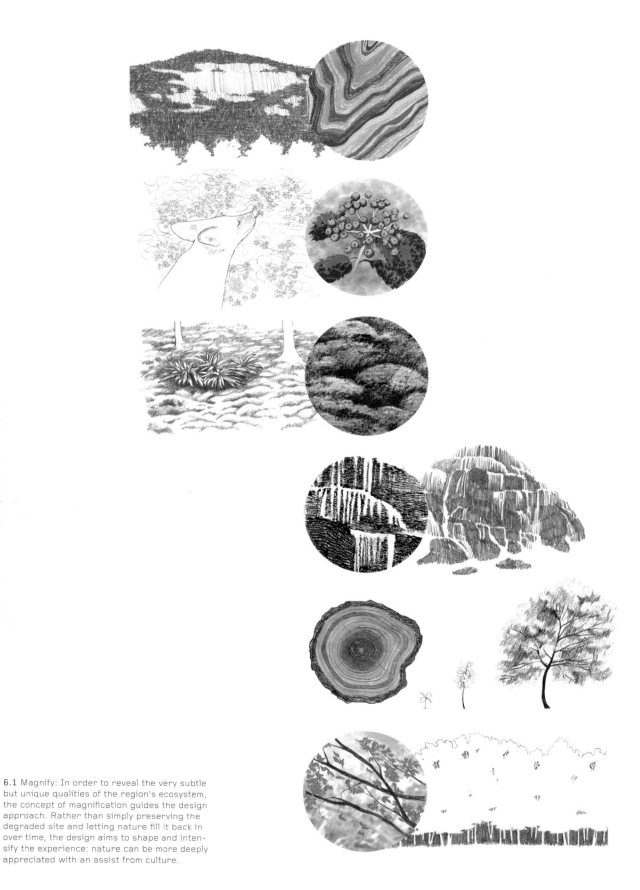

6.1 Magnify: In order to reveal the very subtle but unique qualities of the region's ecosystem, the concept of magnification guides the design approach. Rather than simply preserving the degraded site and letting nature fill it back in over time, the design aims to shape and intensify the experience: nature can be more deeply appreciated with an assist from culture.

BLUE WALL CENTER

Native Americans named the Blue Ridge Escarpment "the Blue Wall."
When the Blue Wall Center and Gardens are complete, South Carolina
will have an interpretive center to expand public awareness and
stewardship of the natural wonders of the Upstate Region. Located
at the nexus between Scenic Highway 11 and the Mountain Bridge
Wilderness Trails at the foot of the mountains, the center is ideally
situated to introduce people to this unique environment and to serve
as an outpost for hikers, bird watchers, and nature enthusiasts alike.

OWNERS: Greenville County
LOCATION: HW 11 at Persimmon Ridge Road, South Carolina, USA
SIZE: 175 acre site / 10,000 SF center
COMPLETION SCHEDULED: 2011

PROJECT / BLUE WALL CENTER

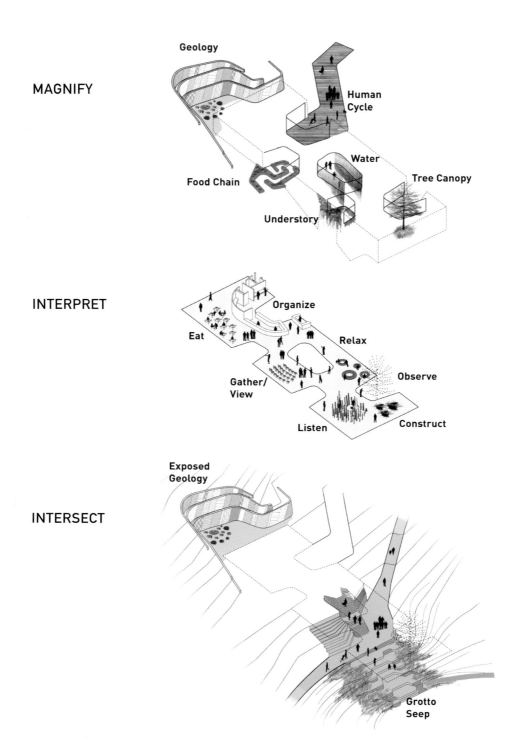

MAGNIFY

Geology

Human Cycle

Water

Tree Canopy

Food Chain

Understory

INTERPRET

Organize

Eat

Relax

Gather/ View

Observe

Listen

Construct

INTERSECT

Exposed Geology

Grotto Seep

6.2 (previous page) Grotto: a place for shade, rest, and events. The cantilevered floor of the building provides a shady respite where understory plants create a carpet for a grotto-like amphitheater. Sunlight and moisture are channeled into the space from the atria "holes" that intersect the building space above.

∧ 6.3 Separating the primary categories of the ecology allows closer inspection and deeper understanding of each one. Dynamic movement into the building, from along the sloping hillside and from below, heightens awareness of the site's section.

MAGNIFY

For regional aficionados, this landscape is a living laboratory, with each season's changes offering opportunities to deepen his or her knowledge of the area's rich ecological palimpsest. The slightest variation in a plant species or avian call can be decoded by local residents who possess a scholarly grasp of nature, some of whom are academics in subjects such as ecology, geology, ornithology, and botany. Visitors, too, travel great distances to the Blue Ridge Escarpment, whether to study it formally or as pure nature enthusiasts who enjoy its unique beauty.

At the other end of the spectrum, however, there are many in this region who know or care very little about its ecology. This is evident in the way land and water are currently being used and abused. Bad practices persist in the logging and mining industries, as well as in the building of dams and residential developments. Somewhere in the middle of these two camps lies a whole segment of the population who truly appreciate the outdoors, but whose view of nature is best represented by a freshly mown golf course.

In this context of extremely divergent perceptions of the importance of the natural world, the charge for the Blue Wall Center project is to heighten awareness of its special ecology. It should inspire visitors with the wonders of the interconnected web of life that exists here, and in doing so fuel the enthusiast, make stewards of the uninformed, and convert the malintentioned. The Center should particularly strive to educate school-age children, because they will inherit the pressing crucible of climate change.

Sloping downward from the eastern edge of the Blue Ridge Mountains, the Blue Ridge Escarpment is home to over 400 endemic species and more tree species than can be found in all of Europe. This biodiversity is the result of the complex geologic history of the Appalachian Mountains (of which the Blue Ridge form part of the southern section) coupled with the specific hydrology and climate of the Escarpment edge. Annual rainfall here is high, averaging 80 to 90 inches. In addition, the Escarpment's elevation change (2000 feet in less than two miles) is the steepest in the eastern United States, and therefore the temperature changes significantly from the base to the top, allowing for a multitude of specific habitats for plants and animals. Within this rich life are reminders of the area's more ancient past: exfoliating domes of rock that are home to many of the rare plants in the area.

One challenge to the task of engaging visitors here is the stubborn subtlety of this landscape's aesthetics. Unlike the immediately awe-inspiring scale of nature in the West, with its giant sequoias and towering Rocky Mountains, the wonders of the Blue Ridge Escarpment reveal themselves only through closer and more careful inspection—if visitors were only given microscopes, they would be duly awed. Calling attention to the site's subtle ecological diversity through magnifying its architecture and landscape became the design idea.

Conceived of as a lens to enlarge and intensify nature, the Center interprets the Escarpment's ecosystem, enhancing visitors' experience of the site and increasing their knowledge for future visits farther afield. A unique characteristic of the Blue Wall Center's structure is its series of interpretive "holes." Each hole is an atrium open to the sky above, the ground below, the landscape adjacent, or combinations of the three. Together, the holes pierce the concrete volume of the building, animating the interior space with natural daylight. The strategy is to intensify the ecological context by creating exhibit spaces that enter the perimeter of the building from the outside, where they are then magnified within the building interior. Functioning as living dioramas, the holes isolate particular aspects of the ecosystem so that they can be understood on a deeper level. A living tree growing up from below though the one of the holes, for example, allows visitors to get up close to the arbor zone in the canopy of the tree. Seen against the backdrop of the building interior, the canopy (normally only viewed from afar) is given scale and becomes perceived in a new way. Another hole

6.4

6.5

6.6

cuts into the adjacent hillside, revealing the complexity of the rock strata and its plant life that combine to form a unique habitat.

These piercings along the different axes are made possible by the building's long cantilever from the steeply-sloped hillside. The hillside position makes the building a sectional nexus, facilitating access from the valley to the hilltop. When it is approached from the valley, the first encounter is a grotto-like amphitheater shaded and protected by the building above. When approached from the hilltop, the structure's perforated volume is the first element seen. Immediately adjacent to the building, outdoor spaces are designed to work in tandem with the interior, accommodating a range of activities.

The site and its surroundings were once occupied by a large summer camp. Removal of the camp buildings, roads, and other infrastructure—all of which were built too close to sensitive ecological areas such as a stream and mountain seeps—will be the first step in rehabilitating the area. Once cleared, it will then be replanted to highlight the region's native flora. A series of "garden rooms" of closely spaced native trees and other plantings will become outdoor living exhibits like those in the building. By also focusing in on and magnifying the experience of the landscape's subtle qualities, these gardens extend the concept of magnification from the building into its surroundings. In this way, intensive reclamation will not only help restore the natural ecosystem but will also work to create meaningful destinations attracting visitors to the site.

Research on many aspects of the region, including its geology, ecology, cultural assets, and contemporary tourism, was conducted as part of the design process. Consultation with many experts in these fields, coupled with ideas put forth from previous studies, helped to build a context for this project. Revealing the ecology of the unique Escarpment environment to its diverse visitors is the most important task of the Blue Wall Center. S/G/A

6.4 An early concept sketch for the project shows the idea of a frame capturing the most potent aspects of the landscape within a rectangle of the building.

6.5 Outside enters inside through piercings in the structure.

6.6 A series of "garden rooms" are defined by densely planted native trees and plantings. Within each clearing, specific aspects of the region's ecology are highlighted.

> 6.7 Amphitheater Level: The outdoor amphitheater is shaded by the cantilevered structure hovering above it. Access to the exhibit level is possible from multiple elevations along the walking path.

6.8 Exhibit Level: The multi-functional exhibition space is pierced by open-air atria—living dioramas that bring light into the space and organize its contents.

6.7

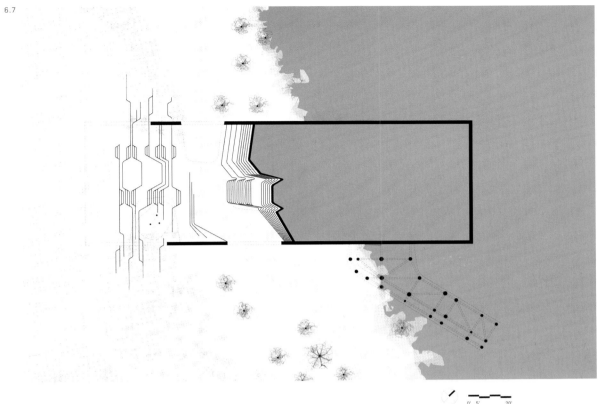

0' 5'   20'

6.8

0' 5'   20'

6.9 A romanticized Yankee notion of Southern moonshining is seen in this illustration from an 1867 issue of Harper's Weekly.

UNSOLVED MOUNTAIN MYSTERIES: A TALE *from* THE DARK CORNER

IT'S EASY TO GET LOST WITHIN THE FAR NORTHWEST CORNER OF GREENVILLE COUNTY, WHERE THE FEW NARROW ROADS THAT LEAD UP GLASSY MOUNTAIN WIND THROUGH OLD, DENSE FOREST ALIVE WITH THE RUSTLING OF LEAVES AND ANIMALS AND THE CALLS OF RARE BIRDS.

by Alissa Anderson

The deeper you wander into this country, the more you begin to lose not only your sense of direction but your sense of time as well—for the Dark Corner (as this place is locally known) is equally as rich with stories as it is with flora and fauna. Many of its best-known tales are those of moonshiners and the bloody violence surrounding their activities—and one of these stories in particular is as dark as a moonless night spent beneath the dense Blue Ridge canopy...

Jim Sudduth was an average man of the Dark Corner at the turn of the century: a subsistence farmer with a wife and three children who made cash money by illegally turning his extra corn crop into liquor. His family didn't have much, but they shared what they could with their friend and neighbor Ed Hayes—or at least they did until one day in early August 1899, when Hayes informed the federal revenue officers in Greenville of Jim Sudduth's illegal still. The "revenuers" rode up Glassy Mountain, hunted down the still and store of moonshine, and destroyed it; they also raided the Sudduths' house. Hayes had violated the sacrosanct code of the Dark Corner: he had broken the trust between himself and Sudduth, and had eliminated the Sudduth family's only source of cash income. He was a marked man.

GLASSY MOUNTAIN TOWNSHIP
Greenville, S.C. 1882

6.10 (page 223, on fold) Today's Dark Corner residents often treat the area's moonshining legacy playfully, as seen in this truck owner's creative signage.
6.11 (above) A local mapmaker plotted all the homes of Dark Corner residents in 1882.
6.12 (below) The October 21, 1907 The New York Times headline from the story of Sudduth and Allen's escape.

POLICE SEARCH HERE FOR BOLD FUGITIVES

Murderers Who Escaped from Southern Prison Thought to be in This City.

SGA

came out carrying a whip and a pistol, and threatened to whip Hayes—at this, Hayes turned and ran toward the Tiger River. Sudduth shot him twice in the back, killing him, and hid the body somewhere on his property. That night, under the cover of darkness, Sudduth removed the body and cut off its head with an ax. He buried the head in his neighbor's nearby field. Then he picked up the remainder of Ed Hayes' body and began to carry it through the trees to the river. It was a windy night, and Sudduth didn't travel far before he began to hear a strange tone—low but distinct, like a ghostly whistle—that seemed to be just at his back, following him. Unnerved, he dumped the body to the ground and checked to make sure that its wounds were true, realizing as he did so that it was the wind blowing through the bullet holes and severed windpipe that was creating the eerie sound. Spooked but determined to carry out his plan, he slung the body over his shoulder again and carried it to the river, all the while struggling to block the ghostly whistle from his mind. When he reached the Tiger he weighted the body with stones and heaved it into the water. His revenge seemed complete.

Little more than two weeks had passed, however, when Hayes' skull was discovered in the neighboring field, and his body washed up on the banks of the Tiger. Condemned by this evidence and haunted by the memory of the whistling corpse, Sudduth turned himself in to the authorities in Greenville and was indicted for first degree murder. In April of 1901 he was found guilty by the state judge and sentenced to life in prison in the South Carolina State Penitentiary—notorious for its terrible conditions. Over the course of the next six years, Jim Sudduth was a model prisoner. He and his good friend Walt Allen (who was also from the Dark Corner, and had murdered another man because of moonshine) became a trusted pair for the guards and Superintendent, who relied on them to do errands and chores around the prison. Sudduth and Allen even became friendly with the prison dogs, to whom they often gave scraps.

All this model behavior paid off for the two when they escaped in broad daylight on October 15, 1907, from a barn lot adjoining the Penitentiary fence. (They had been trusted to begin work there by themselves, and when a guard followed them minutes later, he was too late—they had disappeared.) A manhunt was immediately put in motion, but it was stalled by the fact that the prison dogs wouldn't follow their scents.

Fifteen days later Walt Allen was caught and returned to the Penitentiary. Jim Sudduth, however, was never found. He remained a fugitive until June 1914, when a prominent Greenville County lawyer (at the request of Jim's brother, Peter) petitioned for his pardon, which was granted by the governor on June 12. But despite his official status as a free man, no record exists of Jim Sudduth ever showing his face in that part of South Carolina again—a mysterious absence, compounded by the strange fact that Peter was not only Jim's brother, he was also his identical twin.

What really happened to Jim Sudduth after his escape? The truth seems buried under years and the deep shadows of the Dark Corner, unlikely to ever be revealed.

BIBLIOGRAPHY

Blocker, Jack S., Jr., David M. Fahey, and Ian R. Tyrell, eds. Alcohol and Temperance in Modern History: An International Encyclopedia. Santa Barbara, CA: ABC-CLIO, 2003.

The Dark Corner: A Documentary. DVD. Directed by Campbell Walters. Greenville, SC: Dark Corner Films Inc., 2008.

"Pardons, Paroles and Commutations" (Governor Blease Papers, South Carolina Department of Archives and History. Columbia, SC. S552009, Box 55).

New York Times. "Land of the Crystal Moonshine in South Carolina's 'Dark Corner' a Haunt of Primitive Men." September 8, 1907.

New York Times. "Police Search Here For Bold Fugitives." October 21, 1907.

Snowden, Yates, ed. History of South Carolina. Vol. 4. Chicago: Lewis Publishing Company, 1920.

South Carolina Department of Corrections. Central Register of Prisoners 1899–1913. Document no. S152001, volume 5. Columbia, 1914.

PROJECT / BRICK WEAVE HOUSE

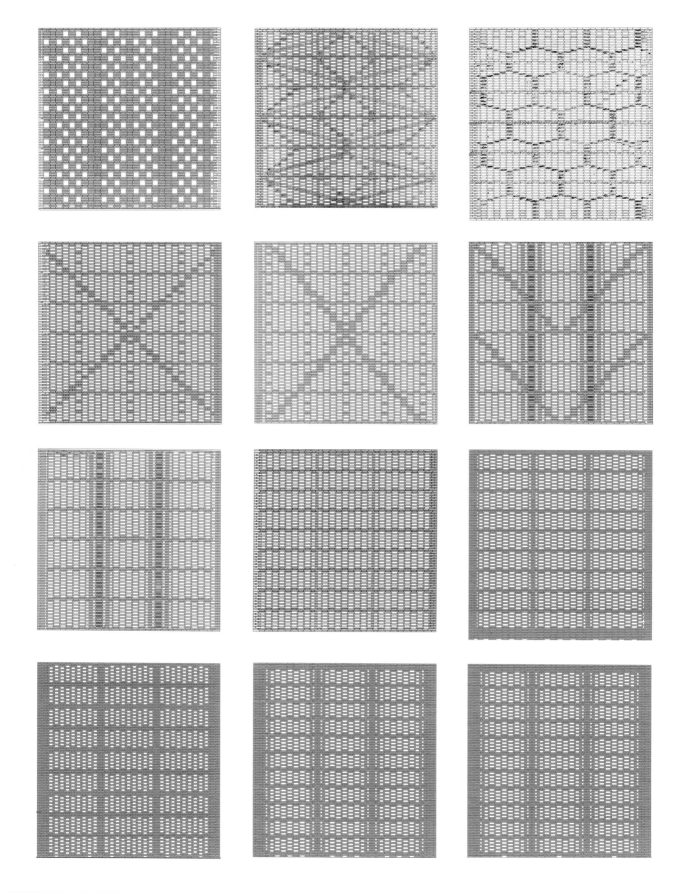

CUT-AWAY, WEAVE-IN

The urban house-plot is often referred to as an "infill site." The term makes this type of plot seem like an anomaly, a blank slot between an otherwise complete and cohesive set of buildings. Building a structure on an "infill site" suggests that it is necessary to fill the gap like a missing tooth, using a material, color, and size consistent with neighboring structures. "Infill" implies that an established context exists, but unlike the fabric of old European cities, many contemporary North American cities are in a constant state of flux. This continuous change renders a so-called contextual design misleading. From which context should one take cues?

7.4 (previous page) At night the house's light pattern reverses and the screen becomes a lantern.

‹ **7.5** Sequential studies of solid-void in the screen wall. Solid areas provided opportunities to stiffen the wall against lateral forces. The last five versions represent small changes and the iterative step-by-step refinements.

Urban neighborhoods in North American cities are relatively young and gain density only through a process of subsequent demolition and re-building. Typically, urbanization begins as agricultural lands are divided into smaller plots accommodating small bungalows. These single-family homes are followed by the construction of larger houses and, later, multi-family dwellings. As the neighborhood matures and the value of the land increases, the last generation of buildings become teardowns, making way for new construction.

This process is uneven and not necessarily progressive because change does not always move a neighborhood toward higher density. In some cases, the last generation of buildings is replaced with fewer, larger homes with fewer occupants. Large single-family luxury homes have recently popped up in urban neighborhoods, replacing contiguous teardowns on multiple lots, thus decreasing the neighborhood's density.

Nonetheless, in this context of constant and variegated change, a snapshot of a neighborhood at any point in time will reveal many different house types and dozens of styles. The different styles combined with different scales produce the antithesis of an imagined homogenous context; there really is no prevailing style or pattern.

In Chicago neighborhoods, a narrow separation is maintained as a walkway or gangway along plot lines. These spaces function as fire separations and access, keeping each house structurally independent. The buffer space at the plot line diminishes the pressure to make houses match. It also makes the sides of the individually designed houses especially pronounced because of the various scales and the occasional presence of a vacant lot. The visible sides of the houses further differentiate the architecture and contribute to the diversity of urban neighborhood homes. Often, in both new and old buildings, facing material is applied only to the street facade, while the sides of the buildings are rendered in raw, common brick. It is as if the buildings are in denial that their sides are clearly visible.

Unstable Stable

The owners of the property tried to renovate the existing structure:

> David: "As for our history with the property, I purchased it over twelve years ago, before Tereasa and I even met, with the dream of someday renovating it. It was a run-down horse stable, with a random assortment of lean-tos and sheds that were all haphazardly tied together over the last hundred-plus years. In spite of this being perhaps the ugliest house in the world, I loved the large footprint it offered. I've been a car and motorcycle geek for a while, so the old stable space offered up plenty of room to store vehicles and wrench on projects. When I started dating Tereasa, I was so embarrassed by the property that the first time she drove me home, I had her drop me off a block away so she wouldn't see it! Later we found it was too far gone and had already been too compromised to pull off a period-correct renovation. That's when we considered a complete re-invention of the space instead."

CIRCA 1890

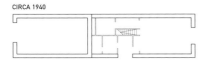

CIRCA 1940

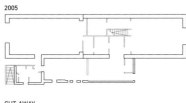

2005

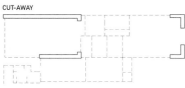

CUT-AWAY

WEAVE-IN

7.6

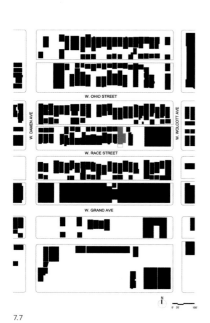

W. OHIO STREET

W. RACE STREET

W. GRAND AVE

7.7

At first glance, the Brick Weave House does not appear to fit with its neighborhood. The site and its original structure seemed to have missed the last wave of upgrades entirely; the nineteenth-century horse stable sat still while neighboring buildings evolved. Its block epitomizes the excitement of a city in flux, in which every stripe of architecture is represented: single-story wooden bungalows, vinyl-clad walkups with Doric columns, anonymous three-flats, and brand-new "developer-modern" speculative townhomes populate the block. The block offers a pure representation of a most impure context.

The Brick Weave House injects a new paradigm into the flow of upgrades that define these changing neighborhoods. Rather than simply adding to the rich diversity of architecture by presenting yet another style, it reverses the wave of tear-down and trade-up and uses its predecessor as a host for a new structure. Instead of completely demolishing the stable, which predates most of the structures on the block, it uses the old shell in new ways. In doing so, the building leapfrogs its neighbors, simultaneously recycling and becoming more contemporary.

Some walls were subtracted and cut away, while new elements were woven into the building's fabric, maintaining 30 percent of the original structure. Initially even more of the building was meant to be reused, but it was later discovered that the stable had sustained fire damage that had to be replaced.

At the entry, subtracted walls and roof create a garden surrounded by the "brick-weave" screen that sits upon the old building outline. This walled garden maintains the former building's height and position on the site but is open to the sky above. The screen walls present a diaphanous veil, replacing the opaque former wall. Entry to the house occurs within the garden that is accessible to the street. Mediating between the public way and the private interior space, the masonry screen walls filter dappled light into the garden, dining room, and the bedroom above.

In section, the house cascades from two stories at the front to one tall volume at the back that serves as the living room and office. The stair and kitchen serve as connecting elements, allowing for access to the larger volumes, including the dining space, living room, and primary bedroom.

Variation in spatial qualities heightens the sensation of a passage through the house. The second floor is set at three ascending elevations via the straight stair along the east edge of the house. Light is delivered to the stair through clerestory glazing at each step in elevation. The primary bedroom at the front of the house ties back to the brick-weave screen and garden below.

7.6 The house sits on the footprint of a century-old stable. Strategic cutting-away of damage and weaving-in new construction allowed 30 percent of the original structure to be reused.
7.7 Any building's context is merely a snapshot in a continuum of constant change.

7.8 Achieving the single-wythe, 26'-high screen challenged engineers—who wanted the masonry rigidly secured to its steel frame—and masons, who wanted movement for mortar's expansion and contraction. The solution was found by customizing anchoring hardware embedded in the mortar joints. Double-ties slotted into columns, rebar every twelfth course, and detailed mortar-joint specifications were required to achieve the wall.

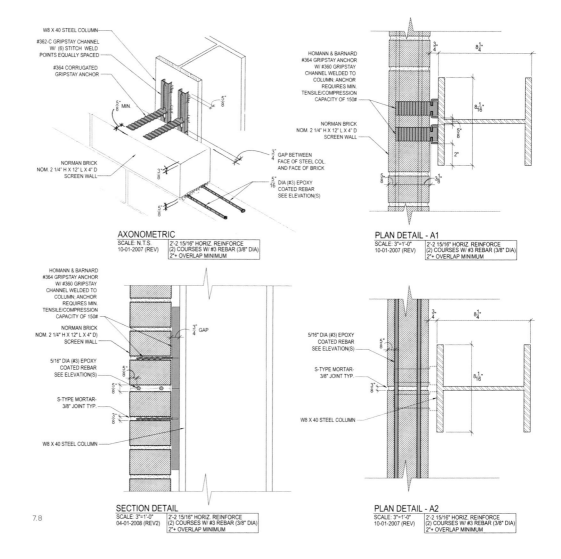

W8 X 40 STEEL COLUMN

#362-C GRIPSTAY CHANNEL W/ (6) STITCH WELD POINTS EQUALLY SPACED

#364 CORRUGATED GRIPSTAY ANCHOR

5" / 8 MIN.

5" / 8

NORMAN BRICK NOM. 2 1/4" H X 12" L X 4" D SCREEN WALL

3" / 8

3" / 8 GAP BETWEEN FACE OF STEEL COL. AND FACE OF BRICK

5" / 16 DIA (#3) EPOXY COATED REBAR SEE ELEVATION(S)

5" / 8

AXONOMETRIC
SCALE: N.T.S.
10-01-2007 (REV)
2'-2 15/16" HORIZ. REINFORCE (2) COURSES W/ #3 REBAR (3/8" DIA) 2"+ OVERLAP MINIMUM

HOMANN & BARNARD #364 GRIPSTAY ANCHOR W/ #360 GRIPSTAY CHANNEL WELDED TO COLUMN; ANCHOR REQUIRES MIN. TENSILE/COMPRESSION CAPACITY OF 150#

NORMAN BRICK NOM. 2 1/4" L X 12" L X 4" D SCREEN WALL

3" / 4   8 1/4"

8 1/16"

5" / 8

2"

5" / 8   3" / 8

PLAN DETAIL - A1
SCALE: 3"=1'-0"
10-01-2007 (REV)
2'-2 15/16" HORIZ. REINFORCE (2) COURSES W/ #3 REBAR (3/8" DIA) 2"+ OVERLAP MINIMUM

HOMANN & BARNARD #364 GRIPSTAY ANCHOR W/ #360 GRIPSTAY CHANNEL WELDED TO COLUMN; ANCHOR REQUIRES MIN. TENSILE/COMPRESSION CAPACITY OF 150#

3" / 4 GAP

NORMAN BRICK NOM. 2 1/4" H X 12" L X 4" D) SCREEN WALL

5/16" DIA (#3) EPOXY COATED REBAR SEE ELEVATION(S)

5" / 8

5" / 8

S-TYPE MORTAR- 3/8" JOINT TYP.

3" / 8

W8 X 40 STEEL COLUMN

5/16" DIA (#3) EPOXY COATED REBAR SEE ELEVATION(S)

S-TYPE MORTAR- 3/8" JOINT TYP.

W8 X 40 STEEL COLUMN

3" / 4   8 1/4"

5" / 8

8 1/16"

3" / 8

7.8

SECTION DETAIL
SCALE: 3"=1'-0"
04-01-2008 (REV2)
2'-2 15/16" HORIZ. REINFORCE (2) COURSES W/ #3 REBAR (3/8" DIA) 2"+ OVERLAP MINIMUM

PLAN DETAIL - A2
SCALE: 3"=1'-0"
10-01-2007 (REV)
2'-2 15/16" HORIZ. REINFORCE (2) COURSES W/ #3 REBAR (3/8" DIA) 2"+ OVERLAP MINIMUM

Building the Screen

While open and delicate in appearance, the masonry screen walls are structurally ambitious. Their scale is achieved by combining structure and craft, two forces that were seemingly at odds at the start of the project. Achieving the single-wythe, 26-foot-high screen challenged engineers who wanted the masonry rigidly secured to its steel frame and masons who wanted movement for mortar's expansion and contraction. Design hit a stumbling block when the structural engineer recommended stabilizing the wall against lateral movement using steel rods embedded into the brick that would be welded to the steel frame behind the screen. The steel frame's role is to resist lateral movement for the structure, but the masons and architects feared the rod imbeds would unnecessarily stiffen the mortar joints and induce cracking. Embedded rods were rejected.

The solution was found by customizing hardware embedded in the mortar joints. Double-ties slotted into columns, rebar every twelfth course, and detailed mortar-joint specifications were required to achieve the wall. Ties, ladder trusses, and slotted connections stitch together and reinforce the brick screen like stitches in a fabric garment.

Animating the garden and interior with dappled sunlight, the screen also reestablishes visual access to and from the street. Its gossamer appearance is visible deep inside the house. Rectangular voids in the screen cast various patterns of light inside during the day; at night the light pattern reverses, and screen becomes a lantern. **S/G/A**

PLAN & SECTION

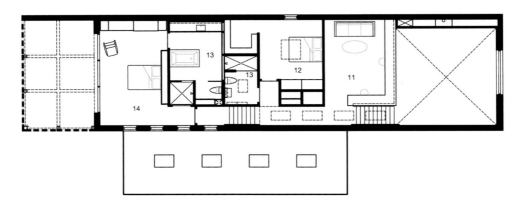

1 Garden
2 Dining
3 Kitchen
4 Library
5 Living
6 Powder
7 Laundry
8 Storage
9 Mechanical
10 Garage
11 Family
12 Study/Bedroom
13 Bath
14 Bedroom

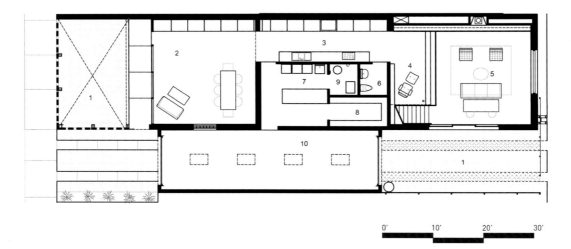

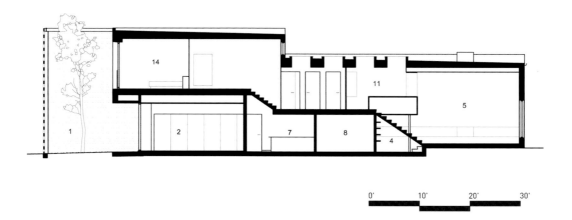

7.9 Second floor plan

7.10 Ground floor plan

7.11 Section: Variation in ceiling heights and floor levels weaves together the two-story garden at the front with a single-story volume in the back through a cascading section.

7.12

7.12 The screen animates the garden and interior with dappled sunlight, establishing a visual connection to and from the street.

(overleaf)

7.13 By decreasing wind pressures, the screen moderates the house's interior temperature in cold weather.

7.14 Carefully placed windows and clerestories fill the interior with light.

7.15 The compressed kitchen visually expands to the diaphanous brick screen at the entry.

7.16 A garden beyond the screen is open to the sky.

7.17 Rectangular voids in the screen throw hexagonal patterns of light inside.

7.18 As captured by aerial photographer Georg Gerster in 1982, the oldest part of the city of Fes, Morocco (known as Fes el Bali) is a striking example of the spatial potential of the courtyard house typology. This walled medina's construction began in the ninth century CE. Created for livable density and privacy, and evolved over time, today Fes el Bali is one of the largest car-free urban areas in the world. © Georg Gerster/Photo Researchers.

7.21 Fresh air, natural daylight, and the presence of water make the interior courtyard of a traditional home in Fes el Bali, Morocco, a tranquil and comfortable place: an oasis in the midst of a dense city.

BIBLIOGRAPHY

Blaser, Werner. Mies van der Rohe: The Art of Structure. New York: Whitney Library of Design, 1994.
Keister, Douglas. Courtyards: Intimate Outdoor Spaces. Layton, UT: Gibbs Smith, 2005.
Macintosh, Duncan. The Modern Courtyard House: A History. London: Lund Humphries for the Architectural Association, 1973.
Sherwood, Roger. Modern Housing Prototypes. Cambridge, MA: Harvard University Press, 1978.

MATERIAL REPORT: COMPRESSED EARTH BLOCKS; IPRO COURSE AT IIT FALL 2009

Instructors: Jeanne Gang with Monica Chadha, Linda Pulik, and Akhil Badjatia

It's not every day that undergrads in the confines of IIT are given the chance to tackle some of the world's most pressing problems while also getting their hands dirty. Students enrolled in this Inter-Professional (IPRO) course, however, were able to do just that. Hailing from a variety of different majors, IIT students take IPRO courses to learn teamwork and address real-world problems with real clients. Their assignment for the semester was to design a safe house for sexually trafficked girls to be built near Mumbai; the client, Robin Chaurasiya, the director of the non-governmental organization Kranti, had requested a sustainable design approach. The IPRO class took on this complex challenge at both macro and micro scales. Employing user-based research, they studied the house's future inhabitants and gathered impressions of the city and its social conditions. Then they experimented with building materials to construct the Kranti safe house. Addressing the comprehensive nature of design in this way, they were able to use what they learned about the organization and Mumbai in developing a series of sustainable design concepts using ecological building materials and methods of fabrication.

The IPRO students focused their material studies on Compressed Earth Blocks (CEBs)—an excellent solution to problems both human (as 25 percent of the world population does not have access to decent housing) and environmental (the ever-increasing demand for concrete is irreversibly warming the planet). Earth as a building material is more abundant and less expensive than either concrete or wood, and its low production cost has long made it a common choice for construction in remote areas. In fact, 40 percent of the world currently lives in earth-built homes.[1] Traditional adobe buildings made from earth and fibrous materials like straw, however, lack structural precision and strength. Fired mud bricks are far stronger and more durable than adobe, but their high-temperature firing and transport to and from the kiln increase cost and produce carbon dioxide. CEBs, on the other hand, are perhaps the "greenest" materials possible, as they can be made directly from the building site's soil. They also require no firing—only the inclusion of a bit of cement to speed the sun's natural drying process. When completed, the blocks offer quality insulation, keeping out the summer heat and, with proper sealing, maintaining a comfortable indoor temperature throughout the winter.

The first mechanical CEB press was invented in 1950; significant improvements have since been made, resulting in the efficient production of stronger and more dimensionally uniform mud blocks. Today a 10-person team (five operators each working a hand-cranked press, and five others gathering the raw materials and overseeing the drying processes) can manageably make 500 blocks a day—enough to complete the walls of a small dwelling within one week. With a more expensive hydraulic press, a small house can be completed in a single day.

The ideal soil used for CEBs worldwide is comprised of 15–40 percent non-expansive clay, 25–40 percent silt powder, and 40–70 percent sharp sand and small gravel. Because these component spreads are so common, there is a great chance that soil from a variety of regions will be usable for CEBs; however, it also mandates repeated soil testing at every build site. One of the final measurements of a soil sample's feasibility for use in CEBs is its plastic index, a measurement of the amount of water present in the material ingredients before they exhibit behavior associated with plastics (the higher the PI, the more clay present). For CEBs, a plastic index measurement of 25–30 for the clay component, and no more than 15 for the soil, is acceptable.

To put these statistics to the test, the IPRO students experimented with an Auroville 3000 mechanical press and materials largely donated from Chicago-area building industry members. Looking to achieve the correct moisture content of the block (ideally between four and twelve percent), the students began with a mixture of soil and clay from a local site, then added water and more dry material. With this composition complete, additives such as cement, gypsum, and lime were added to the blocks in the final steps to increase their stability, strength, and durability. With the introduction of these additives, CEBs become formally known as CSBs: Compressed Stabilized Bricks. Using the knowledge gained through these experiments with local Chicago soil, the IPRO students then began to formulate a plan for CEB fabrication and construction within the context of Mumbai. Here, with input from engineers from Arup, the International Masonry Institue, and IIT advanced materials faculty, they examined how best to design CEB structures to withstand the region's monsoons and unpredicatable seismic activity, and to improve performance.

With a preliminary design for the Kranti safe house drawn at semester's end and their full-scale mock-up of compressed earth block complete, the students had made a significant contribution to the future safe house for Kranti. By combining their diverse backgrounds and knowledge sets to address a real-world issue, they demonstrated the value of teamwork. Through their experimentation combining the low-tech and high-tech ends of the technology spectrum, their work has the potential to have significant real-world impact. [S/G/A]

Notes
1 United Nations NGO Committee on Urban Settlements

7.22 Students experimenting with a mechanical press to create Compressed Earth Blocks (CEBs). Though CEBs are considered low-tech, the course aimed at improving a technology that could have a positive impact on large populations. Forty percent of the world currently lives in earth-built homes, the majority of which are sub-standard. Made from earth on site, CEBs offer a sustainable, high-performance alternative.

BIBLIOGRAPHY

Auroville Earth Institute. "Earthen Architecture in the World: Compressed Earth Blocks." http://www.earth-auroville.com/maintenance/uploaded_pics/7-compressed-earth-blocks-en.pdf.

CRATerre. The Basics of Compressed Earth Blocks. Eschborn, Germany: Deutsches Zentrum für Entwicklungs Technologien (GATE), 1991.

Farnsworth, Christina B. "Earth Building Takes New Shapes." Home Energy Magazine Online, May–June 1999. http://livepage.apple.comwww.homeenergy.org/archive/hem.dis.anl.gov/eehem/99/990514.html.

Austin Energy Green Building. "Materials: Earth Construction." Sustainable Building Sourcebook. 3rd ed. http://www.austinenergy.com/energy%20efficiency/Programs/Green%20Building/Sourcebook/earthConstruction.htm.

McHenry, Paul, Jr. "Adobe: A Present from the Past." Building Standards, September–October 1998. http://www.greenhomebuilding.com/pdf/buildingstandards_adobe.pdf.

Powell, Dan. "The Vertical Press vs. The Horizontal Press." Powell & Sons Earth Construction Machinery. http://www.adobemachine.com/vervshor.htm.

Rigassi, Vincent. Compressed Earth Blocks: Manual of Production. Eschborn, Germany: Deutsches Zentrum für Entwicklungs Technologien (GATE), 1985.

BEFORE BRICK WEAVE: ARCHAEOLOGY OF THE HOUSE IN WEST TOWN

Houses in the midst of demolition provide a rare glimpse of domestic history. With the delamination of their walls, colorful smears of previous residents become visible. What were once painted or wallpapered private interiors become, for an instant, exteriors. These sites are also records: documents of a previous era's construction techniques, or even its shoddy repairs.

PROJECT / BRICK WEAVE HOUSE

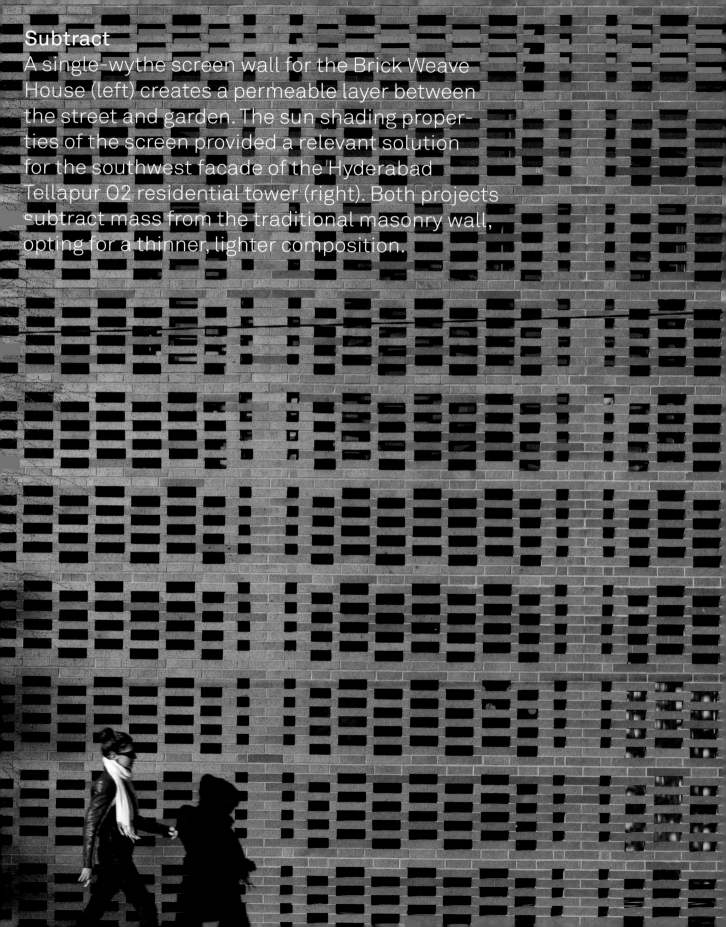

Subtract

A single-wythe screen wall for the Brick Weave House (left) creates a permeable layer between the street and garden. The sun shading properties of the screen provided a relevant solution for the southwest facade of the Hyderabad Tellapur O2 residential tower (right). Both projects subtract mass from the traditional masonry wall, opting for a thinner, lighter composition.

PROJECT

HYDERABAD TELLAPUR 02

OWNERS: TSI Ventures/Tellapur Techno-City Private Ltd.
LOCATION: Hyderabad, Tellapur, India
SIZE: 1 million SF
COMPLETION DATE: 2014

Plan and unfolded elevations showing unit types. The Hyderabad 02 residential tower transforms the traditional Indian courtyard house into a new porous building type with both a higher degree of density and more sunlight. The 25-story cube is eroded with a large central courtyard and a system of "cracks" implemented to create cross ventilation for public space and natural ventilation for the private apartments.

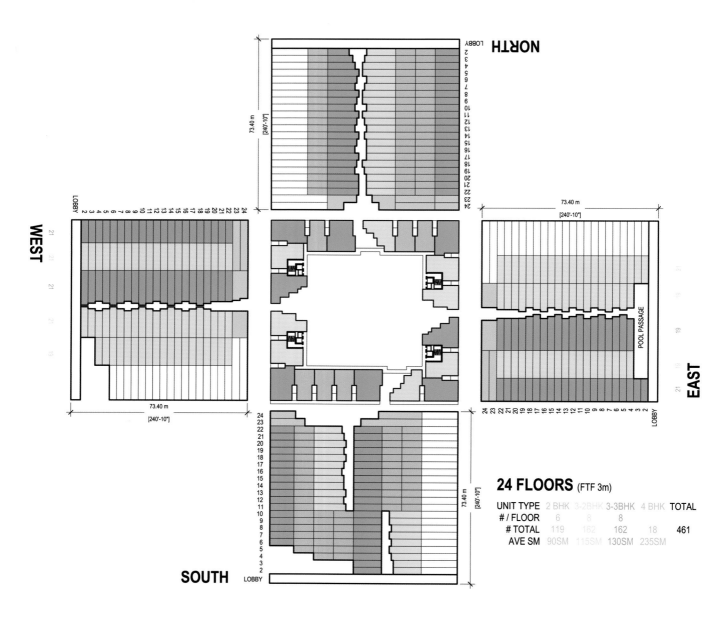

24 FLOORS (FTF 3m)

UNIT TYPE	2 BHK	3-2BHK	3-3BHK	4 BHK	TOTAL
# / FLOOR	6	8	8		
# TOTAL	119	162	162	18	461
AVE SM	90SM	115SM	130SM	235SM	

A street in Jaisalmer, India, lined by havelis (right) and the view
between the cracks that separate the tower's building volumes (left).
Both are similarly animated by outdoor balconies and porches.

Self-shading techniques demonstrated by Indian havelis or courtyard houses are employed to produce comfortable and engaging outdoor spaces.

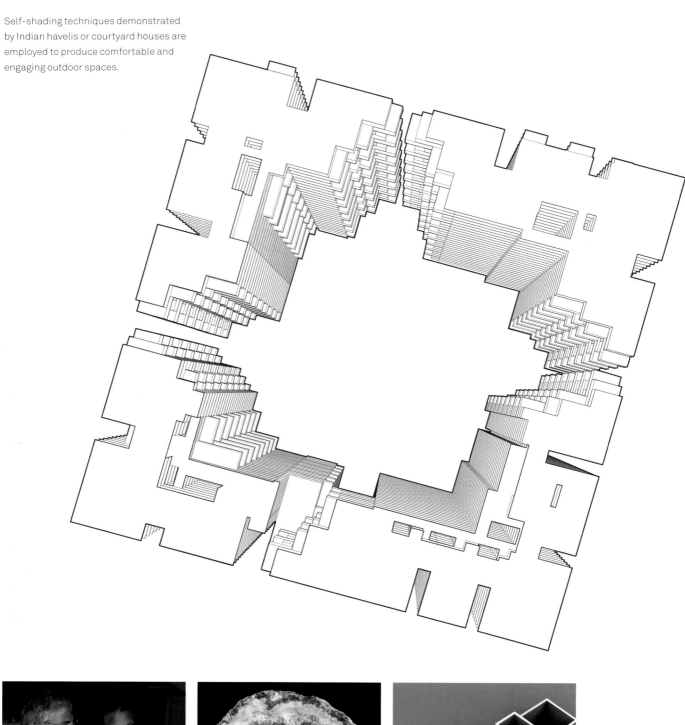

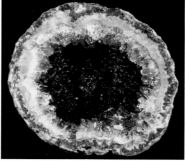

Outdoor terraces along the building's cracks offer breathing space for individual apartments and lend a sense of community to the overall development.

(opposite page, left) Rajeev Kathpaliaat and
Dr. Balkrishna Doshi at a workshop reviewing
the courtyard tower design.

(opposite page, center) A geode serves as a
paradigm of a simple exterior with a faceted interior.

(opposite page, right) Iterations of courtyard models
studying proportion

PROJECT – CHICAGO
WALKER – MINNEAPOLIS
NEW ART, NEW IDEAS
RESTAURANT / CAFE
WAYFINDING

MAKING IS THINKING
TRANSCRIPTS FROM AN OFFICE WORKSHOP HELD IN SGA'S MODEL SHOP

Mark Schendel, Principal, Studio Gang Architects

The Concept/Schematic Moment

Concept and schematic design phases present designers with the opportunity to use their minds, eyes, and hands in conceptualizing, idea-generating, and experimenting. Unfortunately, many architecture schools have abdicated physical model-making in favor of digital explorations, but during the concept and schematic design phases there is opportunity for designers to sketch, collage, and make models—study models—with their own hands. Instead of being a static, finished product, every study model must be a design tool.

Spatial Ideas and Scale

The ease with which digital lines can transform ideas directly to digital production is heralded as a great benefit, but when making models, it actually reduces the range of design options made visible to us and cripples our ability to understand space. Digital laser-cut modeling frequently leads to a loss of scale and the use of inappropriate materials. Cutting by laser requires materials to be robust and resistant to fire, so laser materials are heavy, thick, and limited in range. Using three-dimensional digital printing methods also results in limited material output.

The first model for a campus building for the University of Kentucky, made on a laser cutter and then hand-assembled, exemplifies two of the main problems that arise from using a laser cutter (fig. 1). First, the materials are dull, and there are only two of them: chipboard and Plexiglas. They are also too thick—the Plexiglas "windows" would be 12" thick at scale. Most importantly, the designer spent time building the CAD file rather than sketching or modeling the solution. He focused his mind and energy on two-dimensional lines instead of on choosing modeling materials and deciding on an appropriate building method. As a result, this model is boring—even off-putting. It is ugly, but not in an instructive way that might make its ugliness acceptable. And, since it is built of heavy materials, it is heavy and solid and cannot be easily manipulated after the fact. In other words, it cannot be used as a design tool.

In contrast, the next model for this project was made entirely by hand (fig. 2). It departs from its CAD-conceived origins in a very good way. The modeler drew and sketched over the CAD drawings in order to improve and evolve the design as it was being modeled. The modeling is fast, but intelligent: the eye looks for design opportunities that only the model can reveal,

and the hand responds. The modeling was done with light materials that were chosen for their physical properties: their stiffness, lightness, finish, color, and texture. These qualities can attract the eye, make a reference to an actual building material, or offer diagrammatic clarity.

The entire model is light, yet precise. The thickness of the windows, walls, and beams indicate an appropriateness of scale. There is space—and are spaces—in this model. Most importantly, the model, which is a work in progress, can easily be manipulated and changed. Made by hand, its parts are lightly connected, and even left loose in some places so that it can be used as a design tool. It is susceptible to accidental design discoveries as pieces of it are rearranged. This is what allowed the model to be modified in a meeting. This design change could not have been done with the CAD and laser-cut model, could never have happened digitally, and could never have happened as quickly in any other medium.

The first model made for the Stuart Reading Room project also exhibits an inappropriate dependence on digital tools (fig. 8). This should be a study model, but it is not. Made with CAD and a laser cutter, its potential usefulness as a design tool is lost, crushed under the model's literal self-weight (notice the failing columns). The initial design concept called for light, transparent group-study rooms floating in the ornate, neo-Gothic Stuart Hall. Doesn't that sound like a great idea? Why did the designer waste the opportunity to realize and even further that idea by hand? How did he not even think of doing it? Using inappropriate tools robbed him of the fun and potential of designing with his eyes and hands.

In sharp contrast to these (anti) study models, the base model of the Harper and Stuart Reading Rooms does benefit from the use of CAD and laser cutting technology in some ways. It could have been made by hand, but that would have been a waste of time and effort when the laser cutter can offer such precise detail so quickly. The use of the laser cutter enables this base model to be a scaled expression of the ornate qualities of the old room, and the burned edges of the chipboard simulate the stone and wood materiality of the rooms themselves. The laser cutter speeds the making of the base model, allowing the team to move quickly on to designing. The base model also contrasts perfectly with the modern design intentions. Because of the detail of the base model, it became possible to imagine the insertion of a quick "ready-made" (an empty blue ice-cube tray) into the Hall—ingeniously articulating the desire for a design option that contrasted strongly with the surroundings (fig.10).

Materials and Construction

Bond paper is perhaps the most amazing modeling material there is: it has a very high strength-to-weight ratio, and a high stiffness-to-weight ratio when folded. Indeed, almost any idea can be modeled with paper; see, for example, the model of the Hyderabad tower (fig. 6). The first-ever Starlight Theatre model was made from paper: figure 4 presents an early study model. The joy and conceptual impact of this model requires no explanation.

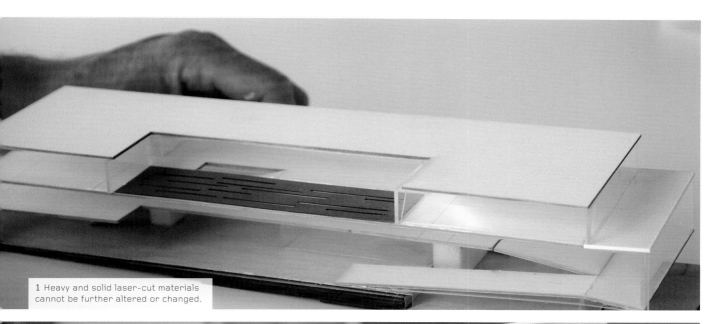

1 Heavy and solid laser-cut materials cannot be further altered or changed.

2 Lightweight, lightly connected paper materials give designers the freedom to manipulate in real time.

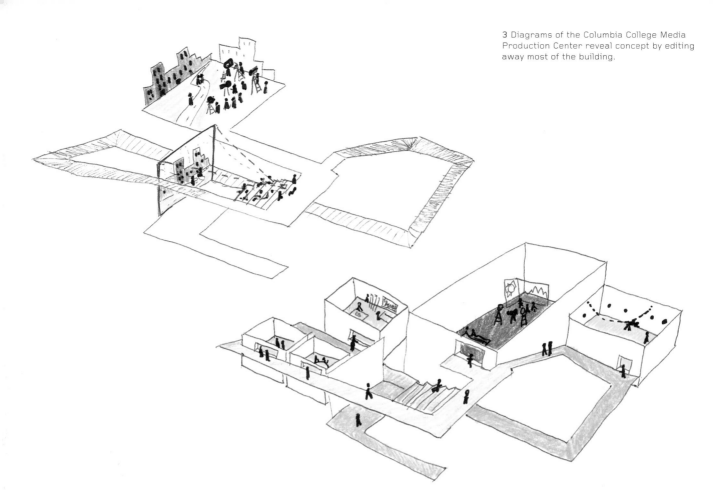

Study models can be constructed out of almost any material, and can take many different forms; here, for example, are three study models that each serve their purpose as a design tool, but could not be more different. Figure 7 presents a handmade model for a concrete spiral stair at the Aqua Tower. Over the course of two to three hours of modeling, many small adjustments were made to the design using scissors and tape. It was the first time that we actively understood the geometry of the stair, and it was the first time the client understood its spatial beauty. The fear of descending fifty feet to the park was relieved—the model made it possible to trace the elegant route down with a finger.

Finally, figure 5 is a concept model of "wind." Here, we were attempting to simulate the movement of solar sequins (individual solar panels mounted on a wall, like a sequin billboard) under wind load. To do this, we draped glimmering fabric over concentric paper rings attached with tape to a sheet of Plexi.

Sketching

Hand sketches can have the same power as models, especially when they simultaneously serve as diagrams. The selective use of colored pencil and shading makes the sketches of the Columbia College Media Production Center in Figure 3

compelling, the editing away of most of the building makes them clear diagrams that reveal a complex system of movement, and the careful, minimal application of pencil scratches makes them elegant. Their message is immediate.

Like a physical model, sketches can offer multiple views of a design, but they can also selectively focus the eye on key details or concepts. The sketch series for an advertising agency (fig. 9) explores a wide variety of design applications for their pin-up space using simple 4' x 8' x 1" grid-core easels. The easel base is shown in detail, but also in application as furniture. The easels are shown alone and in series, always with human-scale context. Columns and doors are explored as easel supports and even the attachment clips are sketched in detail. The sketches are graphic and high-contrast. Created quickly—in one session—the sketches capture the rush of option-making. Each 8.5" x 11" sketch page is the result of two or three traced redraws, with each redraw correcting initial mistakes in layout, line weight, or content. Sketches are rarely good enough to become presentation sketches for clients on the first iteration—they require redraws and corrections to convey the ideas to others. In the case of these particular sketches, the clients loved them!

Train your eyes and hands. It takes practice: find a sketch you know has quality and sketch it over and over again until your hand can almost do it alone. The next sketch you do will unconsciously reveal the lessons of that practice. By using every means available to you when modeling and sketching, you can come up with every possible option. The schematic moment is rare and brief, and when a designer is presented with the opportunity to engage in concept and schematic design, he or she must seize it with all of his or her facility. **S/G/A**

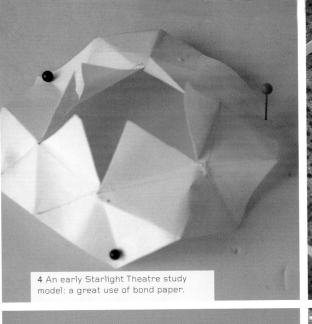
4 An early Starlight Theatre study model: a great use of bond paper.

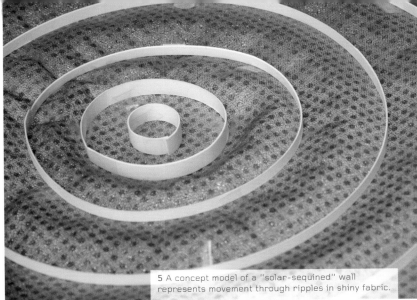
5 A concept model of a "solar-sequined" wall represents movement through ripples in shiny fabric.

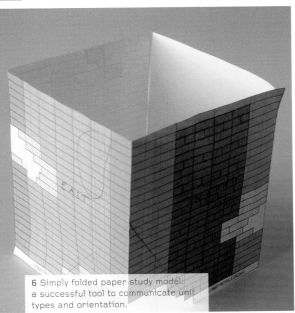
6 Simply folded paper study model: a successful tool to communicate unit types and orientation.

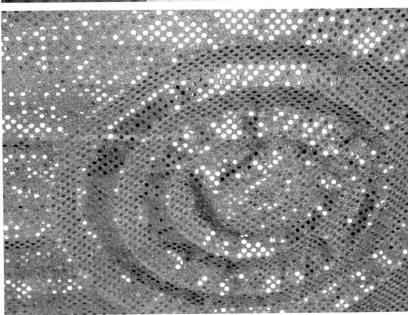

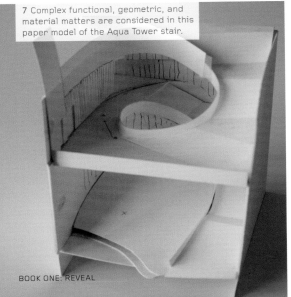
7 Complex functional, geometric, and material matters are considered in this paper model of the Aqua Tower stair.

8 A failed concept model of Stuart Hall that used dark, heavy chipboard to represent "floating" study rooms.

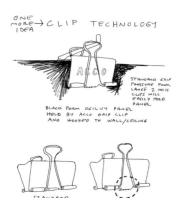

ONE MORE IDEA → CLIP TECHNOLOGY

STANDARD GRIP PRESSURE FROM LARGE 2 INCH CLIPS WILL EASILY HOLD PANEL

BLACK FOAM OGILVY PANEL HELD BY ACCO GRIP CLIP AND HOOKED TO WALL/CEILING

STANDARD ACCO CLIP

MODIFIED ACCO CLIP WITH GRIP TEETH
2 2 JAN. 2004
STUDIO GANG

THE OGILVY BASE: LIGHTWEIGHT WOOD (OR ANODIZED METAL OR ACRYLIC) FREESTANDING BOXES.

360°

THE OGILVY BOARD: BLACK FOAM GATOR BOARDS, 4'X8'

STORAGE BASE ON WHEELS

360° ROLOFRAME ROLLO BOARDS PRESENTATION AND STORAGE MEDIUM
2 2 JAN. 2004
STUDIO GANG

BLACK FOAM BOARD COMES IN BLACK
WHITE FOAM BOARD COMES IN WHITE
WHY NOT ONE BOARD WITH BOTH

WHITE ON ONE SIDE

BLACK ON THE OTHER

THE WHITE REVERSE REFLECTS LIGHT AND IS AN ALTERNATE PIN-UP BACKGROUND

BLACK

WHITE

360° MEETING IN ACTION

B&W BOARD
WE CAN EITHER REQUEST IT TO BE MADE BY MANUFACTURER
OR EASILY HAVE IT MADE LOCALLY
2 2 JAN. 2004
STUDIO GANG

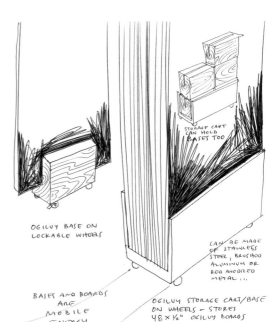

STORAGE CART CAN HOLD BASES TOO

OGILVY BASE ON LOCKABLE WHEELS

CAN BE MADE OF STAINLESS STEEL, BRUSHED ALUMINUM OR RED ANODIZED METAL...

BASES AND BOARDS ARE MOBILE ENERGY

OGILVY STORAGE CART/BASE ON WHEELS - STORES 48 X ½" OGILVY BOARDS

2 2 JAN. 2004
STUDIO GANG

10 Effective use of laser cutting for Stuart Hall's existing Gothic interior contrasted with a provocative ready-made that better represents the idea of "floating" study rooms.

I. Architecture continuously takes a position on material, irrespective of whether its importance is extolled or diminished.

II. There is no relevant building whose material choice is immaterial.

III. "Because all architecture engages material, the question is only at which point in the design process is it engaged—toward the beginning or toward the end?"

IV. It is the one who is thoroughly curious about a material who has the potential to instill it with surprising traits. This is because surprise is dependent upon discovery; discovery on experimentation; experimentation to some degree on chance; and chance on a willingness to fail.

V. A master is thoroughly acquainted with materials; however, a master is the most unlikely candidate to attempt surprise. The master tends to fall in love with his own mastery and concern himself with refinement.

VI. There are relatively few plausible building materials, but their combinations and possibilities are almost limitless.

VII. Materials can be highly manipulated and radically transformed, though this usually consumes more energy.

VIII. Breaking a material reveals more about it than building with it.

IX. No material's market value reflects its true environmental cost —at least not yet.

X. It is more satisfying to design form having already decided on material. A shape that obeys material is protected from future formal compromises.

XI. It is more difficult to have an idea that stems from material when the design expectation is the image and the intended site lies across continents.

XII. Materials in themselves are not a religion and have nothing to do with morals and truth, but they are bound by the laws of physics.

XIII. Those who dismiss the importance of material are usually the ones who have built the least.

— JG

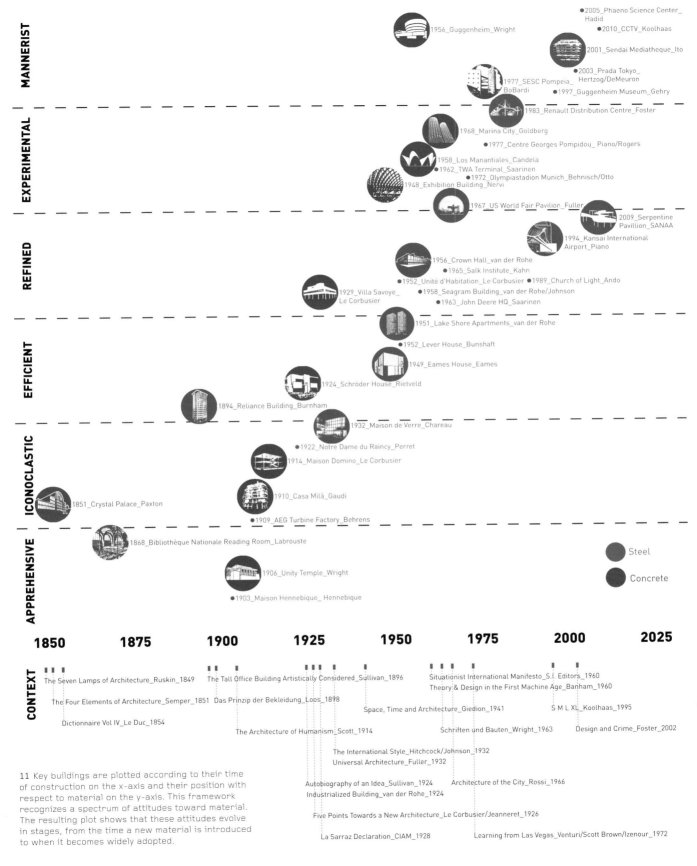

MANNERIST

●2005_Phaeno Science Center_
Hadid
●2010_CCTV_Koolhaas
1956_Guggenheim_Wright
2001_Sendai Mediatheque_Ito
●2003_Prada Tokyo_
Hertzog/DeMeuron
1977_SESC Pompeia_
BoBardi
●1997_Guggenheim Museum_Gehry

EXPERIMENTAL

1983_Renault Distribution Centre_Foster
1968_Marina City_Goldberg
●1977_Centre Georges Pompidou_ Piano/Rogers
1958_Los Manantiales_Candela
1962_TWA Terminal_Saarinen
●1972_Olympiastadion Munich_Behnisch/Otto
1948_Exhibition Building_Nervi
1967_US World Fair Pavilion_Fuller
2009_Serpentine
Pavillion_SANAA
1994_Kansai International
Airport_Piano

REFINED

1956_Crown Hall_van der Rohe
●1965_Salk Institute_Kahn
●1952_Unité d'Habitation_Le Corbusier ●1989_Church of Light_Ando
1929_Villa Savoye_
Le Corbusier
●1958_Seagram Building_van der Rohe/Johnson
●1963_John Deere HQ_Saarinen

1951_Lake Shore Apartments_van der Rohe

EFFICIENT

●1952_Lever House_Bunshaft
1949_Eames House_Eames
1924_Schröder House_Rietveld
1894_Reliance Building_Burnham

1932_Maison de Verre_Chareau

ICONOCLASTIC

●1922_Notre Dame du Raincy_Perret
1914_Maison Domino_Le Corbusier
1910_Casa Milà_Gaudi
●1909_AEG Turbine Factory_Behrens
1851_Crystal Palace_Paxton

APPREHENSIVE

1868_Bibliothèque Nationale Reading Room_Labrouste

Steel

Concrete

1906_Unity Temple_Wright

●1903_Maison Hennebique_ Hennebique

1850   1875   1900   1925   1950   1975   2000   2025

CONTEXT

The Seven Lamps of Architecture_Ruskin_1849   The Tall Office Building Artistically Considered_Sullivan_1896   Situationist International Manifesto_S.I. Editors_1960
Theory & Design in the First Machine Age_Banham_1960

The Four Elements of Architecture_Semper_1851   Das Prinzip der Bekleidung_Loos_1898   Space, Time and Architecture_Giedion_1941   S M L XL_Koolhaas_1995

Dictionnaire Vol IV_Le Duc_1854   Schriften und Bauten_Wright_1963   Design and Crime_Foster_2002

The Architecture of Humanism_Scott_1914

The International Style_Hitchcock/Johnson_1932
Universal Architecture_Fuller_1932

Autobiography of an Idea_Sullivan_1924   Architecture of the City_Rossi_1966
Industrialized Building_van der Rohe_1924

Five Points Towards a New Architecture_Le Corbusier/Jeanneret_1926

La Sarraz Declaration_CIAM_1928   Learning from Las Vegas_Venturi/Scott Brown/Izenour_1972

11 Key buildings are plotted according to their time
of construction on the x-axis and their position with
respect to material on the y-axis. This framework
recognizes a spectrum of attitudes toward material.
The resulting plot shows that these attitudes evolve
in stages, from the time a new material is introduced
to when it becomes widely adopted.

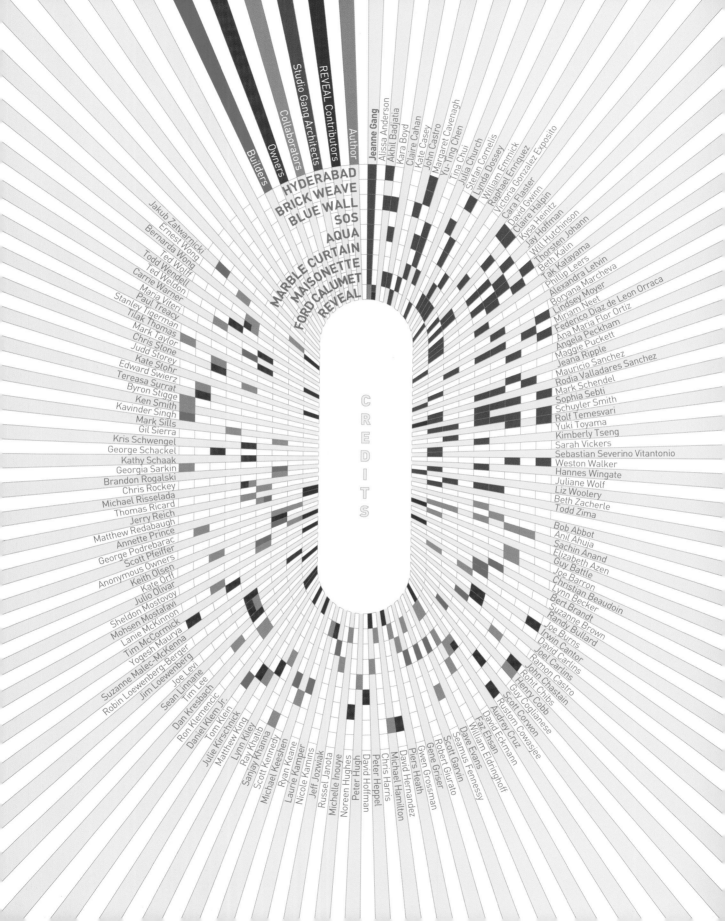

CREDITS

Builders
Owners
Collaborators
Studio Gang Architects
REVEAL Contributors
Author

Jeanne Gang

HYDERABAD
BRICK WEAVE
BLUE WALL
SOS
AQUA
MARBLE CURTAIN
MAISONETTE
FORD CALUMET
REVEAL

Alissa Anderson
Akhil Badjatia
Kara Boyd
Claire Cahan
Kate Casey
John Castro
Margaret Cavenagh
Yu-Ting Chen
Tina Chui
Julia Church
Stefan Cornelis
Lynda Dossey
William Emmick
Raphael Enriquez
Victoria Gonzalez Exposito
Cara Flaster
David Gwinn
Claire Halpin
Kysa Heinitz
Jay Hoffman
Will Hutchinson
Thorsten Johann
Beth Kalin
Tak Katayama
Phillip Leers
Alexandra Letvin
Boryana Marcheva
Lindsey Moyer
Miriam Neet
Federico Diaz de Leon Orraca
Ana Maria Flor Ortiz
Angela Peckham
Maggie Puckett
Jeana Ripple
Mauricio Sanchez
Rodia Valladares Sanchez
Mark Schendel
Sophia Sebti
Schuyler Smith
Rolf Temesvari
Yuki Toyama
Kimberly Tseng
Sarah Vickers
Sebastian Severino Vitantonio
Weston Walker
Hannes Wingate
Juliane Wolf
Liz Woolery
Beth Zacherle
Todd Zima

Bob Abbot
Anil Ahuja
Sachin Anand
Elizabeth Azen
Guy Battle
Joe Barron
Christian Beaudoin
Lynn Becker
Bert Brandt
Suzanne Brown
Randy Bullard
Joe Burns
Irwin Cantor
David Carlins
Joel Carlins
Ramon Castro
John Chastain
Rohit Chibbs
Henry Cobb
Guy Coglianese
Scott Corwon
Scott Cowasjee
Audrey Cruz
Rustom Cowasjee
David Eckmann
Faiz Ehsan
William Eldringhoff
Dave Evans
Seamus Fennessy
Scott Garvin
Robert Giurato
Gene Griser
Gwen Grossman
Piers Heath
David Hernandez
Michael Hamilton
Chris Harris
Peter Heppel
David Hoffman
Peter Hugh
Noreen Hughes
Michelle Inouye
Russel Janota
Jeff Jozwiak
Nicole Kamins
Laurie Kamper
Ryan Keane
Scott Kennedy
Michael Keeshen
Ray Khalib
Sanjay Khanna
Lynn Kiley
Matthew King
Julie Kirschnick
Tom Klein
Daniel Klem Jr.
Ron Klemencic
Dan Kresbach
Sean Linnane
Tim Lee
Tim Linnane
Joe Levi
Jim Loewenberg
Robin Loewenberg-Berger
Suzanne Malec-McKenna
Yogesh Maurya
Tim McCormick
Lanie McKinnon
Mohsen Mostafavi
Sheldon Mostovoy
Julio Olivar
Kate Orff
Keith Olsen
Anonymous Owners
Scott Pfeiffer
George Podrebarac
Annette Prince
Matthew Redabaugh
Jerry Reich
Thomas Ricard
Michael Risselada
Chris Rockey
Brandon Rogalski
Georgia Sarkin
Kathy Schaak
George Schackel
Kris Schwengel
Gil Sierra
Mark Sills
Kavinder Singh
Ken Smith
Byron Stigge
Tereasa Surrat
Edward Swierz
Kate Stohr
Judd Storey
Chris Stone
Mark Taylor
Tilak Thomas
Stanley Tigerman
Paul Treacy
Maria Viteri
Carrie Warner
Ted Weldon
Todd Wendell
Ted Wolff
Bernarda Wong
Ernest Wong
Jakub Zatwarnicki

ACKNOWLEDGMENTS

Sincere thanks to Elizabeth Azen, Alissa Anderson, Liz Woolery, and Alexandra Letvin for their commitments, talents, and ideas that supported this book project, and also to its publisher, Princeton Architectural Press, and the special attentiveness of editors Jennifer Thompson and Dan Simon. Thanks to Mohsen Mostafavi for his thoughtful foreword, and to Thorsten Johann, Jay Hoffman, Beth Zacherle, and Steve Hall for their high-quality graphic and photographic contributions. The wisdom and encouragement of Gwendolyn Wright was very helpful in shaping the project, as was the thoughtful advice offered by Andrew Blum, Stan Allen, Sarah Herder, and Michael Kubo.

I am grateful to Stanley Tigerman for his ongoing mentorship, and to Susann Craig, Leah Zell Wanger, Jim Loewenberg, Donna Robertson, Helmut Jahn, and Robert Stern, Toshiko Mori, and Rem Koolhaas for bestowing important teaching and practice opportunities. Also thanks to inspiring teachers and colleagues Homa Fadjadi, Peter Land, Sadhu Johnston, David Reynolds, and the late Marian Byrnes.

In addition, I am indebted to my partner Mark Schendel for championing this project and instilling it with a sense of urgency, as well as to the continued moral support of Marj Gang, Nancy Hatten, Susan Kasten, Kathy Gang, and Tristan Schendel.

Finally, I would like to thank the Graham Foundation for its early support of this project through a funding grant.

STUDIO/
GANG
/ARCHITECTS

STUDIO/
GANG
/ARCHITECTS